Stephan Sonnenburg · Laura Baker (Eds.)

Branded Spaces

Experience Enactments
and Entanglements

 Springer VS

Editors
Prof. Dr. Stephan Sonnenburg
Karlsruhe, Germany

Dr. Laura Baker
Graz, Austria

ISBN 978-3-658-01560-2
DOI 10.1007/978-3-658-01561-9

ISBN 978-3-658-01561-9 (eBook)

The Deutsche Nationalbibliothek lists this publication in the Deutsche Nationalbibliografie; detailed bibliographic data are available in the Internet at http://dnb.d-nb.de.

Library of Congress Control Number: 2013932217

Springer VS
© Springer Fachmedien Wiesbaden 2013

Printed on acid-free paper

Springer VS is a brand of Springer DE.
Springer DE is part of Springer Science+Business Media.
www.springer-vs.de

Managem  :erpretation

Edited by
Andreas P. Müller
Stephan Sonnenburg

The book series of the Karlshochschule International University explores new ideas and approaches to management, organizations and economy from a cultural and interpretive point of view. The series intends to integrate different perspectives towards economy, culture and society. Therefore, management and organizational activities are not seen as being isolated from their context, but rather as context-bound and dependent on their surrounding cultures, societies and economies. Within these contexts, activities make sense through the allocation, the interpretation and the negotiation of meanings. Sense-making can be found in performative processes as well as the way social meaning is constructed through interactions. The series seeks innovative approaches, both in formulating new research questions and in developing adequate methodological research designs. We welcome contributions from different interdisciplinary and collective ways of thinking and seeking knowledge which focus on the integration of "Management – Culture – Interpretation".

Edited by
Prof. Dr. Andreas P. Müller
Prof. Dr. Stephan Sonnenburg

Karlsruhe, Germany

Contents

Approaching Branded Spaces

Stephan Sonnenburg / Laura Baker

Why is it worth studying branded spaces now? First of all, as brands and branding are radically transforming, brand owners have begun to perceive the relevance and booster qualities of space for branding brands. In a global and fast changing world, branded spaces are becoming icons, cornerstones or lighthouses for brands, for their image and for their relationship to their agents. Space "increasingly becomes (de facto if not de jure) the brand" (Sherry 1998: 112). Even more, as Arvidsson (2005: 236) argues, we are on a way to "end up living in a well nigh all-encompassing brand-space". Brands are enacted and entangled in space more regularly and must be considered with space in mind to be convincing and successful. Branded spaces emplace agents to have an experience that is in multisensual and multisensory association with a brand. Therefore, brand and marketing research has begun to shift its perspective to spatial dimensions (e.g. Hollenbeck et al. 2008, Kozinets et al. 2002, Ponsonby-McCabe and Boyle 2006, Sherry 1998) and scientists who focus on space have gained interest in relating brands and space (e.g. Kirby and Kent 2010, Klingmann 2007, Moor 2003, Pike 2011).

In this context space has become increasingly important for many people, brand owners and scientists alike, because there is a warranted need to conquer space for brand staging. While it is clear that people are interested in the topic of branded spaces, we are interested in not only how but also to what extent branded spaces are approached in a critical way and to what degree branded space affords success. Hence, in a story-like framework we wonder if people are approaching branded spaces as lovers, friends, mutual acquaintances or even enemies and if there are embraces, open arms, a handshake, the cold shoulder or the knife in the back. We believe that branded spaces can be applied to good uses and bad ones as well as take on the characteristics of being progressive and regressive.

Although theoretical preconditions are given, they are not yet to our knowledge combined in a synergetic way in the literature. Inspired by Soja (1989), space has been studied with renewed interest across social sciences since the 1990s which helps to approach, theoretically, branded spaces from the spatial perspective. On the other hand, brand theory has approached branded spaces through the brand perspective but without sufficient implementation of spatial science. Up until now, there has been no known attempt to close this gap in order to better understand and apply branded spaces.

We believe that nowadays space and brand are in a productive interdependency which leads to new forms of interaction between brands and people in spatial settings. Consequently, this concept is one of the main theses of this book. It is also worth exploration because a multidisciplinary (additive) approach with a theoretical basis is still in the beginning phase and lags behind the practical, concrete developments although it is quite necessary. One may think of examples, mentioned in this volume, like Guggenheim Museum in Bilbao, Burj Khalifa in Dubai, Eiffel Tower in Paris or Elbphilharmonie in Hamburg (a branded space still under construction). Additionally, neither brand nor space literature has taken the relationship between brand and space into account through a fundamental much less a higher level transdisciplinary (holistic) approach. If we are allowed creative licence, a love story that needs to be told is definitely emerging here with a relationship between theoretical approach and practical application. Hence, this book will begin with a multidisciplinary approach and leave a transdisciplinary approach as a possible sequel.

By now, the reader might be puzzled as we use the term 'branded spaces' as pre-existing and en passant. As far as we know, Elizabeth Moor (2003) uses the term for the first time but not as a spatial manifestation of a brand. She constitutes a branded space as the consumer-body and its everyday movements. Before we continue with our approach to branded spaces, we would like to introduce this term as our identifier and label for the unfolding of brands in space. We have not chosen this term by accident. We purposefully use this term knowing that it is tautological as a space itself is by definition already branded. Without branding in the sense of a marking or localisation, there is no space at all. Branding determines space. Each spatial entity needs to be branded to become and to be observed as a spatial entity. However, to be a branded space the 'basic' branding is not enough. There has to be more. We believe that meaning is necessary as an addition to the basic sense of observing or sensing so that a space becomes a branded space. To speak in metaphor, without meaning a space is nothing more than a container, a meaningless vessel of stone and glass.

Furthermore, there are branded spaces, which can be labeled as branded spaces without any kind of managed brand being involved. One may think of public spaces like streets or squares which gain political importance in times of revolutions like the Tahrir Square during the Arab Spring or city squares on Monday evenings in East Germany in 1989 and 1990 where a series of peaceful political protests against the government of the German Democratic Republic took place. Such spaces are politically branded at least for a specific period of time. This is the reason why we avoid the term 'brand space' or 'brand land' (Mikunda 2004), 'brandscape' (Sherry 1998), 'brand store' (Kozinets et al. 2002) and 'brand place' (Ponsonby-McCabe and Boyle 2006). The decision would have been problematic as these terms connote a reduction to consumer brands and, hence, lead to equalization with 'spaces for consumption' (Miles 2010). Brand space implicates the misleading assumption that every kind of branded space can be managed. Branded spaces can emerge spontaneously and develop in an uncontrolled manner as well as are owned by no one or the mass.

The core of this contribution, which comprises theoretical guiding principles for branded spaces, is presented in four sections. First, we introduce our understanding of 'brands' to make a connection to space possible. Second, we unfold approaches to space in due consideration to the spatial turn. Third and based on the conflation of brand and space, we develop our concept of branded spaces which is a springboard for the contributions in this book that are then introduced. As already mentioned, we would like to emphasize that branded spaces in this volume is considered from different perspectives with an eye towards cultural, social, philosophical, architectural and managerial perspectives to branded spaces with knowledge being drawn from different disciplines although the disciplines stay within their own boundaries for the most part. We regard this as an essential and open-minded multidisciplinary discourse as this book enters unknown territory.

Brand

The phenomenon 'brand' has developed into a global key issue as it is nowadays difficult to imagine social, cultural and consumer life without brands. On the one side, brands are cornerstones which provide faith and orientation in the daily jungle of information overload. On the other, almost everything today can be branded like products, services, organizations, people, events, buildings, streets, cities, regions or nations (Coomber 2002). Hence, brands are engraved in our everyday and it is not clear any longer who 'owns' the brands.

Brands are omnipresent and made to be interesting. Therefore, it seems logical that more disciplines than just marketing as the original one deal with brands and branding with social sciences and cultural studies leading the way (e.g. Escalas 2004, Hellmann 2003, Holt 2002, 2004, Liebl 2006, Woodside et al. 2008). It is also important to note that the understanding of brands as a trademark has changed over the last decades whereby the following concepts can be observed as influential. Focusing on a managerial and making aspect, brands are regarded as techniques (Domizlaff 1992), personalities (Aaker 1997), or identities (Elliott and Wattanasuwan 1998). Focusing on an emergent aspect, brands are regarded as symbols (Liebl 2006), archetypes (Holt 2004), social creations (O'Guinn and Muniz 2010), performances (Singh and Sonnenburg 2012) or cultural resources (Arvidsson 2005). From our perspective, brands have a story to tell.

Parallel to the above mentioned developments, it can be additionally observed that there is a shift from the owner's perspective, which means that he/she manages the brand, to the agent's perspective, which means that the agents 'make' the brand. In this regard, we quote Liebl who differentiates between owner and possessor of a brand:

> "Brands may legally 'belong' to companies and be 'managed' based on decisions taken by management, yet they are 'in the possession' of consumers, because the latter exploit and experience brands, interpret them in their own way, compare them with other brands, and share their experiences and fantasies with other consumers. And the way a brand is perceived often has little to do with the ideal image of the brand's essence in the heads of the marketing managers." (Liebl 2006: 29)

Before the advent of new media, brands were solely created by the brand owner and mass advertising used to profile a brand image in the agent's head. Brand communication was considered a monologue and people were trapped as a passive recipient of the content. The development of new media has begun to dissipate the boundary between brand owner and brand agents, hence, influencing all kinds of communication from face-to-face to digital. In the course of their increased communicative power, brand agents become an active part in the brand communication. Therefore, brands "are created by interactions of multiple parties, institutions, publics, and social forces" (O'Guinn and Muniz 2010: 133, Ind et al. 2012), which we term 'co-creative'. Consequently, brand owners lose their claim to leadership and are in a 'dilemma' as the brand image dilutes and the brand takes on more a life of its own in the imaginations and in the behaviors of the agents.

It can be stated that new media democratizes brand communication. Particularly, the brand monologue progresses to a brand 'polylogue' (Sonnenburg 2009) or a "process of interagency" (Kozinets et al. 2004: 658) between brand owner and agents. The active role can be described accordingly: Brand agents can be regarded as 'prosumers' (Toffler 1980), 'produsers' (Bruns 2008) or 'bricoleurs' (Holt 2002). In the polylogue, they create and swap brand content in conformist and even nonconformist ways. Agents "tend to be tricky wild things who find their own uses for marketed things and brands to be more interesting than those intended by marketers" (Sherry et al. 2006: 18). They are motivated to engage themselves as brand content carries meaning and gives meaning to their lives and (inter)actions:

> "Meaning defines brands, and people make meaning. People make meaning through social means: they make meaning through their interaction, through the institutions they have created and maintained, through accommodation and negotiation with marketers, through rumors, through politics, and often in reaction to a disruption in the social sphere. Brands are meaning." (O'Guinn and Muniz 2010: 133)

The other way around, meaning helps to structure agents' physical and mental worlds and their interactions with brands. The relation between brand and meaning is based on a high incidence in current brand theories plus models (e.g. Arvidsson 2005, Holt 2002, Liebl 2006) and resonates as well in authors' contributions of this volume. O'Guinn and Muniz (2010: 135) put it nicely into a nutshell by using a spatial metaphor which describes a brand as a vessel of meaning. Previously stated in our own words, a brand as a container or vessel carries various content but is only a branded space when meaning is added to the space. Staying with this metaphor, the main 'role' of the brand owner is then to pre-structure or design the initial shape of the vessel and fill it with intended meanings to evoke responses from desired agents.

Once again, we have to emphasize that a brand owner can only try to evoke a specific meaning from the agents. The brand permeates the 'polylogue' between the brand owner and agent and meaning is created or 'co-created' in our terms between the two even if the brand owner did not intend it. Branded spaces are one manifestation to evoke brand meaning. Before we dive into this topic, we would like to approach 'space' to better understand the concept of branded spaces in this volume.

Space

It is common sense to say that space has become a common place in many social sciences, with geography leading the way, due to the renewed interest and transformation of interpretation of what a space is. Under the umbrella term "spatial turn" (Soja 1989: 39), a new understanding of space has developed which regards space as a social category: "(Social) space is a (social) product." (Lefebvre 1991: 30) Following this thought, space is an everyday life phenomenon.

Therefore, space is not only a 'real' thing or a container but also, even more, a social construction and an entity for cultural practices and change as well as social relationships. Space emerges and permeates by movement and perceptions as well as action, interaction and usage of various agents. With regard to cultural practice, Lefebvre (1991: 38-39) formulates a conceptual triad of spatial practice (perceived space), representations of space (conceived space) and representational spaces (lived space) showing the socially constructed multidimensionality of space. However, "if no localization can be determined, the space concept is used only metaphorically" (Löw 2008: 43).

It is, hence, important to mention that we do not want to play physical space against socially constructed space in this book. To the contrary and as a trend for the contributions of this volume, space is neither an absolute given nor a mere construction. Space is an interdependency between the two. This leads to the question how could space be conceptualized to approach branded spaces? The spatial theory of Martina Löw (2008) is a fruitful way as she focuses on the duality of the physical and social dimension treating "spaces as products of action which at the same time have structuring power" (Löw 2008: 33). We briefly introduce her spatial understanding which comprises the two basic and concurrent processes of 'spacing' and 'synthesis' to create a space.

> "*Spacing* means erection, building, or positioning. Examples are the display of wares in a supermarket, the self-positioning of people in relation to other people, the construction of buildings, the surveying of national borders, the networking of computers to form spaces. It is positioning in relation to other positionings. In the case of mobile goods or of people, spacing means both the moment of positioning and movement to the next positioning. Second, the constitution of space also requires *synthesis*, that is to say, goods and people are connected to form spaces through processes of perception, ideation, or recall." (Löw 2008: 35)

The process of spacing is more related to the physical dimension of space whereas synthesis is more connected to the socially constructed dimension of space. It has to be pointed out that Löw narrows the synthesis to single human beings which means that synthesis is a psychological process. We would like to widen this understanding of space to include social processes, and not just a singular psychological process, by drawing from our ideas of brands and applying them to space. First, we do so by asking you to recall the polylogue and co-creation of meaning between the brand owner and the agent in the previous section. Next, we do so by borrowing from Liebl's concept of brand, who differentiates between owner and possessor of a brand because the latter exploits, experiences, interprets, compares and shares fantasies about brands with other agents. Likewise, we now ask you to extend these ideas to agents who could co-creatively synthesize space in their interaction. Specifically, we highlight the fact that interpretation is not stressed by Löw. Only through the social interpretation of space, can agents construct meaning which is a prerequisite for action or interaction.

To summarize briefly and concisely, there are the social processes of co-created synthesis and interpretation to be added to Löw's understanding of space which could be seen as second and third processes, respectively. Spacing, synthesis and interpretation are influenced by physical objects perceived by agents such as buildings, goods or people. "In brief, the day-to-day constitution of spaces involves perceptions that are grounded in both the external effect of social goods and other people and in the perceptual activity of the constituting agent." (Löw 2008: 41) This external effect can be described as an 'atmosphere' which is connected to a specific place. Each place has an atmosphere provoking and instantiating perception and, hence, space-building of diverse agents. Atmospheres are common realities between the perceiver and the perceived (Böhme 1993: 122).

In contrast to spaces, places do not disappear. Places are mainly branded by architecture and design. Therefore, they are prepared for perception and space-building. Places emplace spaces. In other words, if the rhyming is somewhat distracting, places put spaces into position. A concrete place can have different spaces with different practices by different agents superimposed upon it, either one after the other or at the same time as well as in relation to each other or not in relation. While seeming incongruous, there is actually, according to Foucault simultaneity of offerings, a 'heterotopia', that is "capable of juxtaposing in a single real place several spaces, several sites that are in themselves incompatible" (1986: 25). Equally addressing simultaneity, we will add an exaggerated but plausible element for maintaining interest that a place is a vessel for spaces which are vessels for meanings.

Branded Spaces

We will now approach branded spaces for our readers using, first, a qualitative and then a more equation-like method. The first one has been alluded to already and that is the story-like framework. Stories and storytelling are ubiquitous in our world and branded spaces are dependent upon stories and the situations out of which stories emerge. No matter where they are, branded spaces are created in the mind and in communication just like stories. Additionally, meaning is mixed or co-created among brand owners and/or the social milieu and the agents. The next approach is presented as an equation. While it may appear that two ways have been taken in our approach, we see the two as being interrelated. Especially the concepts of spacing, synthesizing and interpreting in the equation lead to story creation. However, we are getting ahead of ourselves in this story and we will return to a sequential narration.

A branded space consists of two defining dimensions, place and space, as well as processes which bring them into being. Place is the more physical dimension of a branded space which becomes a branded place through branding and perceiving. Space is the more social dimension of a branded space which emerges through spacing, synthesizing and interpreting. It has to be said that dimensions and processes are not mutually exclusive but rather distinguished by interdependency and co-occurrence as well as by the idea that the "constitution of space ... generates places, just as places are prerequisite to the coming into being of space" (Löw 2008: 42). The following semantic equation encapsulates the correlation between dimensions and processes:

Branded Space = Place (Branding, Perceiving) + Space (Spacing, Synthesizing, Interpreting)

Branding a place is a complex task as the history of the brand has to be regarded and different people are involved in the branding process like brand owners, architects or designers but also consumers, journalists or demonstrators who occupy a place. While the brand owner's brand meaning is embodied in the branded place, we can also state that the branded place takes on more a life of its own in the imaginations and in the behaviors of the agents. No one is in total control of a branded space. Although the brand image from the owner could be defined as being diluted, it could also be argued that what the brand owner thinks about its branded place could offer people, first, an experience of pure form. The place of a branded space could be regarded as an "inter-textual commodity" (Arvidsson 2005: 245) that anticipates and pre-structures the agency (at least perceiving) of agents. They are "given contours of and raw material for the exercise of their productive agency" (Arvidsson 2005: 247).

The agents' first exercise is *perceiving* of the place especially the raw material like architecture and design. However as mentioned earlier, it is not the raw material itself but the atmosphere of a brand connected to its place that provokes the perceiving of the agents. "The primary 'object' of perception is atmosphere. What is first and immediately perceived is neither sensations nor shapes or objects or their constellations, as Gestalt psychology thought, but atmosphere ..." (Böhme 1993: 125) The fact that branded places pre-structure or manipulates the perception, and hence the emotional and personal reaction, does not automatically imply that branded places discipline the perceiving entirely. They open up atmospheric possibilities without defining how they will be perceived. With an eye towards the equation, perceiving of a branded place is the initial process which is dependent on the specific situation of the agents. Without perceiving of the branded place, there is no branded space at all.

The triad of *spacing*, *synthesizing* and *interpreting* finally creates a branded space. Spacing means that an agent or a group of agents position themselves in the branded place so that 'their' branded space can emerge. It is a social act as an agent positions himself always in relation to other positionings like architecture, design, or other agents. To form a branded space, agents have to connect or synthesize the positionings respectively their perceived atmospheres. During the process of synthesizing agents interpret the spatial configuration of the positionings and make meaning or a story out of it. The process triad to create a branded space is a personal, social and situational experience. The objective of the brand owner is to set more or less precise brand coordinates so that the brand is not diluted too much and experienced consistently up to a certain degree. Within those brand coordinates, agents are free to create their (shared) branded spaces. To summarize briefly, brand owners try to influence and orchestrate the agents' perceiving of the branded place. However without spacing, synthesizing and interpreting by agents, a branded space would not come into being. Therefore, branded spaces are co-created between brand owners and different kinds of agents. Our conceptual approaching to branded space offers guidance for the premises that follow and a springboard for the authors' contributions of this volume.

A Sketch of this Volume

Branded spaces is a complex theoretical and practical phenomenon so that a variety or relationship of current concepts, precepts and interpretations of brand and space is reflected in this volume as well as in the diverse practical and disciplinary backgrounds of the authors. Some contributions explicitly clarify what their understanding of this relationship is. Others have an implicit understanding of branded spaces which arises by reading them. Even if the authors do not constitute some homogeneous whole, their perspectives, concepts and contents of branded spaces coalesce in this volume. One idea that emerges quite often, however, is that stories or narratives are inherently in juxtaposition with branded spaces. Subsequently, we not only wonder how people are approaching branded spaces through use of a story-like framework but also corroborate through the authors' contributions that story-telling is embedded in branded spaces. These two former elements, consequently, lead us to the creative attempt to weave a story-like framework in this section. Hence, a multiplicity of story-telling unfolds.

To address the complexity and the multidisciplinary challenge of branded spaces, we approach this topic via different categories. The decision for the specific categories and under which category we place a contribution is not easy and we acknowledge that others could dispute our categorization with their own reasons which we would applaud and actually encourage. These categories are not definitive or mutually exclusive, as there is considerable overlap in the ways that problems and challenges are defined and theorized. However, we believe there is an inner arguable logic which leads to our setting of the following categories:

- Places and possibilities
- Facts and figures
- Senses and sensualities
- Stories and situations
- Critiques and consequences

Places and Possibilities

Shakespeare said the world is a stage and sooner or later a story unfolds on a stage. Since stories are embedded in branded spaces, then why not conjecture that the world is branded spaces. After all this is the section for possibilities and why not draw this inference. Housing, buildings, communities, cities, states and countries, places by any other name, are often seen as branded places, whether by the condition of purposeful architecture and design or even when there is the avoidance or lack of any kind of design. Branded spaces have dual, sometimes paradoxical elements, and are, consequently, real and imagined or real and not real. Albeit with poetic license, we refer to Shakespeare again and soliloquize 'to be or not to be real'. So even though branded spaces have real boundaries, they do not conform to nature but are symbols. How is this possible with a natural place within destinations? The understanding lies in the principle that the branded spaces concept is not related to nature, in the case of some natural destinations, but rather the experience of the destination as a co-construction of meaning between agents. This section will explore branded spaces as related to destinations among other possible relationships that have their ups and downs between brand owners and agents known as viewers or tourists.

Stephens Balakrishnan and *Kerr* identify in their contribution *The 4D Model of Place Brand Management* the branding of places and nation branding in particular as risky business while warning at the same time that lack of a purposeful design is just as uncertain. They use examples of the United Arab

Emirates to propose and support a four phase model for place branding and place brand management which incorporates the fundamental concept that brands communicate. Place brand management must consider finances, politics and culture because, ultimately, brand management is about managing meaning which in turn have impact on a nation financially, politically, and culturally.

Related to symbols, architecture has a role in a destination's image. Furthermore, according to *Specht*'s contribution *Architecture and the Destination Image: Something Familiar, Something New, Something Virtual, Something True*, architecture can be icons as they can connote or give meaning to the environment, thus, making it worth the while of a tourist's visit. The idea of 'can give meaning' is relative. Not all architecture encourages consumption as a tourist destination. The features on the continuum of unusual to usual tap, respectively, into the tourist's emotional need for uniqueness and orientation. Specht emphasizes and differentiates architecture from other destination symbols as real or physically present which is catching the attention of many stakeholders.

In their contribution *Branding Views Marketing: Lessons to Learn for Destination Management*, *Gronau* and *Adjouri* continue the quest to explore the uncertainty about the application of brand principles to places. Among other intentions, they focus upon the questions about branding tourist destinations and the complexity of identifying a symbol for a country. They are adamant about stressing the emotional or unperceivable elements of a destination as opposed to specific products in order to go beyond the dilemma of the life cycle of a specific product. Additionally, they offer a model for branding tourist destinations and discuss its ramifications.

Housing as a concept for city branding with their built in risks is a current topic. *Klein* and *Rumpfhuber* take another step into risk or possibility in their contribution *The Possibility of a Social Imaginary: Public Housing as a Tool for City Branding*, by considering if social housing with their defined mode of sustainability and resilience is a tool for city branding. The focus is upon Vienna and considers the post-war welfare state as well as recent developments that include the current financial crises and cuts in social programs. They explore Vienna's social housing as an integrated part of the rental market which is argued to keep the rent in the free market relatively low and the quality of housing relatively high.

Facts and Figures

In our material world people usually want the 'real' facts and figures to be convinced. We always want to see something in black and white because this is our collective mind as human beings. Allow us now to be a little overdramatic in the storytelling. While facts and figures are seen as safe, uncertainty lurks. As a matter of fact, no pun intended, facts and figures can be manipulated or just be downright confounding. Consequently, why is this section here? While branded space is not black or white according to theoretical guiding principles but about being more or less branded, we also know branded space is designed space with design solutions with predetermined parameters. Consequently, facts and figures are required for the predetermined parameters. Drama aside, we continue to build our argument for 'facts and figures' by a guiding principle that states branded spaces are 'real' albeit not real at the same time, which allows us to work outside the paradoxical box structure or at least on the peripheral. Aristotle's adage that the whole is greater than the sum of its parts is also applicable to the contributions in the facts and figures section.

As figured out in *Bielzer*'s contribution *Corporate Branded Spaces: A Glance at Today's Diversity and Some Historic Origins*, the experience society clearly plays a critical role in the narration of corporate branded spaces. Specifically, corporate branded spaces are 'built' because they are concisely planned in the corporate marketing for the visitor to contribute to the experience and give meaning to the space by being actively involved in the experience. Social interaction and relations are needed to facilitate success. Likewise, these interpersonal relationships add to the concept that the space is real and not real because it is symbolic space. The types and dimensions of corporate branded spaces are very complex in contrast to usual branding. The customer, financial investments, heterogeneous target groups, multiple stakeholders and profes-sionals working in and visiting the space all add to the complexity of corporate branded spaces.

The value of branding for consumer business, although recognized for centuries, is lacking in real estate business according to *Ankenbrand, Mussler* and *Mussler*. Albeit a few studies focusing on corporate brands in real estate, they identify in their contribution *Brand Value in Real Estate: The Financial Contribution of Property Brands* a need to examine brands of single real estate properties specifically related to the financial value. Their contribution is to begin to answer how and to what extent single property brands sustain the creation of real estate value. Additionally, they give facts and figures in the terms of euros and cents about how this value can be determined.

The boom in giving naming rights for football stadiums and large multipurpose areas for branding purposes beyond the typical geographical feature or famous person is investigated by *Bezold*. In his contribution *Naming Rights for Sports Stadiums: Sponsor versus Club – Who Makes the Proper Brand?* a comparison of selected examples from Germany, Europe in general and the USA is offered. Specifically, he examines the question of how effective this sponsorship tool is and whether a sponsor or the sport's club has more influence on the brand. The classic advertising value analysis is used to unearth interesting facts about the strategic partnerships that are contemporary and possible for the future.

Senses and Sensualities

This is the section where intimacy emerges from the story. Do not expect, however, gratuitous sex related to see it, like it, buy it. This is a story about nurtured affection in a relationship not to mention a scientific story. The senses, in particular the visual and acoustic, have important roles to play as well as sensuality which is connected to how one is inclined to gratify the senses for the sake of aesthetic pleasure. Appeal, however, becomes a question of individuality and interpretation. No matter the intent of branded spaces, they can have different kinds of impact especially in the embodiment of the retina experience.

Front stage are the London flagship stores of Nike and Apple but do not think that stage setting is the same for these two giants reading out in *Palaiologou* and *Penn*'s contribution *The Branded Experience: Decoding the Spatial Configuration of Flagship Stores*. While sight and sensation are engaged in each store to make a transition of the retina experience to one of embodiment that could in principle be recalled at any time, the spatial configuration is sensationally different in regards to orienting or disorienting the customer for their story or brand narration. Why? Each wants to use space to enhance its individual cultural solidarity with its individual marketing profile. The authors use Depthmap for Visibility Graph Analysis to examine if each flagship store creates, in their own words, a configured branded experience and spatially 'tellable' branded story.

Imagine a management strategy to increase sales by trying not to sell anything! Right, it is an unusual idea but one that *Liu* introduces, substantiates and then implements as a case study in her contribution *Applying Theory of Branding Synergy on Consumer Experience and Spatial Design: A Case Study*. Since the cycle of 'see it, like it, buy it' is no longer singularly vital for retail and the importance of how the customer relates to the brand has surfaced, Liu explores how customers can interact with a brand in an intimate way through physical setting. Specifically, two brands are combined and a synergy is created as an event through spatial design. The brands are able to explore new markets by the management process of having the brands be consistent and innovative at the same time by using experience and space. Paradox!? Maybe, maybe not. It is certain, however, that the consumer has been encouraged to participate in the story by telling their own stories with space.

In her contribution *The Conceptual Design of Branded Spaces by Means of Sonic Branding Kastner* leads us into the acoustic arena in the story-like framework of branded spaces and focuses our attention on the impact of sonic branding. Just as there can be processing of the optic nerve experience into one of embodiment, so does the auditory nerve experience lead to a physiological, emotional and cognitive incorporation which we could describe as sensual. Kastner is not a proponent of a noisy stage setting, which would include muzak and jingles, because auditory perception is delicate. In an attempt to give a specific character to space that does not produce negative reactions, acoustic orientation should target feelings of completeness, stability and trust. Consequently, brand managers are strongly encouraged to consult with a sound designer.

Stories and Situations

Owners of a branded place tell stories in order to involve people to co-create a story through their synthesis and interpretation of the perceived information about the place and the way in which it is branded. A story is multidimensional. Secondly, a story is situational. A story can also be fictional or non-fictional. The authors in this book understand these ideas and the contributors in this section actually go one step further in this section to tell the story of branded spaces by, actually, telling us stories. In essence we have stories within the story. Although it is necessary for them to begin with 'once upon a time' and turn on the valve of our empathy, it is not necessary to have an ending. You will begin to create branded spaces connected to a branded place. Enjoy.

Emotion over reason is touted as the undisputable influence to purchase a product. Although there is a consumer need, it is, essentially, to achieve a feeling of a certain standard of being loyal to one's values. Therefore, brands generate trust. *Engl* addresses in his contribution *South Tyrol: Destinations Can Be Brands Too* the question if it is possible for South Tyrol as a tourist destination to establish itself as a brand using the same principles as mentioned before. To gain market shares for the region, he explores South Tyrol as 'synergy rich in contrast' while moving beyond concepts of price war competition and the one dimensional story of one of the most beautiful recreational landscapes in the world. The end of the story is still unknown.

Branded spaces are stories and a brand's story is essential according to *Vihinen* and his contribution *A Guggenheim in Every City*. Managing a branded place is story telling business and Vihinen is a story teller who has experience, battle scars and suggestions for a happy ending. The building boom of cultural projects in Northern Europe has been woven into a patchwork story in which everyone wants a Guggenheim in their city for destination branding. The plot always thickens when the construction experts enter with the shocking news of the usual overspending of the budget to the tune of 100 million euros. White swans become black swans. In actuality there are no villains or heroes but the moral of the story is that professional culture managers should manage these projects with input from construction experts and not the artists or politicians as the primary sources.

The simplicity of 'once upon a time' that ends with 'and they all lived happily after' is not a target in *Dauscher, Dietrich* and *Schmidt-Bleeker*'s contribution *AAALBANIA: Possibilities and Limitations of Nation Branding Using the Example of Albania* because this represents undesired, complexity reduction. Rather, the approach to branded spaces and Albania in particular is translating complex strategic considerations into a simple story but not a simplistic one. While the story can be simple, diversity and otherness as well as conflict and various values build up the complexity. Hence, an exciting and successful branded space can emerge through a narrative brief that deals with the plurality of life. Interest, sympathy, excitement, joy as well as empathy and perhaps even shock are diverse elements that could emerge and reach a diverse audience instead of a limited target audience. Fasten your seatbelt for some twists and turns.

Critiques and Consequences

Following the story-like framework we know that every literary piece, not to mention scientific work, has critics and critiques. This also holds true for our contributing authors on branded spaces because they are quite vocal, so to speak, in their critiques of how to approach branded spaces. Concurrently, we see that they go even one step further with their critical thinking and point out consequences according to choices taken in branded spaces. Each reader must also become a critic himself and decide if there is agreement or not with the premises stated. The content of the readers' critiques as well as the critical reflections of the authors are neither right nor wrong but necessary, in our eyes, in order to approach branded space. Needless to say that complexity arises as necessary ingredient in the story just to add one more 'C' to the section. On second thought, we will warn you about the 'cannibals'.

Miles expresses serious concern about contemporary cities as spaces for consumption in his contribution *Branded Space; Branded Consumers: Spaces for Consumption and the Uncomfortable Consequences of Complicit Communality.* He critiques consumer consumption that draws attention to dissimilarities between social groups that indicate one is flawed or a loser. He argues that some residents' relationship with the city implicates a compromise of a moral nature. Limitless choice as well as 'bottomless pit' consumption is questioned in the branding of space and particularly in galleries and museums. In these branded spaces created by star architects on high-end real estate, 'real' is presented as themes and interactive experiences that are neither real nor in-depth. Nonetheless, people choose to take advantage of the consumer lifestyle offered so there is complicit communality. While branded space has power, there appears to be lack of social responsibility.

The contribution *Cannibal Architecture Hates BANANAs: Post-Communist Rebranding of Historical Sites* focuses attention on the dilemma of branding spaces in urban spaces with historical sites, particularly, in the case of Budapest. Conflicts in the relationship between those who want transformation and those in favor of conservation are examined. *Mureşanu* and *Mureşanu* critique the ideas of the transformationists known as the cannibals and the conservationists referred to as the bananas as well as the consequences that are obtained. The cannibals and the bananas are neither inherently good nor bad characters in this framework but their compromises lead to dissatisfaction and disappointment with the results, ultimately, that they vilify each other.

Leontiadis adds a strong transdisciplinary approach to the narration of branded spaces in her contribution *Syntax of Intervention in Historically Significant Public Open Urban Spaces.* Psychology, anthropology, philosophy and spirituality are woven into a tapestry to harmoniously fit new architectural elements inside public spaces with historical significance. Before taking pen to paper for a plan, one must consider the evolutionary moments of man with his levels of artistic and literary brilliance that are expressed by the historical space. Any architectural outcome ought to be branded rhythms and patterns germane with the heritage space. Leontiadis draws attention to the idea of historical layering that could even bring in the culinary discipline with the idea of layered cakes or strudel although one should be aware of the complexity in this approach. A unified conceptual whole is never simple but always a space to make inhabitants feel at home.

The contribution *Branding as Enabling Knowledge Creation: The Role of Space and Cognition in Branding Processes* takes the reader into the perspectives of cognitive science which are then transposed to ideas that constitute branded spaces. Specifically, branding involves generating some kind of new knowledge in the perceiver. *Peschl* and *Fundneider* go beyond the usual critique that branding is or could be manipulation because the environment controls or determines the mental state, into the constructivist concept that the environment modulates internal knowledge. They explore the question of how branded spaces could trigger the creation of new knowledge regarding a brand. While it may not initially be appealing for the business environment that wishes to manage and calculate, a joint journey of the perceiver, the brand designer, the brand and networks is predicted to be more effective. The key is to enable.

We believe we have successfully entered with this book the unknown territory of branded spaces. It is interesting to note that very few contributors have used the terminology branded spaces but have danced around it with various terms and definitions while staying within the conceptual boundaries of branded spaces. In the introduction we stated our use of a story-like framework and wondered if people would approach branded spaces as lovers, friends, mutual acquaintances or even enemies and if there would be embraces, open arms, a handshake, the cold shoulder or the knife in the back. As is true with all complex relationships, it usually takes time to make a commitment even if the relationship is solid. We believe we have seen this story-like framework of relationships and commitment with the phenomena of terminology usage. Staying within it, the contributors have taken various approaches to branded spaces in their 'storytelling'. Nonetheless, the authors have implicitly or explicitly focused on different aspects of our semantic equation consisting of two dimensions, place and space, and the processes of branding, perceiving as well as spacing, synthesizing, and interpreting in approaching branded spaces. Collectively they explain or tell the complex story of branded spaces. Thanks to all the authors for their contributions and commitment to this volume. We hope that we motivate readers to accompany us in exploring this territory in the future. Indeed, the topic of branded spaces is an inspiring 'playspace' for practice and theory to create a transdisciplinary approach to branded spaces.

References

Aaker, J.L. (1997): Dimensions of brand personality. In: Journal of Marketing, 34(3), 347-56.

Arvidsson, A. (2005): Brands: A critical perpective. In: Journal of Consumer Culture, 5(2), 235-258.

Böhme, G. (1993): Atmosphere as the fundamental concept of a new aesthetics. In: Thesis Eleven, 36, 113-126.

Bruns, A. (2008): Blogs, wikipedia, second life, and beyond: From Production to produsage. New York: Peter Lang.

Coomber, S. (2002): Branding. Oxford: Capstone Publishing.

Domizlaff, H. (1992): Die Gewinnung des öffentlichen Vertrauens: Ein Lehrbuch der Markentechnik. Hamburg: Marketing Journal.

Elliott, R. and Wattanasuwan, K. (1998): Brands as symbolic resources for the construction of identity. In: International Journal of Advertising, 17(2), 131-144.

Escalas, J.E. (2004): Narrative processing: Building consumer connections to brands. In: Journal of Consumer Psychology, 14(1&2), 168-80.

Foucault, M. (1986): Of other spaces. In: Diacritics, 16(1), 22-27. First published (1984): Des espaces autres. In: Architecture, Mouvement, Continuité, 5, 46-49.

Hellmann, K.-U. (2003): Soziologie der Marke. Frankfurt am Main: Suhrkamp.

Hollenbeck, C.R., Peters, C. and Zinkhan, G.M. (2008): Retail spectacles and brand meaning: Insights from a brand museum case study. In: Journal of Retailing, 84(3), 334-353.

Holt, D.B. (2002): Why do brands cause trouble? A dialectical theory of consumer culture and branding. In: Journal of Consumer Research, 29(1), 70-90.

Holt, D.B. (2004): How brands become icons: The principles of cultural branding. Cambridge, MA: Harvard Business School Publishing.

Ind, N., Fuller C. and Trevail, C. (2012): Brand together: How co-creation generates innovation and re-energizes brands. London: Kogan Page.

Kirby, A.E. and Kent, A.M. (2010): Architecture as brand: Store design and brand identity. In: Journal of Product and Brand Management, 19(6), 432-439.

Klingmann, A. (2007): Brandscapes: Architecture in the experience economy. Cambridge, MA: MIT Press.

Kozinets, R.V., Sherry, J.F., DeBerry-Spence, B., Duhachek, A., Nuttavuthisit, K. and Storm, D. (2002): Themed flagship brand stores in the new millennium: Theory, practice, prospects. In: Journal of Retailing, 78(1), 17-29.

Kozinets, R.V., Sherry, J.F., Storm, D., Duhachek, A., Nuttavuthisit, K. and Deberry-Spence, B. (2004): Ludic agency and retail spectacle. In: Journal of Consumer Research, 31(3), 658-672.

Lefebvre, H. (1991): The production of space. First published (1974): La production de l'espace. Paris: Anthropos.

Liebl, F. (2006): From branding goods to hacking brands: A beginner's guide to the brand universe. In: Heusser, H.-J. and Imesch, K. (eds.): Art & branding: Principles – interaction – perspectives. Zürich: Swiss Institute for Art Research, 25-42.

Löw, M. (2008): The constitution of space: The structuration of spaces through the simultaneity of effect and perception. In: European Journal of Social Theory, 11(1), 25-49.

Mikunda, C. (2004): Brand lands, hot spots & cool spaces. London: Kogan Page. First published (2002): Marketing spüren: Willkommen am Dritten Ort. Frankfurt: Wirtschaftsverlag Carl Ueberreuter.

Miles, S. (2010): Spaces for consumption: Pleasure and placelessness in the post-industrial city. London: Sage.

Moor, E. (2003): Branded spaces: The scope of new marketing. In: Journal of Consumer Culture, 3(1), 39-60.

O'Guinn, T.C. and Muniz, A.M. Jr. (2010): Toward a sociological model of brands. In: Loken, B., Ahluwalia, R. and Houston, M.J. (eds.): Brands and brand management: Contemporary research perspectives. New York, NY: Routledge, 133-155.

Pike, A. (2011) (ed.): Brands and branding geographies. Cheltenham: Edward Elgar.

Ponsonby-McCabe, S. and Boyle, E. (2006): Understanding brands as experiential spaces: Axiological implications for marketing. In: Journal of Strategic Marketing, 14(2), 175-189.

Sherry, J.F. (1998): The soul of the company store: Nike Town Chicago and the emplaced brandscape. In: Sherry, J.F. (ed.): Servicescapes: The concept of place in contemporary markets. Lincolnwood, Ill.: NTC Business Books, 109-146.

Sherry, J.F., Kozinets, R.V. and Borghini, S. (2006): Agents in paradise: Experiential co-creation through emplacement, ritualization, and community. In: Carù, A. and Cova, B. (eds.): Consuming experience. London: Routledge: 17-33.

Singh, S. and Sonnenburg, S. (2012): Brand performances in social media. In: Journal of Interactive Marketing, 26(4), 189-197.

Soja, E.W. (1989): Postmodern geographies: The reassertation of space in critical social theory. New York: Verso.

Sonnenburg, S. (2009): Markenmodelle des Involvements: Von der Mission zur Transmission. In: Sonnenburg, S. (ed.): Swarm Branding: Markenführung im Zeitalter von Web 2.0. Wiesbaden: VS Verlag, 73-86.

Toffler, A. (1980): The third wave. New York: Bantam Books.

Woodside, A.G., Sood, S. and Miller, K.E. (2008): When consumers and brands talk: Storytelling theory and research in psychology and marketing. In: Psychology and Marketing, 25(2), 97-145.

Places and Possibilities

The 4D Model of Place Brand Management

Melodena Stephens Balakrishnan / Greg Kerr

Place branding is receiving increased practitioner and academic attention. While the need and benefits are becoming more widely accepted, there is uncertainty as to the application of brand principles to places. Both the similarities and differences between corporate brands and place brands have been given attention in the literature with the consensus being that place branding is more complex. This work identifies some of the issues and processes relative to place brand management. While not purporting to be a definitive model of place branding, a model consisting of four sequential stages is proposed. The 4D model consists of the stages of *deciding, designing, delivering,* and *determining* and is supported by relevant literature and examples from the United Arab Emirates. It is anticipated that the model will contribute to academic work and as well be of benefit to practitioners charged with place branding.

Introduction

It has been established that a place name is a brand and, similar to other types of brands, people can share *a consistent group of characters, images, or emotions* (Simeon 2006) when they recall or experience the place. Location names or place names as brands can identify and differentiate a place from other places (American Marketing Association, 2005 definition of brand). In introducing their *Country Brand Index*, Future Brand (2006: 3) advises:

> "Countries are brands, by design or default. A country brand can be a generic label or ubiquitous wrapper, or can become the compelling glue between political, social and economic pillars of a nation. Brand, when properly conceived, and executed, can elevate a country, focus its tourist offering, fuel its outbound and inbound investment, reframe its reputation and create renewed pride among its citizens."

Not only are country names brands, all place names are brands, and if managed, can potentially deliver the types of benefits proposed by Future Brand for countries. Brands are created (Morgan 1999) and can be managed to influence the meaning of the entity it represents. Brands have a role of communication

(Hankinson and Cowking 1995, Hankinson 2003) and can influence the meanings of identity, image and reputation (Balmer and Greyser 2003). As communicators, corporate brands for instance, compete with communications from an array of sources, including media, customers, employees, competitors and governments. Brand management, therefore, is about managing meaning. With regard to places, Gilmore (2002) claims, it is now a risk *not* to apply a brand strategy to a place name. She suggests that locations that do not seek to brand manage themselves run the risk of being positioned by competitors or other interest groups. As with corporations, the media and even movies can influence the meaning of a place brand. For example, the effect of the movie *Midnight Express* upon the reputation of Turkey (Mutlu 2005) is an example of a movie 'managing the brand'. Effective place brand strategies can counter negative communications (Avraham 2004). Kerr (2007) defines place brand management as "the act of communicating the place brand in a manner to deservedly influence the meaning of the location in the minds of the people who matter to the future of the location".

Academic and practitioner literature has compared and contrasted corporate branding and place branding (Olins 1999). Green (2005: 280) states that while working with stakeholders is a familiar concept, "the stakeholder matrix is considerably more complex in a place branding project". Place brands require multilateral alliances throughout the community and beyond. In addition to the number and nature of stakeholders, it is more difficult to select partners as well as exclude partners. Further, there is not a formal organisational structure and places do not have the same rigid control mechanisms which exist in organizations (Hankinson 2001). Potential partners may decide not to participate or even develop a separate and competing place brand strategy. When compared to corporations, places are less able to exclude groups of users or stakeholders (Kavaratzis and Ashworth 2007).

The need for place brand management is becoming more widely accepted in an environment of more competition and mobility of place markets, particularly corporations and residents (Mommaas 2002). The function of place marketing is increasingly being argued for as a role of government in the era of the "competitive state" (Dickinson 2007). A number of leading authors have called for more research into place branding. Dinnie and Melewar (2008) for instance, state:

> "The field of nation branding is characterised by an increasingly large amount of real world activity, but relatively little rigorous theory building. The domain of nation branding remains under-theorised."

In order to better understand place brand theory and practice, we reviewed the literature on place branding and branding generally and examined place branding issues in the United Arab Emirates (UAE). Although the UAE study was a matter of convenience for the authors, the UAE was chosen for its rapid economic growth and, hence, the attention it draws to marketing and branding. In particular, we were interested in, *what were the issues faced in managing the place brand* and second, *what governments were doing about place branding.* The consolidation of the literature, as well as an examination of issues in the UAE, allowed us to reflect on what might be essential components of place brand management. These are introduced and discussed in the next section.

A Model of Place Brand Management

While not purporting to be a definitive model of place brand management, we identified four essential stages. The 4D Model shown as Figure 1 consists of the stages of *deciding, designing, delivering,* and *determining.*

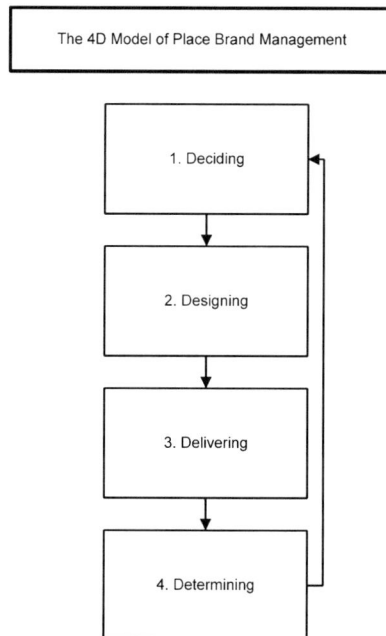

The 4D Model of Place Brand Management

1. Deciding

2. Designing

3. Delivering

4. Determining

Figure 1:   The 4D Model of Place Brand Management. (Authors)

Each of the stages is now introduced and discussed.

Deciding

The *deciding* stage is linking strategy for a place to its brand, that is, its name. The strategic direction of a place should be linked to the brand. The brand orientation argument suggests that brands can be "the starting point for the formulation of a new strategy and an important precondition for a new direction" (Urde 1994: 18). The arguments for a brand orientated corporation put forward by authors including Urde (1994, 1999) and Urde, Baumgarth and Merrilees (2011) are seemingly just as relevant to a place. Important questions include: *What issues are important for the future of a place and why are these issues important?* We argue that some governments in their enthusiasm to implement what they interpret as a brand, such as the hypothetical tagline 'city of flowers', do not commence with strategic planning for the future of a place but seem to take the view 'a brand will save us'. Our point is similar to that of corporate strategy, in that the place strategy and the brand strategy should be aligned. The place brand strategy may be the executive summary of the desired positioning of a place and may be pivotal in driving a new place strategy (see the City of Innovation discussed by Kerr et al. 2007).

In Dubai and Abu Dhabi, the brand strategies have been underpinned by extensive strategic planning in the *Dubai 2015 Strategic Plan* (Government of Dubai 2007), the *Plan Abu Dhabi 2030* (Government of Abu Dhabi 2011) and the *Abu Dhabi Strategic Plan 2008-2012* (Government of Abu Dhabi 2011). The Abu Dhabi Government (2011) states:

> "The process involved two years of coordinated work across 26 of the Abu Dhabi Government entities. Tens of government workshops and 350 meetings have been held, and so far eighteen goals, 202 priorities, 636 targets and 1,499 initiatives have been identified."

Abu Dhabi has a focus on diversification by looking at sustainable industry and infrastructure, urban planning, hospitality, environment (ecology), retail, and culture. Dubai identifies its opportunities as being financial services, professional services, logistics, trade, hospitality, storage, construction with a strong focus on education, particularly at the university level. Once these issues are decided, it is then possible to *design* a brand strategy which may be used to lead the future direction of a place. With regard to places, Van Ham (2001: 2) refers to the changing role of politicians:

"To do their jobs well in the future, politicians will have to train themselves in brand asset management. Their tasks will include finding a brand niche for their state, engaging in competitive marketing, assuring customer satisfaction, and most of all, creating brand loyalty."

The role of government extends from *deciding* to *designing*.

Designing

The design stage should determine which brands will be used to achieve the desired outcomes. Designing the brand strategy is far more than creative design. While creative design is important, Petromilli et al. (2002: 23) remind us that *logos, taglines, jingles,* and *spokespeople* are merely representations of the brand. It should be remembered that with the exception of renaming a place, most place brands, that is the names, have existed for many years and some for thousands of years. Also, similar to diversified corporations, nations have a portfolio of brands. This portfolio can be discussed in terms of brand architecture. Petromilli et al. (2002: 23) state that in the context of a business, brand architecture is the external face of business strategy and must be aligned with and support the business goals and objectives of the business. Different business strategies may require different brand architectures. Petromilli et al. (2002) suggest that strategies for brand architecture fall along a continuum ranging from a *branded house, such as* the dominant brands McDonalds and Sony, to a *house of brands* represented by Unilever and Proctor & Gamble. Nations could be seen as a conglomeration of many brands, consisting of place brands, corporate brands (Dinnie 2008 regarding country of origin effect) and even people brands such as politicians and celebrities. Figure 2 provides examples of place and corporate brands in the UAE. The UAE as a country is not a branded house using the nation brand (UAE) as the one dominant brand as reflected by the examples of McDonalds and Sony, but is more aligned to a house of brands consisting of an array of place and corporate brands. This shows the national brand of the UAE as well as brands relative to Abu Dhabi and Dubai. Examples of relevant corporate brands include Etisalat, Emirates, Emaar with examples of events being Dubai Shopping Festival and Dubai World Cup. An important consideration in place brand management is identifying the brand(s) within the portfolio that may be relevant to a place brand strategy and even drive the strategy.

The brand design considers relationships between brands as well as relationships between the stakeholders. In the case of a place brand, not only the brand portfolio and brand architecture are a way of defining relationships, the opportunity (necessity) exists to build relationships with people behind the brands as well as the consumers of the brand. Jansen (2008: 134) points out:

> "Nation branding is a monologic, hierarchical, reductive form of communication that is intended to privilege one message, require all voices of authority to speak in unison, and marginalize and silence dissenting voices. The message itself is, by design, hyper-visible, but the decision making involved in arriving at it and the multiple agendas incorporated within it are neither legible nor visible in the classic liberal sense."

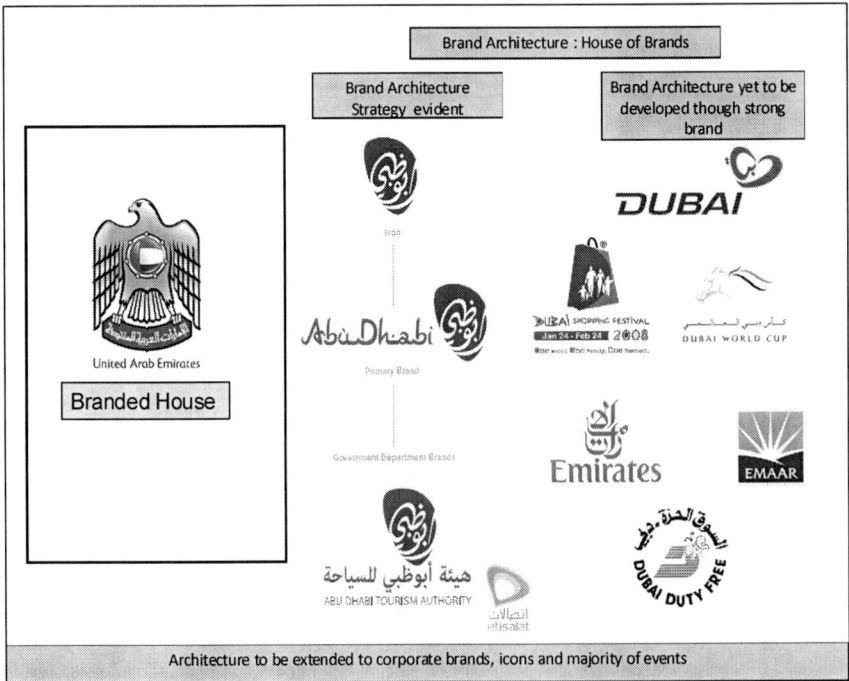

Figure 2:   Examples of Place and Corporate Brands in the United Arab Emirates. (Web Pages)

By way of example, Dubai and Abu Dhabi are part of the brand architecture of the UAE. As global brands, these cities might be seen as strategic brands within the nation's brand architecture.

The identification of the national brand portfolio and the determination of the objectives and the target segments should aid the formulation of the brand design strategy; that is, *which brands can be best managed to achieve the desired objectives?* Identification of the sectors in which a place is to compete is an important consideration which was done by the Abu Dhabi and Dubai governments. Demand analysis should include the identification of existing and likely consumers of the brand, that is, using the brand to appeal to the target segments of place markets, including corporate headquarters, new residents, investors, exporters and tourists (Kotler et al. 1993). It is after *deciding* and *designing* have taken place that consideration can be given to the creative aspects of the brand such as symbols, colours and taglines.

Delivering

As discussed in the introduction, place brands are in many ways more difficult to manage than corporate brands because of complexity of the stakeholder matrix and the less rigid control systems. Morgan and Pritchard (2004: 4) refer to the "political act of place branding". Schwartz (2004) suggests that the point of advertising is often not to provide consumers with useful decision making information, but to sell brands. We suggest however that the selling concept is insufficient for successful brand management. Brand management should at least be more in line with the marketing concept of delivering value to satisfy the wants and needs of members of targeted segments. It is in the context of creating brand loyalty through the value enhancing role of brand management that the brand experience is important.

Brand value derives from how the brand is managed and delivered, not just the name. Ultimately the name should 'mean' some type of value in the minds of place consumers. Included in Kerr's (2007) definition of place brand management is reference to the requirement to *deservedly influence* the meaning of the location in the minds of the people who matter to the future of the location. The brand must deliver on what is promised (and what is decided). Hall (2008: 239) claims that:

> "Place branding is dependent on both hardware: the architectural design of buildings and use of space, which can be used as a differentiator and to communicate an image to a target audience; and software which incorporates marketing strategies to create a place identity through the use of slogans, brand identity programs, and other traditional marketing tools being applied to a place."

Agreeing with Hall's claim, place managers need to deliver on the promise as it relates to the physical environment. This might include attention to landscapes, streetscapes and infrastructure. This tangible hardware not only satisfies functional needs but communicates meanings about a place. While also agreeing with the importance of the 'software' which we argue is included in the *deciding* and *designing* stages of our model, there is also a need for internal stakeholders to deliver the brand. In corporations, employees' ability to deliver on the communicated brand promise is suggested to be dependent on the employees' awareness of the brand (Harris and de Chernatony 2001). Importantly, there is no point projecting a brand to existing and potential customers if the employees of the company do not champion the values of the brand, or worse still, are openly critical of the corporate brand strategy. The ability to link the promise of the corporate brand to the corporate culture is a challenge for managers and marketers. A reduced brand-culture gap can be a source of competitive advantage (de Chernatony 1999, Hatch and Schultz 2003). A similar scenario is evident in the tourism marketing literature where one challenge facing destination marketers is to encourage the host population, that is residents and business proprietors, to deliver on the brand promise (Buhalis 2000). For place branding, therefore, it is important that internal stakeholders are aware of the brand strategy and their role in delivering the brand promise. Kerr et al. (2007) in their study found that even community leaders, the 'senior management' of the community, disagreed on the merits and worth of their place brand. It is argued that acceptance of a place brand requires 'buy-in' on the part of stakeholders, particularly internal stakeholders. In their brand management study of a city, one respondent commented, "it is not just a council initiative, it is a city initiative". Managers of the place brand need to ensure that the brand promise is delivered by its population.

By way of example, the document Abu Dhabi Brand Identity (Office of the Brand of Abu Dhabi 2007) identified the word 'respect' as summarising: "A cherished past and good fortune, Abu Dhabi has nurtured a rich, live and proud culture that delights people that crave authenticity." The document goes further to discuss "Delivering our Promise" and advises:

> "This promise must exist at every stage of conversation with the outside world – from watching a cinema commercial in Berlin, to experiencing a taxi ride to Abu Dhabi Airport to Emirates Palace. Even to the way we brief architects on new buildings." (Section 1.0)

Determining

The fourth stage of our model is *determining* the effectiveness of the stages of *deciding, designing* and *delivering* the brand. This should consider the economic and social objectives set by the leaders of the place. Not only should the objectives be set, the items and measures which can be used to determine the success of the brand strategy also need to be specified. Kerr and Braithwaite (2011) provided a list of key performance indicators for a place. They classify these as being *tangible* and *intangible* outcomes and are shown in Figure 3.

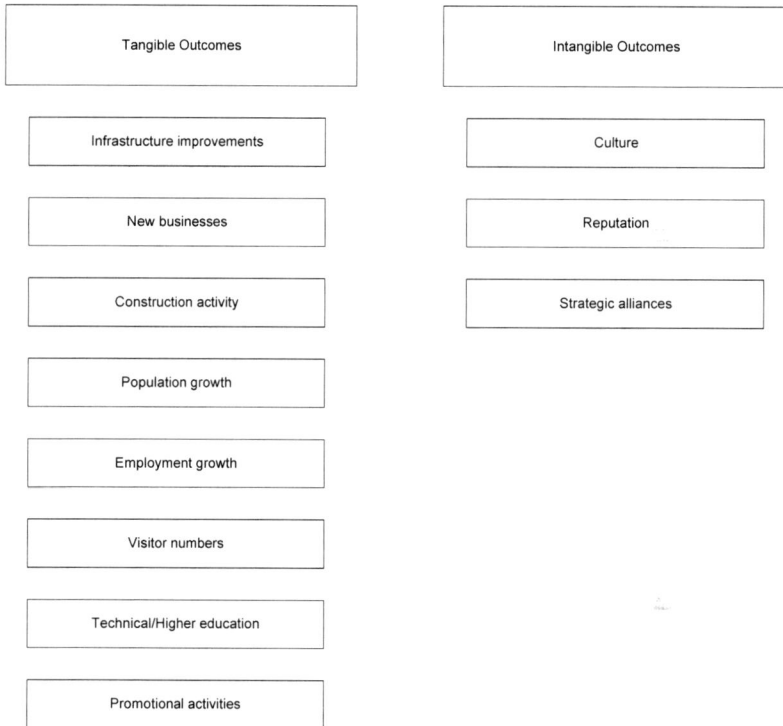

Tangible Outcomes	Intangible Outcomes
Infrastructure improvements	Culture
New businesses	Reputation
Construction activity	Strategic alliances
Population growth	
Employment growth	
Visitor numbers	
Technical/Higher education	
Promotional activities	

Figure 3:   Examples of Measures Which Can Be Related to Brand Strategy and Brand Performance. (Kerr and Braithwaite 2011)

These tangible outcomes shown in Figure 3 can be measured and longitudinal data is often readily available from government departments or business associations. With regard to the intangible outcomes, culture has a focus on the internal stakeholders and instruments can be developed to measure constructs such as commitment to and confidence in the place. Florek (2011) and Hidalgo and Hernandez (2001) provide literature and recommendations regarding place attachment. Reputation has a focus on the summary of images held by external stakeholders. Baxter and Kerr (2010) provide explanations and examples as to the measurement of place identity and place image. Strategic alliances or partnerships formed by a place internally and externally can be identified although their value may be difficult to measure and quantify. Examples of strategic alliances may be public-private partnerships, projects across government departments, as well as corporate joint ventures.

In the case of the UAE, we were not able to find public evidence of steps taken to determine the effectiveness of the stages of brand management proposed in our model. This seems to be consistent with most place brand strategies where measurement of performance of the brand is neglected. Brand tracking studies similar to that used in corporate and product brand management (Keller 2008) are warranted to demonstrate the effectiveness of place brand strategies.

Conclusion

Jansen (2008: 134) points out, "nation branding is, in short, a risky business that can backfire financially, politically, and culturally". It is for this reason that theories of place brand management are needed. While not purporting to be a definitive model of place brand management, we suggest that based on our review of relevant literature and using examples from the UAE, the stages of *deciding, designing, delivering,* and *determining* are necessary for effective place brand management. It is anticipated that the 4D model will contribute to existing works and provide the foundation for more academic work and as well be of benefit to practitioners charged with place branding. To support our claim, we use Stuart's investigation of the then current 1999 models of corporate image formation and corporate identity management and the proposal for a more definitive model of the corporate identity management process. It is both pleasing and exciting to see the increased interest in place brand management not just for the sake of academic pursuits, but also for the importance of the real world economic and social benefits which we and our academic and practitioner colleagues believe can result from place brand management.

References

American Marketing Association (2005): Dictionary of marketing terms. http://www.marketingpower.com/mg-dictionary-view329.php?, 20.06.2007.
Avraham, E. (2004): Media strategies for improving an unfavorable city image. In: Cities, 21(6), 471-479.
Balmer, J. and Greyser, S. (2003): Revealing the corporation. London: Routledge.

Baxter, J. and Kerr, G. (2010): The meaning and measurement of place identity and place image. European Regional Science Association Congress, August 19-23, Jönköping, Sweden.

Buhalis, D. (2000): Marketing the competitive destination of the future. In: Tourism Management, 21(1), 97-116.

De Chernatony, L. (1999): Brand management through narrowing the gap between brand identity and brand reputation. In: Journal of Marketing Management, 15(1-3), 157-179.

Dickinson, S. (2007): Urban regeneration: UK practice. In: Diamond, J., Liddle, J., Southern, A. and Townsend, A. (eds.): Managing the city. Abingdon: Routledge, 16-31.

Dinnie, K. (2008): Nation branding: Concepts, issues, practice. Oxford: Butterworth Heinemann.

Dinnie, K. and Melewar, T. (2008): Call for papers: International perspectives on nation branding: Current trends and future directions. In: International Marketing Review, http://info.emeraldinsight.com/products/journals/call_for_papers.htm?id=146, 15.04.2008.

Florek, M. (2011): No place like home: Perspectives on place attachment and impacts on city management. In: Journal of Town and City Management, 1(4), 346-354.

Future Brand (2006): Country brand index. http://www.docstoc.com/docs/3390366/future-brand-design, 01.03.2009.

Gilmore, F. (2002): A country – can it be repositioned?: Spain – the success story of country branding. In: Journal of Brand Management, 9(4/5), 281-283.

Government of Abu Dhabi (2011): Abu Dhabi 2030. www.dot.abudhabi.ae/download.do?loc=stmp/&file=PlanAbuDhabi2030.pdf, 13.06.2009.

Government of Abu Dhabi (2011): Abu Dhabi strategic plan 2008-2012. http://www.abudhabi.ae/egovPoolPortal_WAR/appmanager/ADeGP/Citizen?_nfpb=true&_pageLabel=P42001137912184442608398lang=en, 09.06.2011.

Government of Dubai, (2007): Dubai strategic plan 2015. http://www.dubai.ae/en.portal?topic,hm_dxbstgplan,1,&_nfpb=true&_pageLabel=3, 13.06.2009.

Green, S. (2005): Defining West London: A case study of the initial stages of a strategic place branding exercise. In: Co Design, 1(4), 277-287.

Hall, C.M. (2008): Servicescapes, designscapes, branding, and the creation of place-identity: South of Litchfield, Christchurch. In: Journal of Travel & Tourism Marketing, 25(3), 233-250.

Hankinson, G. (2001): Location branding: A study of the branding practices of 12 English cities. In: Journal of Brand Management, 9(2), 127-143.

Hankinson, G. (2003): Relational network brands: Towards a conceptual model of place brands. In: Journal of Vacation Marketing, 10(2), 109-121.

Hankinson, G. and Cowking, P. (1995): What do you really mean by a brand? In: Journal of Brand Management, 3(1), 43-50.

Harris, F. and de Chernatony, L. (2001): Corporate branding and corporate brand performance. In: European Journal of Marketing, 35(3/4), 442-456.

Hatch, M. and Schultz, M. (2003): Bringing the corporation into corporate branding. In: European Journal of Marketing, 37(7/8), 1041-1064.

Hidalgo, M. and Hernandez, B. (2001): Place attachment: Conceptual and empirical questions. In: Journal of Environmental Psychology, 21(3), 273-281.

Jansen, S. (2008): Designer nations: Neo-liberal nation branding – brand Estonia. In: Journal for the Study of Race, Nation and Culture, 14(1), 121-142.

Kavaratzis, M. and Ashworth, G. (2007): Partners in coffee chops, canals and commerce: Marketing the city of Amsterdam. In: Cities, 24(1), 16-25.

Keller, K. (2008): Strategic brand mangement. Upper Saddle River, NJ: Pearson Prentice Hall.

Kerr, G. (2007): Location branding of a city: Formulation to implementation. Location Branding Conference, May 10-11, Barcelona, Spain.

Kerr, G. and Braithwaite, B. (2011): A framework for preparing and implementing economic development plans for local government areas in Australia. ANZRSAI Conference, December 6-9, Canberra, Australia.

Kerr, G., Noble, G. and Glynn, J. (2007): The role of community leaders as 'senior managers' in place brand implementation. ANZMAC Conference, December, Dunedin, New Zealand.

Kotler, P., Haider, D. and Rein, I. (1993): Marketing places: Attracting investment, industry, and tourism to cities, states, and nations. New York: Free Press.

Mommaas, H. (2002): City branding: The necessity of socio-cultural goals. In: Patteeuw, V. (ed.): City branding: Image building and building images. Rotterdam: Nai Uitgevers Publishers, 34-47.

Morgan, A. (1999): Eating the big fish. New York: John Wiley & Sons.

Morgan, N., Pritchard, A. and Pride, R. (2004): Destination branding: Creating the unique destination proposition. Oxford: Elsevier Butterworth-Heinemann.

Mutlu, D. (2005): The midnight express (1978): Phenomenon and the image of Turkey. In: Historical Journal of Film, Radio and Television, 25(3), 475-496.

Office of the Brand of Abu Dhabi (2007): Abu Dhabi brand identity. Abu Dhabi.

Olins, W. (1999): Trading identities: Why countries and companies are taking on each others' roles. London: The Foreign Policy Centre.

Petromilli, M., Morrison, D. and Million, M. (2002): Brand architecture: Building brand portfolio value. In: Strategy and Leadership, 30(5), 22-28.

Schwartz, B. (2004): The paradox of choice. New York: Harper Collins.

Simeon, R. (2006): A conceptual model linking brand building strategies and Japanese popular culture. In: Marketing Intelligence & Planning, 24(5), 463-476.

Stuart, H. (1999): Towards a definitive model of the corporate identity management process. In: Corporate Communications, 4(4), 200-207.

Urde, M. (1994): Brand oriemntation: A strategy for survival. In: The Journal of Consumer Marketing, 11(3), 18-18.

Urde, M. (1999): Brand orientation: A mindset for building brands into strategic resources. In: Journal of Marketing Management, 15(1-3), 117-133.

Urde, M., Baumgarth, C. and Merrilees, B. (2011): Brand orientation and market orientation: From alternatives to synergy. In: Journal of Business Research, Article in Press.

Van Ham, P. (2001): The rise of the brand state: The Postmodern politics of image and reputation. In: Foreign Affairs, 80(5), 2-7.

Architecture and the Destination Image: Something Familiar, Something New, Something Virtual, Something True

Jan Specht

Linked to the image of a destination, signs and symbols are important instruments in tourism with architecture playing a dominant role in this context. Recognition value might be one reason, the tourist's search for the photogenic, another. "Environments which are not visually distinct in some way or other are very unlikely to be consumed." (Urry 1995: 189) Konrad thus argues, "for the masses, architecture is a major element of the semiotics of tourism leading to the connotation of a place ... and because of expanding tourism the construction of architectural icons has become an increasingly popular phenomenon" (2010: 228). However, a valid differentiation only works if architecture provides an emotional and unique selling proposition, something unusual, which stands out from the crowd. As Urbain observes, "one of the oldest and most widespread reasons for travelling was to see the unusual" (1989: 107). Yet, architectural symbols carry out a number of further functions in tourism, among those the need to satisfy a tourist's desire for orientation. Hence, to discover the unusual and the unknown is complemented by the requirement to find the familiar (Specht 2009: 100). "The implications and impact of promoted image can affect tourists through the creation of expectations and the desire for image verification." (MacKay and Fesenmaier 1997: 541)

The article investigates the role of architecture as a destination symbol, while demonstrating that, unlike other symbols, it is more than just a virtual ambassador. Physically present as 'real' building structure in a specific place, architecture is impacting a large group of stakeholders.

About the Destination Image and the Role of Signs, Symbols, Icons and Ducks

"Recognition is more important than knowledge." (Auge 2005: 91)

A *symbol* is "something that stands for something else" (Berger 1998: 206). Further defined, it is "anything to which meaning is attributed" (Vernon 1971 cited in Colton 1987: 347). Depending on appearance and context, a cross might, for instance, represent Christianity. Yet, it might have many other meanings too, which ultimately depend on the recognition of individuals and groups of people and their respective behaviours. Therefore, "symbolic interactionism is based on the premise that human society is characterized by the use of symbols and meanings, and that the meanings of various social and nonsocial objects or symbols are derived through the interaction process" (Colton 1987: 346). This interdependency might be as old as the phenomenon of society itself with symbols perceived as such both consciously and unconsciously.

In literature and practice, the terms *symbol* and *sign* are often used in an interrelated or even synonymous way. American philosopher Charles Sanders Peirce (1839-1914), for instance, believed that a *sign* "is something which stands to somebody for something in some respect or capacity" (cited in Zeman 1977: 24). He thus focused on three aspects, the "iconic, indexical, and symbolic dimension" (Berger 1998: 4). The *Oxford English Dictionary*, on the other hand, defines the *symbol* as "a shape or sign used to represent something such as an organization" (Soanes 2002).

Religious and political institutions are represented by all kinds of signs or symbols to which the meaning of power is often attributed. Likewise, those are used by commercial corporations, for instance, in form of brand and product logos, which are also an important instrument in tourism. Depending on type and connotation, they might, under certain circumstances, function as visual ambassadors for a destination, linked to specific values creating desires in a tourist's mind. Such symbols might be humans, such as the *samba dancers,* who stand for Rio de Janeiro and a desired zest for life; or animals, such as elephants and lions symbolising Africa and a spirit of wilderness and adventure. Likewise landscapes, from beaches to mountains, might express natural beauty.

However, when it comes to destination symbols, a dominant role is played by architecture. Recognition value might be one of the reasons, the tourist's search for the photogenic, another. There are only a few landscapes and natural monuments, such as *Ayers Rock* and the *Great Barrier Reef* in Australia, which can be distinctively identified on a photo or a postcard. On the other hand, it is difficult to tell from a picture of a beach or mountainscape where exactly it might be located. However, an important success factor in tourism is to differentiate a destination from its competitors. As Urry argues, "environments which are not visually distinct in some way or other are very unlikely to be consumed" (1995: 189). Ritchie and Crouch point out that both awareness and image of destinations are amongst the most important factors regarding their competitiveness (2003: 243). Hence, if linked to a positive destination image, visually distinct attractions might provide a competitive edge to those who are lucky enough to have them available.

This applies above all to such attractions, whether natural or man-made, that are not reproducible and inseparably connected to their specific locations. Whoever desires to see the *Pyramids* needs to visit Egypt (Figure 1); the *Colosseum* asks for a journey to Rome, and China is the place to go to glance at the *Great Wall*. On the contrary, beautiful beaches or diving spots can be found in many places around the globe and, consequently, there is strong competition between so-called *sea and sun destinations* (Figure 2). And what about destinations that need to enhance their touristic appeal or those which still aspire to become a destination at all, but do not yet have any important attractions? Beautiful and distinctive landscapes are rather 'God-given' opportunities, while it is in the hands of residents and visitors alike to treat them with care and responsibility.

Figure 1:   *Great Sphinx of Giza* (Front) and *Great Pyramid of Giza* (Back). (Author 2007)

Figure 2:   Children at the Beach of French Island *La Reunion*: Appealing,
              but Not Easy to Associate with a Specific Destination.
              (Author 1998)

The human influence in transforming or creating new landscapes is (fortunately)
limited. Architecture on the other hand, can be purpose-designed and
individually adapted or staged, perhaps giving rise to a desired symbol which is
linked to a positive destination image. As Zeman before, also Konrad emphasises
the iconic dimension of the sign as an important aspect for semiotics in tourism
and argues that "because of expanding tourism the construction of architectural
icons has become an increasingly popular phenomenon" (2010: 228). Defined by
the *Oxford English Dictionary* as "a person or thing regarded as a representative
symbol or as worthy of veneration", an icon has thus an inherent positive and
often emotional connotation, while a symbol can also stand for something
negative (Soanes 2002). In the context of architecture and branded spaces,
Klingmann reasons that "because icons have the power to reflect a social system,
they become objects of veneration that are imprinted in people's memory ... so
much so that even after their physical destruction, they leave a permanent trace
in people's minds" (2007: 50). Goeldner and Ritchie, therefore, conclude that
"internationally recognized tourism icons are a powerful draw to any destination
fortunate enough to have inherited or created one ... the challenge for all
destinations is to find 'the stroke of genius' that will uniquely associate the icon
with the destination – and that will, for any number of reasons, become
internationally popular" (2009: 247). As demonstrated for hundreds of years,
such icons will most likely find expression in architectural structures. In an essay

about *Spectacle Architecture,* Smith argues "at the most general level, architecture has for centuries supplied the image economy (the *iconomy,* for short) with key markers, with built stakeholders that seek to arrest the image flow, to tie it down to place, a brand, and a purpose" (2008: 3). Jencks calls attention to the *Seven Wonders of the World* and argues that the practice of the iconic building is old (2005: 23). He believes that after the war, in a period otherwise dedicated to "reconstruction and austerity", the "first modern icon" was Le Corbusier's *Chapelle Notre-Dame-du-Haut,* in the French region of Franche-Comté (Figure 3). In fact, even in the present day, Ronchamp is mainly known for its chapel which long ago became more than a destination symbol but a destination in itself.

The reasons for an (architectural) object to become significant for tourism and eventually a destination symbol, a famous icon uniquely associated with a specific place, are still not clear. However, being photogenic and represented in international media definitely has an impact and interrelates with further factors. Yet, whether historical or contemporary, a valid differentiation only works if architecture provides an emotional and unique selling proposition; or, as Grötsch calls it, a "unique aesthetic proposition" (2006: 280). Once again, while taking Gehry's Guggenheim Museum in Bilbao (Figure 4) and Calatrava's Milwaukee Art Museum as contemporary examples, Schwarzer holds their "iconoclastic form" responsible for being chosen "among other possible designs. At the time of their construction, they looked like no other architecture" (2005: 25). In their book *Learning from Las Vegas,* Venturi et al. name such buildings "ducks" that are structures which are "permeated with naively or gratuitously expressive values", while relying on their mere form. The term derives from a poultry restaurant of this very shape, on Long Island, USA (1978: 130). Yet, while the expressive and often "iconoclastic form" of the "duck" is shaped on purpose, a similar outcome might even result from chance or mistake, as the example of the *Leaning Tower of Pisa* demonstrates. "Completed in 1350, the tower became a tourist icon because of an engineering error." (Judd 1999: 265)

As a matter of course, the types of tourism need to be differentiated. An architectural symbol or icon might not have the same importance or meaning for a *recreational tourist* seeking a beach holiday, as it has for a *cultural tourist* or an *urban tourist.* Still, even *sea and sun destinations* might seek 'the architectural stroke of genius' in the form of an architectural icon that will make them easily recognizable. An example is the Spanish resort island of Tenerife, where Santiago Calatrava designed the *Auditorio de Tenerife 'Adán Martín',* an iconic concert hall with a distinctive and emblematic roof structure. Opened in 2003, this exemplary *duck* is today considered the landmark of the island's capital, Santa Cruz de Tenerife (Borowski 2007: 248). Yet, in his book *The*

Iconic Building, Jencks strongly criticises Calatrava's design and writes it was "meant to do for that port city what iconic architecture did for the ports of Sydney and Bilbao – transform the economy – and it has resulted in one of the biggest empty gestures in architectural history" (2005: 138). In a report about city tourism and culture, the Research Group of the European Travel Commission and the World Tourism Organization, therefore, warns "that the danger is that the context will dominate the content. Only when both the content and the context are of 'signature' level can they succeed over a long(er) period of time" (2005: 43). What is valid for the building itself applies even more to the broader context of the destination. "To rely on the icon is to undermine the accepted value of tourism to the destination. Certainly it can reduce the more nebulous benefits flowing from an appreciation of other people's history, heritage, values, culture, anthropology, cuisines, living and other habits" (Human 1999: 83). Bilbao might be the prime example of a destination focusing only on a few architectural icons. As Lee writes in the *New York Times*, "the city lacks the critical mass of attractions … architecture alone does not a city make. Bilbao is all dressed-up, but hasn't figured where to go" (2007).

Figure 3:   *Chapelle Notre-Dame-du-Haut de Ronchamp*, France. (Author 2010)

Figure 4:   *Guggenheim Museum Bilbao*, Spain (Front): Contemporary "Duck"
              and Controversial Destination Symbol. (Author 2011)

The Tourist's Desire to Go and See Something New, While Also Seeking Something Familiar

"The traveler sees what he sees, the tourist sees what he has come to see."
(Gilbert K. Chesterton cited in Konrad 2010: 227)

According to Urbain, "one of the oldest and most widespread reasons for traveling was to see the unusual" (1989: 107). He quotes Jousset, who observed as early as in the 19th century that since "the common-place spreading nearer and nearer covered everything with a uniform grey color", one had to travel far to find something new (1860: 1). What was true at that time has not lost any of its relevance today. On the contrary, the continuously increasing stimulus satiation provokes a likewise increasing stimulus threshold. What was regarded as spectacular yesterday might today be perceived as trivial. For tourism developers, this leads to the need for ever new attractions which are (and, at best, remain) unique and appealing. Not an easy task as demonstrated by Las Vegas, 'the capital city' of spectacular architectural icons. "Las Vegas might be the prime example of a location where there are only signature buildings, and consequently, the *Eiffel Tower*, *Campanile*, a volcano, *Statue of Liberty* and the *Great Pyramid* become boring once the next new casino is built." (Shaw 2007: 82)

On the other hand, there are also examples of significant architectural landmarks which have not lost any of their appeal for tourism, although the initial triggers for their fame no longer exist. Size, for instance, is a strong force of attraction with historical examples from the *Great Wall of China* to the *Pyramids of Giza*. Architectural 'superlatives' have always been an expression of power and at the same time attractors of floods of pilgrims and other visitors, a convenient synergy which has been appreciated by religious and secular rulers for centuries and might as well have given inspiration to one destination developer or another. Hence, since the biblical *Tower of Babel*, there is a perpetual and increasingly faster competition for the tallest structures (Figure 5 and 6). When in 1889 the *Eiffel Tower* in Paris surpassed the *Washington Monument*, it represented the tallest building in the world. It took over 40 years until the slightly taller *Chrysler Building* at 319 metres in New York City was constructed. However, only 11 months later within the same city, the (without antenna spire) 381-metre tall *Empire State Building* followed. It stood as the world's tallest building for 40 years until the construction of the *World Trade Center* once again in New York City in 1972. In 1998 and many broken records later, the *Petronas Towers* in Kuala Lumpur, Malaysia, represented the tallest buildings in the world, surpassed by *Taipei 101*, Taiwan, in 2004. Since 2010 *Burj Khalifa* in Dubai, United Arab Emirates, holds the record at 829 metres. Yet, Saudi Arabian Prince Al-Waleed bin Talal has already signed the construction contracts for the *Kingdom Tower* which is intended to be the first to break the one-kilometre mark (Reuters 2011).

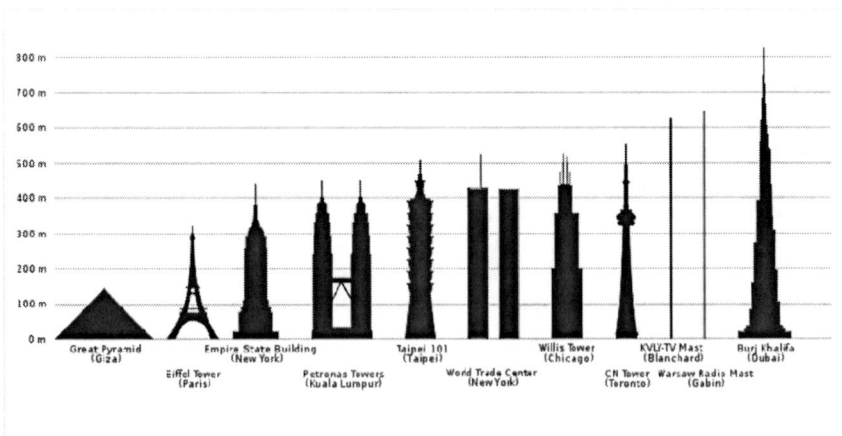

Figure 5:   Examples of Current and Previous Height Record Holders with Significance for Tourism. (Rama 2009)

Skyscrapers are "the iconography of the city" (Gilmore 2004: 173). Whether as single buildings, e.g. *Empire State Building*, New York, or as structural urban ensembles, e.g. *Manhattan Skyline,* New York, skyscrapers stand for the contemporary urban destination like almost no other type of building. And often, being the tallest one also means being the most famous. Yet, sometimes fame lasts longer than merit, as applied to all the previously mentioned towers. Although they might have lost their records as the tallest structures in the world, they never lost their touristic significance. On the contrary, today many of them succeed in attracting more visitors than ever. Urry noted to this effect that "first, there is seeing a unique object, such as the Eiffel Tower, the Empire State Building, Buckingham Palace ... They are famous for being famous, although such places may have lost the basis of their fame" (2002: 12).

Figure 6:   *Burj Khalifa*, Dubai, UAE (Left), and *Petronas Towers*, Kuala Lumpur, Malaysia (Right). (Author 2010, 2011)

In a study about determinants of tourism destination competitiveness in Asia Pacific, Enright and Newton discovered that, for the urban destinations Singapore, Hong Kong and Bangkok, the *well-known landmarks* ranked 4th to 5th while *interesting architecture* ranked 9th to 10th on a scale of 15 attractors ranked by 'importance mean scores' among visitors (2005: 345). In fact, with the overabundance of propositions in tourism, well-known landmarks carry out a number of functions. Among those is also the need to satisfy a tourist's natural desire for orientation. As Specht (2009: 100) points out:

"The tourist ... wants to feel safe in his selected holiday destination – not only safe in a physical manner, but also protected against disappointment. Vacation time is valuable and must not be wasted. Therefore the desire to discover the unknown is complemented and sometimes even substituted by the requirement to find the familiar ... Seen for a hundred times in pictures, movies, books and the internet, the *Eiffel Tower* is familiar long before the tourist has even visited Paris."

Hence, Baloglu and Brinberg claim that "future research should take into consideration an individual's familiarity with the destination because of its potential influence on image formation in tourism literature (1997: 14). MacKay and Fesenmaier state in an article about image formation in tourism that "image is subjective knowledge. The implications and impact of promoted image can affect tourists through the creation of expectations and the desire for image verification" (1997: 541). "Once a consumer decides to travel, he or she expects a rewarding experience from the trip. The traveler's anticipations are derived from the image the traveler has of the destination." (Gartner 1989 cited in Leisen 2001: 51) Yet, a symbol or well-known landmark linked to the destination image does not only satisfy a visitor's expectation, the entire visit might be validated by means of it. Goeldner and Ritchie take Paris' *Eiffel Tower* as an example and claim it "one of the world's most instantly recognizable icons" and a "must-see structure for all visitors to France. A photo taken beside the tower is a lifelong treasure for many tourists" (2009: 247). In fact, a picture alongside the *Eiffel Tower* is the ultimate proof of having been in Paris for the visitor as well as for those who are staying at home but are aware of this specific destination symbol (Figure 7). Even before a visitor's return, his pictures might be uploaded to *Facebook*, *Picasa* or other *Web 2.0* applications. Thus, the visitor is sharing his travel experience with family and friends while at the same time fostering a common understanding of destination symbols and images. Once again, he contributes to the "self-reinforcing 'closed circle of representation' in which tourist photographs both reflect and inform destination images" (Urry 1990 cited in Garrod 2009: 346).

However, photos are not the only popular proof of a tourist's visit to a destination. According to Garrod "like tourist photographs, postcards represent a 'trophy' of the tourist gaze: tangible evidence that the trophy-bearer has visited the destination and in some sense consumed it" (2009: 348). In fact, postcards often carry the same symbols and icons of a destination the visitor is already familiar with and seeks to capture in his own photos. Furthermore, besides postcards, tourists can also get physical replicas of their 'favourite' attractions (Figure 8). "Souvenirs, the material artefacts of tourism" (Benson 2004: 33), are present everywhere and available in almost any form and size. The *Eiffel Tower* made out of metal, glass or wood, in a snow dome, on a t-shirt or as a key ring shows there are no limits to the power of commercial imagination. Contrary to landscapes, architectural icons are ideal to be transformed into tangible memorabilia, while, as a result, not only occupy a virtual position in a tourist's mind, but also a physical place in his living room.

Figure 7:   *Eiffel Tower*, Paris, France: An Easy Recognizable Icon for Tourists. (Author 2010)

Figure 8:   Miniatures of the *Eiffel Tower*: Material Artefacts and Memories of a Visit to Paris, France. (Author 2010)

The 'Virtual' and the 'Real' Symbol – and Why One Is Not Just Like Another

"Among the various things that make an iconic building successful, one ... is its relationship to local society." (Jencks 2005: 48)

Nowadays most corporations employ a so-called logo which is described in the *Oxford English Dictionary* as "a symbol or other small design adopted by an organization to identify its products, uniform, vehicles, etc." (Soanes 2002). Hence, the design of a bitten-into apple stands for a technology company, the image of a jaguar for a car manufacturer and a shell represents a multinational oil and gas company. The success and sustainability of such logos depend on their recognition value and the perception and ability of targeted customer groups to relate them to specific brands and products.

Evans believes that "logos have been used at least since Ancient Greece as a form of shorthand that communicates specific information using a minimum of visual support to refine and condense a range of complex, even disparate, meanings and knowledge in one integrated symbolic image (Lip 1995)" (2003: 421). For tourism destinations, architectural structures often serve as such 'symbolic images'. Yet, in order to become an appealing tourism attraction and, furthermore, to be widely accepted as a destination symbol, architectural structures need to comply with a range of requirements, ultimately depending on each individual context. According to Konrad, "most tourist attractions work with a code that is easy to decipher – height, size, shape, typology, materials, and so on" (2010: 229). Taking the *Sydney Opera House* as an example, he explains, "the major semiotic level is the syntax, the shape. We perceive a shell-like structure in front of an open field of water. The tourist reads this uniqueness as an attraction and that makes the opera house an often photographed building" (2010: 229). A distinctive shape might also facilitate media distribution which might then further intensify the recognition value of the building and, in the long run, turn it into an unquestioned and enduring destination symbol, into a 'must-see icon'. Providing a distinctive form, some architectural icons, as *Sydney Opera House* and the *Eiffel Tower* in Paris, are now so well established in tourism and media that, even when simplified or displayed in a strongly abstract manner, they can most likely be recognised and linked to a specific destination (Figure 9).

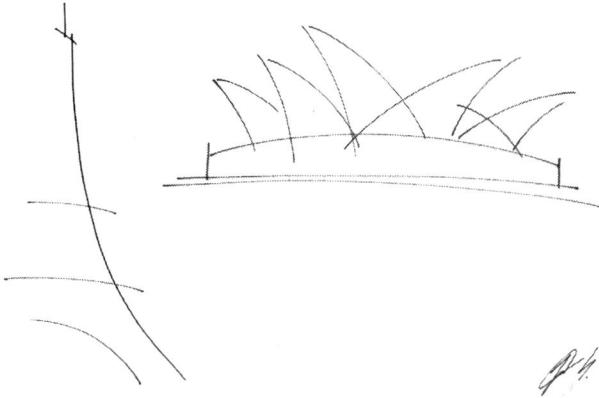

Figure 9:   Simplified Pictograms of the *Eiffel Tower*, France (Left), and the
                 Sydney Opera House, Australia (Right): Remaining Recognition
                 Value Despite Strong Abstraction. (Author 2009)

An example is also the logo of 'KölnTourismus' which is the official tourism
board of the German city of Cologne. The main attraction and an unquestioned
destination symbol of Cologne is the gothic *High Cathedral of Sts. Peter and
Mary* also referred to as *Kölner Dom*. The iconic landmark was classified as a
UNESCO *World Heritage Site* in 1996. KölnTourismus integrated the cathedral
into its logo by means of the transparent simplification of its two characteristic
spires. The resulting umbrella brand links the destination Cologne to its most
famous landmark while still allowing space for other content (Figure 10).

Figure 10:   Umbrella Brand of KölnTourismus on a Panorama Picture of the
                City of Cologne, Germany. (KölnTourismus GmbH 2011)

Yet, despite many examples of architectural destination symbols used in tourism
marketing and branding, such physical structures are very different from virtual
symbols used for other consumer products. When Belgian artist René Magritte
creates 'La Trahison des Images' [The Treachery of Images], showing a pipe, he
writes below it, "Ceci n'est pas une pipe" [This is not a pipe] (Figure 11). He
later explains, "Could you stuff my pipe? No, it's just a representation, is it not?
So if I had written on my picture 'This is a pipe', I'd have been lying!" (Magritte
and Miller 1977: 71).

     In fact, as Magritte expresses, a painted pipe does not fulfil any function of
a physical one apart from having a similar appearance. Hence, it is not 'real', not
'true', but just a sign, an image of an object, which does or does not physically
exist. As Eco writes, "a sign is everything that can be taken as significantly
substituting for something else. This something else does not necessarily have to
exist or actually be somewhere at the moment in which sign stands for it" (1976:
7). Yet, unlike other symbols, architecture does physically exist and is located
somewhere which eventually has a major impact on its application as a
destination symbol and within a logo.

Figure 11:   La Trahison des Images. (Magritte 1929)

Companies might choose amongst almost any kind of sign to represent their brands and products. Sometimes these symbols do not even logically correspond to the products they stand for, as is the case of Apple using the image of bitten-into fruit to represent consumer electronic products. As long as the targeted consumers make the link between the sign and the product, its original meaning becomes irrelevant. The same applies to the American restaurant chain and international franchise Pizza Hut which uses a red hat to represent its brand and products. Yet, while the connection between the image of a piece of headgear and American fast food might not be obvious, the company's name and word mark of the logo 'Pizza Hut' are directly linked to the physical place of consumption, the pizza 'hut' or pizza restaurant. Depending on its strategy, the target markets and the general *Zeitgeist*, Pizza Hut might at any time decide to relaunch its logo, to adapt the form or colour or even to use a completely different design. Ultimately, it is just a virtual symbol owned by a specific company while impacting a fairly limited group of stakeholders. Things change when it comes to the related architecture(s). Hence, while the 'virtual' hat serves representational functions only, the 'real' hut (or restaurant) consists of physically existing architecture thus providing, first and foremost, space to process and consume the company's products. Located in a specific place, it has to adapt to an individual built environment as well as to a specific cultural context. At the same time, its physical presence and any related change might impact a large range of stakeholders from owners to customers to employees to neighbouring residents.

Figure 12:   'Virtual' Logo of Pizza Hut (Left: Pizza Hut Germany 2011) and a 'Real' Pizza 'Hut' in Zhuhai, China (Right). (Author 2011)

Conclusion

What applies to corporate architecture, applies a fortiori to architecture as a destination symbol. Such a symbol is not only linked to a specific destination, it represents it together with its residents and the related culture. Hence, in general a destination symbol concerns a much larger group of stakeholders than corporate architecture does which is involving visitors and residents from far beyond the object's direct neighbourhood. As a matter of course, just as with corporations, destinations can also relaunch their logos, whether containing architectural elements or not. Yet, the physical architectures behind them cannot be changed as easily or be adapted to a new style or *Zeitgeist*. On the contrary, any intrusion into the (built) environment might have long-term effects. A company, first of all, has to keep an eye on its customers when choosing an appropriate brand or product symbol. Yet, a destination cannot only focus on the customer group of tourists, but needs to consider, first and foremost, the requirements of its own residents. Only a symbol accepted by those whom it represents, the people living and defining the culture of a place, can be successful in the long term which is a fact developers and politicians should keep in mind when intending to copy the 'Bilbao Effect' in order to create a new image of a destination and thus increase the numbers of visitors.

While visitors can leave after having gazed at a destination's architecture, the residents will have to stay and live with it, whether they want to or not. Klingmann concludes in *Brandscapes: Architecture in the Experience Economy* that "architecture is more than an image. Unlike products, architecture is characterized by an enduring public presence that defines our environment more than any other brand as a lived, day-to-day experience" (2007: 327). Hence, whether promoted as a destination symbol or involved in any other way in the branding process of space and place, architecture always needs to be understood and assessed within an individual overall context that is linked to its large group of stakeholders.

References

Auge, M. (2005): Contemporary tourist experience as mis-en-scène. In: Ockman, J. and Frausto, S. (eds.): Architourism: Authentic, escapist, exotic, spectacular. Munich: Prestel, 88-91.

Baloglu, S. and Brinberg, D. (1997): Affective images of tourism destinations. In: Journal of Travel Research, 35(3), 11-15.

Benson, S. (2004): Reproduction, fragmentation, and collection: Rome and the origin of souvenirs. In: Lasansky, D.M. and McLaren, B. (eds.): Architecture and tourism. Oxford: Berg, 15-36.

Berger, A.A. (1998): Media analysis techniques. Thousand Oaks: Sage.

Borowski, B. (2007): Teneriffa. Ostfildern: Karl Baedeker.

Colton, C.W. (1987): Leisure, recreation, tourism: A symbolic interactionism view. In: Annals of Tourism Research, 14(3), 345-360.

Eco, U. (1976): A theory of semiotics. Bloomington: Indiana University Press.

Enright, M.J. and Newton, J. (2005): Determinants of tourism destination competitiveness in Asia Pacific: Comprehensiveness and universality. In: Journal of Travel Research, 43(4), 339-350.

Evans, G. (2003): Hard-branding the cultural city: From Prado to Prada. In: International Journal of Urban and Regional Research, 27(2), 417-440.

Garrod, B. (2009): Understanding the relationship between tourism destination imagery and tourist photography. In: Journal of Travel Research, 47(3), 346-358.

Gartner, W.C. (1989): Tourism image: Attribute measurement of state tourism products using multidimensional scaling techniques. In: Journal of Travel Research, 28(2), 15-19.

Gilmore, F. (2004): Brand Shanghai: Harnessing the inner force of people and place. In: Morgan, N., Pritchard, A. and Pride, R. (eds.): Destination branding: Creating the unique destination proposition. Oxford: Elsevier Butterworth-Heinemann, 169-184.

Goeldner, C.R. and Ritchie, J.R.B. (2009): Tourism: Principles, practices, philosophies. Hoboken: John Wiley & Sons.

Grötsch, K. (2006): Design und Architektur als Instrument der Innovation im Tourismus. In: Pikkemaat B., Peters, M. and Weiermair, K. (eds.): Innovationen im Tourismus: Wettbewerbsvorteile durch neue Ideen und Angebote. Berlin: Erich Schmidt Verlag, 277-287.

Human, B. (1999): Kodachrome icons: Photography, place and theft of identity. In: International Journal of Contemporary Hospitality Management, 11(2/3), 80-84.

Jencks, C. (2005): The iconic building. New York: Rizzoli.

Jousset, P. (1860): Un tour de Mediterranee. Paris: Librairies-Imprimeries Réunies.

Judd, D.R. (1999): Constructing the tourist bubble. In: Judd, D.R. and Fainstein, S.S. (eds.): The tourist city. New Haven: Yale University Press, 35-53.

Klingmann, A. (2007): Brandscapes: Architecture in the experience economy. Cambridge: The MIT Press.

Konrad, D. (2010): Collecting the icon or: Semiotics of tourism. In: Richter, J. (ed.): The tourist city Berlin: Tourism & architecture. Salenstein: Braun, 227-235.

Lee, D. (2007): Bilbao, 10 years later. In: The New York Times, September 23.

Leisen, B. (2001): Image segmentation: The case of a tourism destination. In: Journal of Services Marketing, 15(1), 49-66.

Lip, E. (1995): The design and Feng Shui of logos, trademarks and signboards. New York, NY: Prentice Hall.

MacKay, K.J. and Fesenmaier, D.R. (1997): Pictorial element of destination in image formation. In: Annals of Tourism Research, 24(3), 537-565.

Magritte, R. and Torczyner, H. (1977): René Magritte: Signes et images trans. by Miller, R. (1977): Magritte, ideas and images. New York, NY: H.N. Abrams.

Magritte, R. (1929): La trahison des images. www.shimon-yanowitz.com/art/Magritte, 11.09.2011.

Rama (2009): Wikimedia commons: Cc-by-sa-2.0-fr. http://en.wikipedia.org/wiki/File:BurjKhalifaHeight.svg, 12.10.2011.

Research Group of the European Travel Commission and the World Tourism Organization (2005): City tourism and culture: The European experience. Madrid: World Tourism Organization.

Reuters (2011): Höchstes Gebäude der Welt: Saudis bauen Kilometer-Turm. In: Spiegel Online, September 23. www.spiegel.de/reise/aktuell/0,1518,778180,00.html, 24.09.2011.

Ritchie, J.R.B. and Crouch, G.I. (2003): The competitive destination: A sustainable tourism perspective. Cambridge, MA: CABI Publishing.

Schwarzer, M. (2005): Architecture and mass tourism. In: Ockman, J. and Frausto, S. (eds.): Architourism: Authentic, escapist, exotic, spectacular. Munich: Prestel, 12-31.

Shaw, G.B.C. (2007): Tourism by design: An analysis of architectural tourism and its influence on urban design from 1997 to 2007, PhD thesis. In: ProQuest Dissertations and Theses database (UMI Number: 3329667).

Smith, T. (2008): Spectacle architecture before and after the aftermath: Situating the Sydney experience. In: Vidler, A (ed.): Architecture: Between spectacle and use. Williamstown, MA: Sterling and Francine Clark Art Institute, 3-24.

Soanes, C. (2002): The paperback Oxford English Dictionary. Oxford: Oxford University Press.

Specht, J. (2009): The role of architecture in tourism destination development and branding. In: Krakover, S. and Uriely, N. (eds.): Proceedings of the conference on tourism destination development and branding, held 14-17.10.2009 at Ben-Gurion University of the Negev. Eilat: Ben-Gurion University of the Negev, 98-106.

Urbain, J.-D. (1989): The tourist adventure and his image. In: Annals of Tourism Research, 16(1), 106-118.

Urry, J. (2002): The tourist gaze: Leisure and travel in contemporary societies. London: Sage.

Urry, J. (1995): Consuming places. London: Routledge.

Venturi, R., Brown, D.S. and Izenour, S. (1978): Learning from Las Vegas. Cambridge, MA: MIT Press.

Vernon, G.M. (1971): Aspects of symbolic interaction theory, unpublished manuscript. Salt Lake City, UT: University of Utah.

Zeman, J.J. (1977): Peirce's theory of signs. In: Sebeok, T.A. (ed.): A perfusion of signs. Bloomington, IN: Indiana University Press, 22-39.

Branding Views Marketing:
Lessons to Learn for Destination Management

Werner Gronau / Nicholas Adjouri

A review of the literature on branding in general, and on destination branding more specifically, raises several questions about the branding of tourist destinations. What is clear is that confusion exists in the concept of 'brand' in the tourist destination context. Several propositions will be developed and explored in regards to the lack of clear definitions regarding branding and marketing, the confusion between brand and image, the lack of conception of similarities and differences between branding for consumer products and tourist destinations, the difficulty of identifying one symbol for countries, and the lack of commonly-known brands of tourist destinations. Furthermore, the complexity of generating one specific brand based upon a consensus of various different stakeholders within a destination will be addressed. The paper will propose a model of branding and its ramifications in the tourism destination context as well as providing several methodological, theoretical and practical implications.

Branding versus Marketing

It's a shame. In many cases branding and marketing are stated as the very same thing over and over again. Marketing, design and advertising agencies pride themselves as branding professionals and promise their clients to create a comprehensive and imperishable brand strategy besides a creative advertising campaign. Is this Bullshit-Marketing-Promotion-Bingo or does it contain a grain of truth? Still it is not that simple. Steps, which are common in practice, are not clarified in theory yet. A look back at marketing theory shows that, for a long period, branding was seen as a part of product policy partly because branding could also be found in communication policy, as it also involves creative aspects like symbol creation, packaging or even advertising and public relations. The brand as an integral part of a product strategy was seen as a special way of labeling and presentation of a product. Of course, it also was distributed in a special way and promoted communicatively. This usually happened with great emphasis on advertising to gain a high level of awareness as fast as possible.

Therefore, it is not surprising that this is still willingly seen in the advertising practice. That product and brand development are two very different aspects will not be clear until a second glance. Two examples will prove that. Sony is a famous and successful brand. But when you think about typical products of Sony, many different success stories will come into your mind from the Walkman to the Trinitron TV to the entertaining movies of Sony Entertainment. It is very important to notice that the product life cycle is quite short. Or in other words, products like Trinitron are fading because they come and go. The brand Sony itself remains.

A second example is the Finnish company Nokia which faces some problems but is unquestionably still a global brand. These days Nokia stands for mobile hardware, but in the past, the company also produced products like cables, rubber boots, tires, satellite receivers, etc. In Finland, you can still find rubber boots of this brand but they are a relic from past times. Again, the brand survives its products. It's a natural law.

Despite this, the brand is still designated as a part of marketing and usually seen in connection with a product. The reason is probably that people have a lack of abstract thinking which means they like to hold on to tangible things. In addition, the marketing reality looks different from the theoretical depiction. In the theory, marketing consists of the marketing-mix, mostly the four P's of product, price, place and promotion which is completely different in practice. In enterprises, the marketing department is responsible for the advertising, the presence on fairs and other operational-communicative topics. Often public relations as part of promotion within the marketing-mix and also the Internet or social media are outsourced and, therefore, no part of marketing. Hence, the subject branding is often supervised by the marketing departments, whereas there is the strict rule that the brand should always be under control of the management board.

But as the times changed and the markets became saturated and partly crisis-ridden, branding and marketing had to be adjusted in a different way. The conclusion is that the classical marketing point of view changed slowly in the last years. The background is that the brand is increasingly perceived as a strategy that concerns the entire company and with this, all divisions and departments. So far so good, but what is the exact difference between branding and marketing?

The difference can be found in the basics. The fact is marketing developed as a consequence of economy. Branding by contrast is a result of society. What does this mean? Marketing requires the market economy. A brand on the other hand works in every kind of economy and society. This is a fundamental difference.

A look in history shows the difference. Marketing emerged and developed as the supply exceeded the demand. There simply were more products than consumers. Solutions had to be found to make the products interesting to the customers. Marketing is a wide-range selling tool which contains strategic and operative tools. Thus, the competition between enterprises is both a crucial factor and characteristic of marketing. Certainly, even brands compete. Brands also develop in unsaturated markets as well as in monopolistic markets. Even in the socialistic planned economy, where the demand exceeded the supply by far, brands developed. Along this way some famous brands from the former GDR, like Florena skin care, Rotkäppchen sparkling wine or Radeberger beer were able to pass over successfully into the tough market economy.

This means that branding is primarily a social phenomenon. People tend to build a close and long-lasting relationship to things and objects like products or companies. These do not necessarily have to be economical goods. This implies that for a destination a wise brand strategy does not just affect the economic aspect of a city or region but also the destination as a whole.

A further difference between branding and marketing is that brands are not solely focused on the external target groups. On the contrary, brands develop from the inside to the outside which means that the internal brand involved persons have to be taken into consideration first. Marketing on the other hand focuses on the change of the external view. Admittedly, internal marketing, which focuses on the employees of a company, developed in the recent past. However, this is just a further development of the classic approach.

Hence, it becomes evident that marketing is only a tool to develop a brand and to position it on the market. Marketing with its different instruments is more than strengthening the brand development. It can even support and speed up the process of branding. Hence, branding and marketing often go hand in hand which leads to the fact that many people are not aware of the borders.

What Exactly Is a Brand?

In terms of a brand, it becomes clear that not every well-known product is automatically a brand as well. Awareness indeed is an important, but often overrated aspect, because there are many brands which are solely famous in their region and, therefore, only to a specific target audience. But what exactly is a brand and how can it be defined? To express it as simply as possible, a brand is a name. This concept is easy. There is no brand without a name! This would be sufficient from the legal perspective as a differentiated name can be registered in the patent and trademark register and, thus, gains legal protection towards the competition. Yet, it is not that simple. Many other attributes have to come along with the name to complete the branding process.

Here one can differentiate that every brand consists of two levels. The first level concerns all perceivable aspects. Beside name, logo, color, product design, claim or sound, the logo is another aspect of this first level. The most important features here are the identification of the brand and the differentiation from other brands. For all unperceivable aspects, which are the emotional and cognitive contents, the second level of the brand is of importance. The most important task at this level is the development of a long-term and sustainable relationship to the audience. A stable meaning is needed. One rule applies. Only when both levels are cooperating, an ideal development of the brand can be ensured.

The illustration of the brand into two levels further shows the function of marketing. Marketing acts as a booster. On the one hand, the formal, perceivable aspects like the name, logo, etc. should be presented to the target groups while on the other hand the emotional contents should also be outlined. All things considered, the process of the development of a brand takes at least ten years because no long-term, successful and meaningful relation between the brand and the target audiences is possible before that.

Branding and Marketing in the Context of Destinations

For destinations, several options arise. The first misconception that has to be corrected is that destination brands are completely different from brands of consumer goods. The fundamental principle of the two levels applies for all brands and it does not make a difference if the brand is a product, service or destination. Furthermore, it does not play a role whether the target groups are b2c or b2b. Every brand consists of perceivable and unperceivable components and this rule applies everywhere.

Often, destinations are criticized due to the fact that too many stakeholders are involved in the decision-making process and, therefore, a consistent image of the internal and external perception is rarely possible. However, whoever works for international companies in practice, knows the diversity of options and the hierarchy-oriented decision making, which is often far from stringent and strategic orientation. But what exactly is different in destinations?

The basic problem sounds simple at the first glance because it is the name. Because the name of a product is usually open to choice, there are no limits concerning the creativity except for legal limitations. This is different and also more complex regarding destinations, as the name usually has a historic or at least a traditional background. Two drawbacks can arise when the name of a town is given. The first rule concerns the differentiation of a brand when the name of a town is similar to others or even the same. Therefore, the name Frankfurt is not differentiated enough as Germany has two Frankfurts which are 'Frankfurt am Main' and 'Frankfurt an der Oder'. Names of towns like Rot(h)enburg or Neukirchen are also not differentiated clearly as there are many towns named like this in Germany.

A second problem regarding city names is that many names are being pronounced or written differently in other languages. An example is the German spelling of Köln, which is called Cologne in English. In Finland, many towns still have the historic Swedish name and the new, Finnish name. That is the reason why the tourists are confronted with two names for the south-western Finnish town Turku (in Finnish) and Åbo (in Swedish). Confusion is preprogrammed. This is definitely different for product names as most product names keep the pronunciation in other languages. China constitutes an exception here, as names are often allocated to the meanings.

Regions occasionally have the possibility to develop a name. Unfortunately, the creativity is often limited since already existing parts of regions are combined. The problem is that long names are formed. Though, the rule for a brand name is that it should consist of not more than four syllables to support the commemoration of consumers which is reflected by a major rule for brands in general: 'keep it simple and short'.

Brand level is being treated as an orphan. Regarding the logos of towns, escutcheons or arms are being used for traditional reasons. This is comprehensible but impractical as most arms are everything else than brand suitable. Good logos have to be concise, which means that the principle of 'less is more' applies. Complex, graphical shapes are not recognized or remembered by the target groups. Here, regions have a far bigger scope but the creative designing should be often kept within a limit. Often, characteristic elements that represent the diversity of the region are being visualized such as sun, mountains, water and nature. Plenty of logos, which are combining these elements, can be found and, therefore, they are not differentiated enough. The result is the brand development is complicated. Speaking of diversity! When a region should be marketed, the word diversity emerges again and again. Since every destination claims it for itself, diversity is not a differentiating factor anymore and can even be counterproductive as such. Of course, there are positive examples of cities and regions as well. New York developed the 'Big Apple' as a second name which also works as a visual symbol. Berlin with the bear on the arm is recognized and accepted internally by the inhabitants and externally by the tourists and business people. The bear can be found in very different spots of the Berlin cityscape and is a popular figure beyond the borders because of its simplicity and impressiveness.

The perceivable components of a destination brand must be comprehensible and easy to implement. This is slightly different regarding the non-perceivable emotional and cognitive components. To build up a meaningful relation between the destination brand and the customer, several measures and requirements are needed. This is where the necessity of marketing arises as it helps to develop the brand and to strengthen the brand core. What has to happen in this stage? It is crucial to know that it is about to achieve the identification of a brand and the differentiation from the competitors. This is only possible over a long period which could be ten years or more as already mentioned. This aspect is also the weakest part of the branding, as many decision-makers underestimate the temporal necessity and are not consistent enough considering the marketing of a brand. In other words, many decision-makers tend to emphasize creative attention and change their marketing activities like advertising or the stationary at frequent intervals. Also logos have changed too often so that no continuity can arise or the marketing managers try to realize the diversity in all marketing activities which leads to the result that the brand messages are interchangeable. Marketing and particularly advertising campaigns for typical tourist destinations like Turkey, Spain, Croatia or Tunisia differ only through the name instead of visuals and headlines.

Nevertheless, a brand requires continuity and this means that stability regarding the once defined formal and contextual components of a brand is essential, although this could mean that the enterprise might not receive an award for their creative and attention attracting commercials. The brand manager, therefore, takes over two positions. On the one hand, the right formal and contextual brand components have to be developed starting with the name to the logo through to the emotional-cognitive components. On the other hand, it is more important to pay more attention to the continuity instead of just minding about the creativity. This function concerns the branding. Through this it becomes clear what the main duties of the brand manager are. The manager has to combine different disciplines and competences. He has to work strategically and define long-term goals. Moreover he has to have operative competences and be able to empathize with the brand. That it should not be developed and implemented by one manager is self-evident. However, there has to be at least one decision-making person who is familiar with the brand development. This is not always just a problem of destinations but also in many companies. It is important that the brand and marketing are complementing each other. Only then can a destination be developed into a successful brand.

Framework Conditions for Re-thinking Destination Branding

Based upon the first section presenting the wider theoretic framework of marketing and branding in general and more specifically the context of destination, this second section aims at a more specific discussion on a state of the art destination branding concept. Therefore, the authors propose a conceptual model combining classical marketing as well as branding approaches. As described before, branding should be understood as a reflexive process because the perception of a brand has to be analyzed from an internal as well as from an external perspective. Exactly the alignment of these two perspectives by an iterative reflection of both can, therefore, be seen as the integral part of a branding process. Specifically this integration makes the difference to a one way consumer orientated marketing process, as it is understood by the authors. Based upon such a perception the destination marketing process is understood as a consumer and, therefore, market oriented reshaping of a given destination reality. Based up on such a reshaping process the external destination image is supposed to change as well (Figure 1). Of course the external destination image is influenced by various aspects such as media or one's own experience. Nevertheless active destination marketing is an important factor in the image building process as well. Due to the fact that destination as geographic entities can not be created like some kind of standardised products, the destination marketing process can be seen as a more interpretive process, compromising customer needs and destination reality. By doing so, marketers create an external destination image that forms the base for customer exspectations.

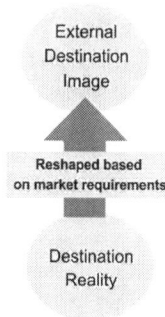

Figure 1:   External Destination Image. (Authors)

Depending on the quality of the given process, an external destination image can vary from a simple stereotype outlining a standardised 'sun&beach-destination' to a very distinguished individualized authentic destination. In any case the aim of a destination marketing process is to influence the external destination image in such a way that the external perception of a destination meets the market requirements. Quite often the long-term result of such a process is an increasing gap in between the external market orientated destination image and the destination reality. Similar to the process of creating an external destination image, a similar process takes place within the destination itself. Stakeholders within a destination also generate an interpretation of the destination reality and by doing so introduce an internal destination image (Figure 2).

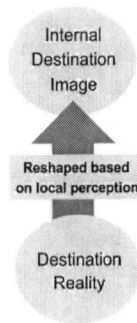

Figure 2:   Internal Destination Image. (Authors)

This process usually is not as structured and organised as a destination marketing process aiming at an external perception as it lacks a responsible body and it is not a direct aim of any stakeholder. Instead it is an unspoken rather hidden process. Nevertheless it plays a vital role due to its influence on local stakeholders, especially if the internal destination image differs dramatically from the external destination image existing in the market. The internal image is rather influenced by local processes, values and individual experiences of key stakeholders than on an analysis of the destination reality. Different from the external destination image, it is rarely analysed or spoken about since it is more a kind of locally accepted destination reality. Based on the stage of a destination within the 'Tourism Area Life Cycle', the gap between the external and the internal destination image of course varies related to the degree of tourism development. It seems that the internal destination image is a more stable one because local stakeholders rooted in the local society tend to downsize the social and environmental impact of tourism development and, therefore, keep a more traditional interpretation of the destination reality. As a consequence the standardization of the local tourism products as well as the specific competitiveness of the destination may not be evaluated realistically any longer. Exactly this variation in the destination perception is often one of the major obstacles for fighting a destination decline.

Based upon their internal destination image, local stakeholders often misinterpret the framework conditions for the management of their destination. In order to be able to successfully guide the destination development, it is crucial that the internal and the external image are aligned in order to have a realistic view of the customer expectations as well as one the destination reality. The destination reality has to satisfy both tourists as well as locals. Therefore, it should neither be a stereotype of customer expectations nor a stereotype of locals but a realistic perception of its reality. Only such a situation gives stakeholders the opportunity to manage the destination in a way that it can ensure a high level of satisfaction amongst locals as well as tourists.

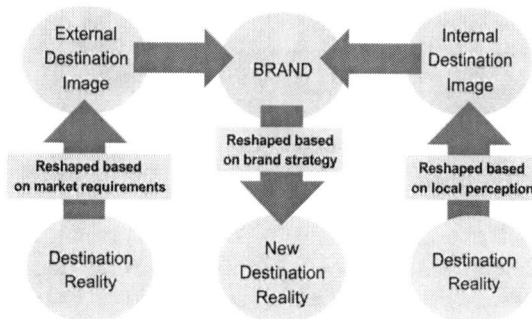

Figure 3:   Destination Branding Process. (Authors)

To establish such an alignment of internal and external image the authors recommend a branding process (Figure 3). The reflexive nature of a branding process by analysing a product or company's external as well as internal image deals with similar framework conditions and can form the ground for an adequate destination perception and, therefore, be the ground for an improved destination management. A destination branding process can be interpreted as a mediation process of the external and the internal destination image. Once both images are analysed, decision-makers have to establish a brand that is able to reflect both images and the existing destination reality as well. Therefore, the brand to be established is in its first phase a theoretic concept combining the internal and external destination image with the destination reality. It is the compromise of all stakeholders on how the destination reality is supposed to be in order to satisfy the multidimensional needs of the specific tourist destination. In the second phase of the branding process, the theoretical concept of the brand will be implemented through destination management as well as as internal and external marketing. By doing so, the theoretical concept will influence the destination reality and the perception of it amongst internal and external stakeholders.

The conceptual model for destination branding as outlined above brings together destination marketing and destination management in a bottom up, reflexive, multidimensional and multi-stakeholder planning process. The generic nature of the model can support on the one hand a broader approach towards destination branding as Echtner and Ritchie are asking for. Destination Branding has "to evaluate not only the perception of individual destination attributes, but also a holistic impression made by the destination" (1991: 326). On the other hand, it can also become more detailed by introducing Biel's concept of the two dimensional nature of a destination image. "In this conceptualization, evoked associations can be either hard (tangible/functional/ attributes) or soft (emotional attributes), whereas the later are interpreted as destination personality." (1997: 204) Especially such an approach can be very beneficial when considering the work of Hosany et al. (2007: 71): "The findings of the study show that destination personality boosts the impact of destination image on the intention to recommend."

Therefore, the evaluation and, based upon those results, the design or re-design of the destination personality can contribute a lot to the overall success of a given destination. Scholars and consultants have to focus on evaluation techniques satisfying the need for a multidimensional and multi-stakeholder analysis of such a complex entity like a destination in order to be able to form the ground for a realistic destination brand modelling process. This can provide the guidelines for a future destination management strategy. Unfortunately there is still a long way to go in order to etablish a branding process in the context of destination which is worth to be called as such. Branding in the every day context of destinations is too often misunderstood as Blain et al. stress. Destination managers "tend to equate the development of destination logos and associated 'taglines' with the more comprehensive process of destination branding" (2005: 332). The understanding of the complexity of destinations as well as the complexity of branding processes have to be stressed more clearly and more awareness has to be created amongst all stakeholders involved in the process of destination management.

Conclusion

Having in mind the confusion when it comes to using the term branding or marketing, this paper outlined the wider sociological background of branding instead of a getting stuck with specific products; branding offers the opportunity to create competitive advantages for a company or destination on the long term far beyond the life-cycle of a specific product. In the context of destinations the specific aspects of a destination rather than its specific products have to be outlined. The emotional or unperceivable aspects contributing to the uniqueness of the destination have to be stressed. The consistency of a brand in the case of a destination has to be centrally controlled and monitored. The way towards a destination brand is understood as a reflexive process involving several stakeholders and comprising the internal as well as the external image of a destination. Therefore, the brand is understood as the amalgam of a destination, those dimensions reflecting the core of the destinations from the demand as well as from the supply side. An established destination brand can even support the development of a new destination reality when being communicated to the external and the internal stakeholders. Accepting branding as bottom up destination planning method offers a variety of opportunities for the future of destination management.

References

Biel, A.L. (1997): Discovering brand magic: The hardness of the softer side of branding. In: International Journal of Advertising, 16(3), 199-210.

Blain C., Levy, S.E. and Ritchie, B. (2005): Destination branding: Insights and practices from destination management organizations. In: Journal of Travel Research, 43(4), 328-338.

Echtner, C.M. and Ritchie, B. (1991): The meaning and measurement of destination image. In: Journal of Brand Management, 9(4/5), 323-334.

Hosany, S., Ekinci, Y. and Uysal, M. (2007): Destination image and destination personality. In: International Journal of Culture, Tourism and Hospitality Research, 1(1), 62-81.

The Possibility of a Social Imaginary: Public Housing as a Tool for City Branding

Michael Klein / Andreas Rumpfhuber

This paper examines social housing as a tool for city branding.[1] We ask whether or not social housing (that is public and subsidized housing) has capabilities for branding the city. The underlying hypothesis is that housing contributes essentially to what is considered the brand of a city, even if it is not part of the established forms of brand-production. We will be investigating the relationship of housing and of branding the city by focusing on the case of Vienna, its history and its recent developments. In doing so, we do not engage in a debate on how to design a city as a competitive consumer brand. We rather aim to go beyond contemporary concepts of branded spaces that seem to be fixed to the iconic, the exceptional and to artificial theme-park-like assemblages of sceneries. The objective of this text is to think beyond upgrading and branding city quarters and its spaces through cultural venues, railway stations and other means of gentrification. In other words this contribution challenges what has become *the* predominant idea of city branding. It questions a mode of governance that confuses running a city with that of running a business. In the lines to follow we propose an alternative approach of branding (space) that fosters structural change and local qualities and not the repetition of a global typology or best practice. In this sense, our contribution questions an approach to city branding eventually oriented towards predatory competition and concurrency; we rather propose a sustainable mode of branding in social housing that pursues an economy of resilience.

The Entrepreneurial City, Social Housing & Branding

The predominant idea of branding a city is based on the concept of the *entrepreneurial city* (Hubbard and Hall 1996). This idea to run cities like businesses has introduced characteristics distinctive to the field of business to the

---

1   The research for this paper is part of the ESF/HERANET funded research project SCIBE – Scarcity and Creativity in the Built Environment.

governing or in the line of business-lingo managing the city. It includes *risk taking, inventiveness, promotion and profit motivation.* Such an economy-based understanding also incorporates *marketing* as a central tool for developing and for governing the contemporary city. This becomes apparent in the literature on city-marketing that adapts key-concepts from marketing and translates them into the urban domain. One example is the take-up of the 4 P's of marketing (Product, Price, Promotion, Place) in the "geographical marketing mix" by Ashworth and Voogd (1990) who translate them into *organizational measures, financial measures, promotional measures and spatial-functional measures.* Another example, given by Kotler et al. (1999), is to build up strategies for place improvement as a mix out of "design, infrastructure, basic service and attraction" (Kavaratzis 2004: 61).

Yet the difference between beauty creams, trainers and cities is an *accidental* and not an *essential* one, as Mattl (2009) rightly points out. Mattl argues that in an international competition of cities, municipal planning departments have been increasingly involved in recent decades. In doing so urban planning issues have become part of consumer culture. Yet the encounter of branding and marketing with municipalities and planning does not necessarily involve the entirety of a city's inhabitants. Following up the argument, we add housing to the list of contemporary consumer goods. Even though it is necessary to state that this development towards consumption in housing is a recent one, particularly in social housing.

We argue that basically all marketing claims of the entrepreneurial city like risk taking, inventiveness, and so on have always been an immanent part in developing social housing programmes. Yet social democratic city politics, corporatism and a Keynesian model of market intervention as it has been practiced in Vienna for several decades differs fundamentally from the approaches along the entrepreneurial city and city-branding with their focus on city-production through iconic global architecture-objects. The production of a state-owned housing complex was not geared to payable profit making. It aimed to distribute wealth to society and was rather, seen from today, an adjustment measure of the welfare state for market economy, so as to balance out social inequality that actually helped to foster a positive image of a city like that of Vienna. Here one can assert that historic practices of urban design and of producing social housing have actually generated branded spaces without already naming them so. Yet not only in matters of market regulation, but also in the concern of branding, has the contemporary situation differed significantly to the Post-war period and the high-time of the welfare model.

From today's perspective, the question is how to learn from these historic practices for the challenges of the contemporary city and its mechanisms. Moreover, we need to ask how to re-actualize housing as a structural tool to create a sustainable branded space – a space that still aspires to the universal project of the distribution of wealth to all.

We base this conceptual examination, therefore, (1) on the assumption that housing has become a consumer good reflected in current discourses and (2) on a need to learn from contemporary discourses in marketing and branding. Together, these promise fruitful options to rethink and restructure the otherwise highly contested and nowadays questioned field of social housing. Yet one needs to be aware that both are part of a neo-liberal discourse with its own value system and ideology.

Considering the established current practices in city branding, social housing is hardly involved. Mass housing and social housing blocks might be way too boring and might have a negative image in the first place. Only a few and then mostly 'classically modernist' social housing projects from the 1920-30s have become part of the architectural 'canon'. The vast majority, however, remains unnoticed, even in the field of architectural history: Siegfried Gideon for example found the housing initiative of Red Vienna, the early beginnings of municipal housing in Vienna, not even worth mentioning in *Time Space Architecture*, his seminal book on 'modern' architecture. And it seems that city branding rather employs fancy museums, temporal sports events, cultural venues, and sometimes converted factory spaces into high-priced loft-like spaces for working and living than the mundane. This is also the case in Vienna's touristic branding of the image of the 'Fin-de-Siècle-Habsburg-Empire-Centre with Lots of Waltz'. Yet housing, notably social housing, has not been considered to create a 'unique selling' point, even in Vienna with nearly half of the real estate market for housing to be social or publicly funded.

For the conception of an alternative tool of city branding along an enhanced notion of welfare, social housing could draw upon the potential of branded spaces for creating coherence and identification through information. Eventually the practice of branding spaces could extend its field of operation into the domain of organizing the social in yet unprecedented ways. This implies a form of branding that goes beyond the simple idea of a consumer brand, and would conceive of the city as a *social form* which means a form of coexistence that is based on equality of all the city's inhabitants and the overall high quality of life for everyone. By retracing Vienna's past in social housing, describing the current status quo of public housing, and by introducing Vienna's actors and experts' self-perception, we will be able to shed light on such a fictitious yet possibly future practice of branding that might trigger a new kind of welfare politics.

Sustainable Branding of the Welfare State

Speaking of the Post-war welfare state of 'Central' Europe, social housing developed on the basis of non-profit rental accommodation. In this context, social housing was particularly considered to be an asset of welfare, a tool for governing society and a social and economic regulative. Nevertheless, in the 1970s, housing came under heavy scrutiny based largely on two reasons. The first reason was related to the structural problems of often too large and poorly equipped and maintained housing schemes. The other more fundamental critique was the questioning of the very idea of the welfare state by neo-conservatives and neoliberals. As a reaction, the 1980s showed a first wave of major sell-outs (e.g. in UK under Thatcher). A second wave of sell out of state-owned public housing estates followed in the 1990s, particularly in former socialist countries of Eastern Europe. And the critique on social housing has not vanished ever since. The European Union's position gives one example. It has accused publicly funded housing to be an intervention distorting the market.[2] Thus the EU rather approves poverty-prevention by subject-oriented housing policies. And very recently the financial crises and its accompanying austerity policy have spurred even more drastic cuts in public housing programs all over Europe.[3]

What is sometimes ignored in these liberal discourses focusing on just one specific economic argument is that social housing has enormous capabilities beyond the provision of shelter (Doling and Ronald 2010: 166). Large stock-shares in housing provide strong means for socio-economic and ecologic policies and can conciliate welfare. Housing can actively shape the 'image' of a city. It can contribute to a city's stability and its resilience without excluding someone. A stable development of rental prices for housing in general, as well as a high quality of life for everyone leading to high satisfaction of all its residents are in fact substantial characteristics – also as indicators - in the global competition of cities. Vienna's high quality of life has been approved in studies.[4] The rather balanced rent market is one quality that has been achieved through the equal distribution of housing over the city. Furthermore, in the current quest for social and sustainable environments, social housing for everyone might again become a significant contribution. Apart from its quantitative factors when it comes to efficient land-use and sustainable energy rate, cheap overheads and running costs, social housing can also create high-quality urban space shared by all.

---

2   For an example concerning the case of the Netherlands see Elsinga et al. (2008).
3   See e.g. the case of the UK (Williams and Ramesh 2012).
4   One example gives the Mercer city ranking on quality of living headed by Vienna (Mercer 2011).

This does not necessarily require branding measures as such. In the face of the widespread scepticism about politics on the one hand, a liberal imperative to retreat from state-interventionism in housing and the austerity measures that accompany the economic crisis on the other, branding (space) might provide a useful tool: to generate a broad acceptance of social and public housing as well as to boost the performance of the location factor by communicating its qualitative and quantitative surplus. This branding strategy is firstly directed towards the societies' 'interior', namely, to the people coexisting in a local environment that live and work there. Only afterwards, is this form of branding directed towards the 'outside' to attract new investors and/or inhabitants, and thus aims to take a stance in the global competition. It is this mode of developing a branding 'from within' that allows for a sustainable mode of branding that pursues an economy of resilience.

The Boring Imaginary

Literature on city branding (e.g. Hubbard and Hall 1996, Kavaratzis 2004) has underlined cities' two-fold status: The *factual* status of a city is accompanied by an *imaginary* or *representational* one. As a reality to operate upon, both are constructed; yet concerning city marketing and branding, particular attention is given to the *imaginary* status when it is about forming an image of a city. Branding engages in planning a set of measures which shape a distinctive and recognizable quality, be it a product, a concept or a commodity. The brand is characterized by its interaction of material and immaterial relations. When examining, therefore, the historical project of social housing and its development in consideration of branding, we will not only have to focus on the built object itself, but as well on the plans and goals purported by the programs and how they were communicated.

Housing has been the 'flagship' of social democracy in Vienna ever since the first social democratic government in the interwar period introduced housing. In this era, which has become known as 'Red Vienna', the housing program was launched above all as a means to raise the poor living quality that had resulted from the rapid growth of the population during the *Gründerzeit*. In only 12 years, from 1923 to 1934, the municipality provided 63,000 flats. The political program to counter the scarcities in housing aimed at rebuilding the city *from within* by distributing housing all over the city. This was enabled by a series of fiscal interventions such as taxes on speculation and luxury goods. As a consequence, landlordism had become highly unprofitable; for the municipality however, it allowed to gain land at low costs. Finally, this lead to a homogenous distribution of social housing in the whole cityscape – no matter whether the neighbourhood was bourgeois upper class in the first place or housing got built in workers districts.

The housing schemes being built all over the city, in empty lots within the existing urban fabric, but also in bigger empty sites at the 'back then' margins of the city, allowed for a strong presence of the new hegemonic power in the city. These buildings, above all the large-scale housing schemes, the so-called superblocks, unveil in strong iconic quality, particularly as a multiplicity. They need to be considered to be clearly visible and unambiguous signs in the cityscape of a new emerging era turning the city upside down. They had, so to speak an *imaginary* quality, showing that a new society actually was feasible and doable. Exactly in this sense one needs to understand the housing program of Red Vienna not only as a means of reforming society through dwelling but also as an integral tool to brand the city completely anew, from the *Gründerzeit*-era and the liberalist imaginary of the city towards the modern and emancipated society. One could call it 'integrated space branding'. By this we mean that the imaginary ideal of society merges with the concrete strategy to realize it. In our case housing exceeds its pragmatic conception to be merely an asset of welfare thus becoming a symbol for the new society. To do so, emphasis of the branding was not so much given to the single object; it was not the hope of the single iconic building's capability to generate more value in a certain urban context. Rather, it was a multi-layered, 'universal' program directed towards one class of society aiming to emancipate and restructure it from its very basis. In the interaction of space, social imaginary and program so as to form a 'new identity', Red Vienna goes beyond other examples of branded spaces.

Decoupled Space Branding

In the decades after WWII, some aspects of such a branding remained an integral part of the political strategy and the housing program at large in Vienna. As in the rest of Europe, these times were coined by the aspiration of the building industry to systematize and standardize planning. It aimed to employ technology to lower construction costs through prefabrication.

Never before or after was more housing built. Housing had become effectively a universal asset in welfare provision and dwelling had become affordable for large parts of society.

The vision and the brand of the 'modern city' had only become feasible outside the historic centre; implementation in decongested, linear urban structures at the city's fringes. Soon, these schemes got criticised for their architectural monotony and their mono-functionality. As in other cities, the modern city outside the historic city mainly covered dwelling, yet it missed the diversity the inner city could provide. The disillusion and critique of the modern city, therefore, was accompanied by the rediscovery of the historic city which had remained partly untouched for decades. Also in social housing provision, after the post-war euphoria of city extension, the focus gradually shifted back to the centre for the refurbishment of the old urban fabric in the 1980s. This allowed the city also to re-invent itself and, moreover, its brand as the 'romantic, historic city'.

At about that time, actual housing production disintegrated from a unique branding strategy for the city. As with the housing production itself, branding got decoupled and out-sourced. The municipality retreated from the active involvement in housing production in the 1990s. Since then, the model of housing provision has undergone a structural shift towards regulated competitiveness. But unlike other European cities selling their estates, the municipality of Vienna rebuilt its provisional system of housing so as to continue social housing. Though the municipality withdrew from active housing construction, it reserved the role of administration of its present real properties securing and controlling new social housing construction by means of regulation, subsidy and land procurement. Embodied by the 'Fund for Housing Construction and Urban Renewal' (*wohnfonds*), a legal subsidiary, the city ensures land provision, coordination and quality and realization measures in social housing. At the new model's core is the so-called developers' competition (*Bauträger-wettbewerb*), a selection procedure for housing schemes larger than 200 dwelling units. In this process, housing projects developed by teams of architects and developers are evaluated according to (1) architecture, (2) economy, (3) ecology and (4) social sustainability. Furthermore all projects are discussed and evaluated by an advisory board, the *Grundstücksbeirat* of experts in the field of social housing.

Despite these instruments of regulation and the advisory board, the change towards a liberalized market brought an end to the former existing notion of an integrated brand. Today, singular projects in the city compete with each other than a whole program aiming to create a universal imaginary for the city. After the expiration of the unique brand of municipal housing, the developers' competition brought a multiplicity of brands seeking to attract possible lifestyles of prospective user groups. The supply range and the variety of unit types have widened; users have become more selective and demanding. Something else has changed with this shift. Developers would advertise their buildings to consumers and target groups and no longer to a certain class or towards society at large.

The Possibility of a Re-actualization

Such a development has doubtlessly generated a new dynamic in the building sector in the city of Vienna, as interviews with stakeholder and experts in the City's housing production have shown (Rumpfhuber et al. 2012: 16-19). These interviews, as well as empirical quantitative data, and an analysis of the popular discourse around housing issues in Vienna indicate that social housing in Vienna is still considered to be *one of Europe's best*. All interviewees agreed that social housing contributes considerably to the social configuration of Vienna and to the city's character. Certain aspects of social inequalities are levelled out by housing not only in a social, but also in a spatial sense resulting in little socio-spatial segregation and modest changes in rent between one district of the city and another. For a large portion of the population, accommodation is quite affordable when compared to other European cities, even though the model of housing provision needs to be reconfigured, as it does not cover lowest income groups, as some interviewees pointed out.

The balanced situation of Vienna's rental market is derived from a structural specificity: The municipality actually owns 27% of the city's housing stock and indirectly controls and influences another 21%, which is owned by limited-profit housing developers (Rumpfhuber et al. 2012: 32), resulting in a so-called 'integrated rental market' (Kemeny 1995: 49, Amann and Mundt 2008: 4).This means that social housing is not considered to be a supplementary, discrete market for a specific user group, such as 'the poor', but rather an integral part of one rental market; social housing that competes with the free market for the same share of potential clients, possible through the large shares of the city's overall housing stock. The sheer amount of social housing in Vienna indirectly influences the private market. Because of the high standards in social housing, the integrated market keeps the prices for rent relatively low and the quality of housing relatively high.

Besides this, one needs to take into account another issue of the social housing practice: the amount of public and social housing in Vienna is able to stabilize the economy (Streimelweger 2009). Interviewees argue that it actually was able to partially absorb the local effects of the global financial crises of 2007. When the financial crisis got worse in 2008, social housing was even employed as a means for counter-steering economic recession. The municipality increased the budget for housing expenses so as to stimulate construction economy. All interviewees have acknowledged this stabilizing effect of interventionist politics into housing markets.

Most important however for our conceptual examination of the possibility of branding space and the city appears to be the strong visual and spatial aspects in housing. Still, housing is the significant determinant when it comes to shaping the city's visual appearance. It is particularly the sheer amount of housing in Vienna and its ubiquity, we argue, which bears the potential for a contemporary social imaginary, namely, for a contemporary society in a contemporary European metropolis.

Revisiting the historic example of Red Vienna, we have shown that the concept of 'profit' has not always been bound to the single individual and its pursuit of happiness, but about the profit of society at large and the imaginary's potential of an emancipating society. Comparing Red Vienna to the four points of the branding-concept of the *entrepreneurial city* (Hubbard and Hall: 1996), we actually find similarities: (1) Red Vienna was highly risk-taking because it invested enormous sums despite of the economic situation, (2) it was inventive in its spatial strategy and (3) the use of architecture and space was at that point unique. It is only Hubbard and Hall's point of profit motivation (4) that differs from the historic example shown. In contemporary idea, 'profit' is increasingly limited to the gains of a single entrepreneurial self. This has actually limited the idea of branding to the iconic object of the global super-star-architect. These developments hinder us to understand the potential of including forms of 'integrated branded spaces' into contemporary urban development. The integrated brand, therefore, is first of all a different understanding, a reinterpretation of 'profit'. This would allow creating sustainable developments which are no longer carried out in a top-down manner. It would no longer be a one-way communication of the development itself, telling us, at its best, 'I am an Icon'[5]. It might include the possibility of a multi-directional process of developing and branding space that includes many. We understand this as a development and a branding of a *social imaginary*. For cities like Vienna this includes 'social housing' as a tool of branding.

In Vienna's recent past, housing is increasingly employed in conveying a 'modern' and 'active' role in urban development and active policing. Mediated above all by newspaper-inserts and billboards, new housing stands for 'development', 'progress' and 'urban quality of life' achieved through the active role of the municipality (Kolmayr 2012: 21-24). This massive presence of social housing in paid newspaper supplements and ads leads to the assumption that

---

5   An architecture only communicating 'I am an Icon' will be and can be discussed only by questions of taste. This has always been the problem of Post-Modern developer architecture of the 1980s and 1990s completely obstructing a discourse on the qualities of architecture as sign and symbol to which Robert Venturi und Denise Scott Brown had contributed so much (Venturi et al. 2003, Venturi and Scott Brown 2004).

social housing is already being used as a tool for branding the city of Vienna. Yet this form of branding rather paints a picture of the investor; but for the time being, social housing is not considered to be a sustainable brand for the city of Vienna itself. The shift towards the so-called 'entrepreneurial city' was "underpinned with a neoliberal business approach to public policy which, in turn, has justified and legitimated substantial reductions in the welfare service provided by the public sector". It has forced cities to "redefine their objectives, their means and institutions and themselves as social-political units" (Ache and Andersen 2008: 3). Part of this development was the sell-out of the public and social housing stock in many European cities. We can even state that precisely because city-branding became increasingly discussed with the introduction of neoliberal ideas, the concept to use forms of welfare for branding to establish more resilient urban conditions was left out of consideration. Since Vienna did not join the sell-out of housing but only gradually adapted to prevailing managerial and fiscal discourses, the city today might be actually in a position to implement a sustainable form of branding spaces focussing on the right of proper living, on quality of life. Branding then, would not be limited to neoliberal practices in urbanism, but it would contribute to an alternative idea of living together.

References

Ache, P. and Andersen, H.T. (2008): Cities between competitiveness and cohesion: Discourses, realities and implementation. In: Ache, P., Andersen, H.T., Maloutas, T., Raco, M., Taşan-Kok, T. (eds.): Cities between competitiveness and cohesion. Dordrecht: Springer Netherlands, 3-18.

Amann, W. and Mundt, A. (2008): Armutspolitische Dimensionen von Gemeindewohnraum, Gemeinnützigem Wohnungsbau und Wohnbauförderung. In: Dimmel, N., Heitzmann, K. and Schenk, M. (eds.): Armut in Österreich. Innsbruck: Studienverlag, 538-557.

Ashworth, G. and Voogd, H. (1990): Selling the city: Marketing approaches in public sector urban planning. London: Belhaven Press.

Doling, J. and Ronald, R. (2010): Home ownership and asset-based welfare. In: Journal of Housing and the Built Environment, 25(2), 165-173.

Elsinga, M., Haffner, M. and Van Der Heijden, H. (2008): Threats to the Dutch unitary rental market. In: International Journal of Housing Policy, 8(1), 21-37.

Hubbard, P. and Hall, T. (1996): The entrepreneurial city: New urban politics, new urban geographies? In: Progress in Human Geography, 20(2), 153-174.

Kavaratzis, M. (2004): From city marketing to city branding: Towards a theoretical framework for developing city brands. In: Place Branding, 1(1), 58-73.

Kemeny, J. (1995): From public housing to the social market: Rental policy strategies in comparative perspective. London: Routledge.

Kolmayr, G. (2012): Lucky Vienna: How an image of housing is cultivated. In: Dérive, 46(Jan-Mar), 20-24.

Kotler, P., Asplund, C., Rein, I. and Haider, D. (1999): Marketing places Europe: Attracting investments, industries, residents and visitors to European cities, communities, regions and nations. London: Pearsons Education.

Mattl, S. (2009): City Brandings. In: Becker, K. and Wassermair, M. (eds.): Phantom Kulturstadt: Texte zur Zukunft der Kulturpolitik II. Vienna: Löcker Verlag, 15-25.

Mercer (2011): Quality of living reports: 2011 edition, Mercer survey, London, UK. http://www.mercer.com/articles/quality-of-living-survey-report-2011, 02.04.2012.

Rumpfhuber, A., Klein, M. and Kolmayr, G. (2012): Vienna housing glossary. In: Dérive – Zeitschrift für Stadtforschung, 46, 30-32.

Rumpfhuber, A., Kolmayr, G. and Klein, M. (2012): Views from within – (self-) perceptions, (self-)descriptions: Experts' prospects, challenges and critique in Vienna housing provision. In: Dérive – Zeitschrift für Stadtforschung, 46, 16-19.

Streimelweger, A. (2009): Eine Insel der Seligen? In: Die Zukunft: die Diskussionszeitschrift für Politik, Gesellschaft und Kultur, 2(3), 14-20.

Venturi, R. and Scott Brown, D. (2004): Architecture as signs and systems: For a Mannerist time. Cambridge, MA: Harvard University Press.

Venturi, R., Scott Brown, D. and Izenour, S. (2003): Lernen von Las Vegas: Zur Ikonographie und Architektursymbolik der Geschäftsstadt. Basel: Birkhäuser und Bertelsmann.

Williams, M. and Ramesh, R. (2012): Housing benefit cuts: "It's not as if we're living in luxury". In: The Guardian. http://www.guardian.co.uk/society/2012/jan/01/housing-benefit-cuts-case-study, 02.04.2012.

Facts and Figures

Corporate Branded Spaces: A Glance at Today's Diversity and Some Historic Origins

Louise Bielzer

Corporate branded spaces as an integral part of corporate marketing communication increasingly contribute to the perception and image of a corporate brand. By providing brand experiences in unique environments, they make the visitors "hold some favorable, strong, and unique brand associations in memory" (Keller 1993: 2) and help to create and maintain a brand's equity. However, branding such unique environments or spaces is a challenge. It is more complex than the usual branding process since the financial investment is often enormous, target groups are heterogeneous and there are many parties involved, and more stakeholders' requirements to be considered like owners/investors, architects, designers, operators, professional users or visitors. Furthermore, corporate branded spaces have to continuously react on and adapt themselves to changes in both their external environment, such as the economic and socio-cultural framework, and the changing expectations of their various stakeholders.

There is often debate in scientific fields about what is the 'correct' definition of an object of study and it is the same for the definition and specification of corporate branded spaces. As in most scientific areas, definitions and explanations of key terms often center on the specific scientific perspectives from which they are looked upon. In the case of corporate branded spaces, important perspectives are marketing (Ponsonby-McCabe and Boyle 2006: 183-184) or often architecture and urban planning or tourism (Hospers 2006: 1017-1018). Sociological, psychological, management or marketing issues may be in the focus of the definitions. Whereas it is not possible to cover or evaluate the numerous definitions within the framework of this article, the author's own generic definition shall be given exemplarily to provide a basis to deal with these special corporate venues:

Corporate branded spaces may be defined as built multi-purpose spaces. They are often architecturally unique which are part of an integrated corporate marketing communication strategy and provide interactive, multi-sensory brand experiences to its visitors. Corporate branded spaces are not only tangible but also symbolic spaces reflecting corporate identity and building or maintaining personal relationships with its customers or visitors.

This article will introduce selected types of corporate branded spaces and show the wide range from corporate museums, branded sports and event venues such as soccer stadiums or arenas to flagship stores, brandlands or brand parks. Whereas some of those corporate branded spaces such as corporate museums hark back to a comparative long history, other corporate branded spaces such as brandlands have developed more recently. In order to show the development towards today's 'landscape' of corporate branded spaces, the following major section of the article will be dedicated to a historical outline of the development of these special venues.

Diverse corporate branded spaces feature various differences. However, they all have some dimensions in common which will be briefly discussed with different practical examples. Key issues will be summarized with an outlook on potential developments at the end of the article.

Historic Development of Corporate Branded Spaces

Many forms of corporate branded spaces are somehow connected with the general development of society and the specific development of marketing activities and the means of corporate marketing communication in use. Especially the boom of corporate experience and event centers in the past decades perfectly matches with the concept of the experience society with concepts of experiential marketing (e.g. Podesta and Addis 2007). In the United States, B. Joseph Pine II and James H. Gilmore published an article titled "The Experience Economy" in 1998, discussing the evolution of society into an experience economy. They developed four realms of experience (the entertainment, educational, aesthetic and escapist realm) in which customers range between active and passive participation on the one hand, and absorption and immersion on the other hand (Pine and Gilmore 1998: 102). In Germany, the sociologist Gerhard Schulze (2005) described the phenomenon of an experience society in his book "Erlebnisgesellschaft" in 1998. He outlines different milieus to which people belong depending on their patterns of experiences, leisure behaviors and lifestyles. Generally, experiences may be gained rather passively 'at home', for instance by media consumption, or more actively by being involved in events, taking part in activities or visiting themed venues, places or corporate branded spaces.

Thus, when considering today's corporate branded spaces as part of corporate marketing communication (see Figure 1), a look at the development of corporate marketing communication itself and the different degrees of active involvement of target groups helps to explain the manifestations of corporate branded spaces:

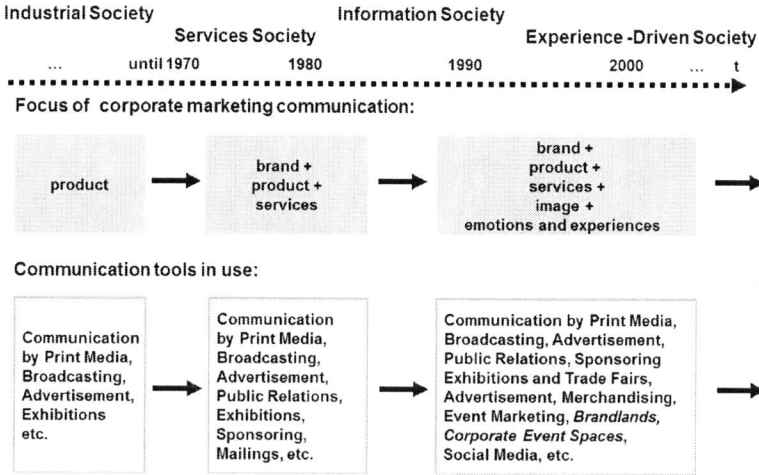

Industrial Society		Information Society	
	Services Society		Experience -Driven Society
... until 1970	1980	1990	2000 ... t

Focus of corporate marketing communication:

| product | → | brand +
product +
services | → | brand +
product +
services +
image +
emotions and experiences | → |

Communication tools in use:

| Communication
by Print Media,
Broadcasting,
Advertisement,
Exhibitions
etc. | → | Communication
by Print Media,
Broadcasting,
Advertisement,
Public Relations,
Exhibitions,
Sponsoring,
Mailings, etc. | → | Communication by Print Media,
Broadcasting, Advertisement,
Public Relations, Sponsoring
Exhibitions and Trade Fairs,
Advertisement, Merchandising,
Event Marketing, *Brandlands,*
Corporate Event Spaces,
Social Media, etc. | → |

Figure 1:   Corporate Branded Spaces as Element of Corporate Marketing Communication. (Author)

Until about the 1970s the product itself was in the focus of corporate marketing communication. With the exception of exhibitions, mainly one-way communication tools were used in order to show the products and make the brand known to its customers. Today, the focus is on the product, the accompanying services, the brand, the image, brand experiences and emotions. Accordingly, the tools used in corporate marketing communication do not only include rather traditional instruments such as advertisement in print media, radio or television, exhibitions or sport sponsoring but also event marketing, experience marketing, the use of social media and corporate branded spaces. The customers or visitors should be as actively involved as possible in order to contribute to the creation of the experiences and give meaning to the spaces. Thus, corporate branded spaces can be seen as 'built' communication spaces or 'built' corporate communication, having both real and symbolic character and meanings. Relating characters to a story framework, they all tell their own stories that have to be related to the master brand and to the overall corporate strategy. The customer or visitor, therefore, is co-creating the story.

Looking back at the historical story, corporate branding is already visible in the 19th century. As early as the 19th century, companies such as Krupp or

Siemens in Germany or Cadbury (Bournville) in the U.K. built their own housing areas for their workers and other deserving tenants which can be considered as a type of corporate branded space. Whole districts or parts of cities became connected with corporate brands such as the 'Kruppstadt Essen' or the 'Siemensstadt Berlin' because distributors, intermediaries etc. needed to know from where a product came. Together with the emergence of advertisement a more holistic view of corporate design saw its beginnings. The architect Peter Behrens is often mentioned as an early example of a corporate designer. In his function as artistic corporate adviser for AEG since 1907 he designed logos, advertisements and products for the German corporation AEG as well as exhibition stands, company buildings and housing estates for the AEG employees. By integrating all those aspects of corporate design, he contributed to a holistic corporate identity of the corporation (Buddensieg and Rogge 1993).

The use of corporate architecture is nothing new; consider examples such as the famous expressionist Behrens building of Hoechst in Frankfurt, Germany, built in the 1920s,[1] Marco Trucco's Lingotto building (Olmo 1994: 151) with the rooftop test track for Fiat in Torino, Italy, that opened in 1923, or the BMW Cylinders at the corporate headquarters in Munich, Germany from 1972. Those historic corporate spaces were usually not open for the public or used for direct marketing activities because they were administrative buildings.

However, corporate architecture has become narrative and provides opportunities for performances and emotional experiences (Klingmann 2007, Messedat 2005). Today, one often mentioned example is Prada and its cooperation with Rem Koolhaas and Herzog & de Meuron for its flagship stores, expensive buildings which finally have become its own brand and represent a landmark at their respective destination. Nevertheless, exterior building architecture should not be seen solitarily. It is always interrelated with the interior design and has an impact on the buildings external environment and, depending on its location, on general urban development.

Taking the development of corporate marketing communication as outlined above into consideration, we may state that specifically brandlands as branded corporate experience centres showed a big boom in the past about 20 years. Compared to that, for example corporate museums, based on product collections and archives, are no new phenomenon, although they have become more interactive in their programs (see the section corporate museums). With regard to brandlands, corporations often took their milestone anniversaries as an occasion to invest in this specific form of permanent marketing, such as Swarovski, Opel,

---

1   http://www.industriepark-hoechst.com/en/index/industriepark/tradition-zukunft.htm# iph_tradition-zukunft pt-Anchor-1925, 17.08.2012.

RWE did on the occasion of their respective centenary. Even though this boom in many European countries started in the 1990s, there are different 'predecessors' such as brand parks that go back in history for several decades or even more than a century.

As further explained below, one of the first corporate leisure parks was Hersheypark in Pennsylvania which opened in 1907 next to Hershey Chocolate Factory (see more detail in the section branded leisure parks). Another established branded leisure park looking back through decades of history is Knott's Berry Farm in Buena Park, California. It is said that the origins hark back to a little fun area which the Knott family developed in order to reduce waiting times for clients at the roadside Knott's Berry Stand and Chicken Dinner Restaurant in Buena Park in the 1920s. Being successfully accepted by the customers, it became a fun park in 1940 which today covers a total area of about 500,000 m² and counts more than 3.6 million visitors per year. Since 1997 Knott's Berry Farm is owned and operated by Cedar Fair Entertainment Company and listed at the New York Stock Exchange.[2] As some further examples we may mention the developments of Walt Disney which opened 1955 in Anaheim, California, USA[3] or the Legoland Billund in Denmark which started operations in 1968.[4] Compared to other forms of corporate branded spaces such as brandlands or branded event venues, the development of corporate leisure parks as well as corporate museums did not see a specific 'boom period'.

Types and Dimensions of Corporate Branded Spaces

When talking about branded spaces in general, we may first distinguish between corporate branded spaces and non-corporate branded spaces such as place brands or destination brands. Non-corporate branded spaces include for example architectural landmarks such as museums like Guggenheim Museum, Bilbao[5] or Tate Gallery of Modern Art, London[6], opera houses like Sydney Opera House[7] or the KKL, Luzern[8] or churches like Cologne Cathedral[9] or St. Peters Basilica,

---

2   http://www.knotts.com/media-center/history and
     http://www.cedarfair.com/ir/company/properties/, 13.08.2012.
3   http://www.justdisney.com/disneyland/history.html, 17.08.2012.
4   http://www.legoland.dk/Documents/About/Press/LL_Presse_UK.pdf, 17.08.2012.
5   http://www.guggenheim-bilbao.es/?idioma=en, 12.08.2012.
6   http://www.tate.org.uk/visit/tate-modern, 12.08.2012.
7   http://www.sydneyoperahouse.com/, 12.08.2012.
8   http://www.kkl-luzern.ch/navigation/top_nav_items/start.htm?client_locale=en_GB, 12.08.2012.
9   http://www.koelner-dom.de/index.php?id=19167&L=1, 12.08.2012.

Rome[10]. They are often a key element in the destination marketing activities of
the respective cities, regions or countries (Ashworth and Kavaratzis 2010,
Gobers and Go 2009, Lucarelli and Berg 2011). In contrast to non-corporate
branded spaces, corporate branded spaces are always purpose-built venues,
consciously planned to impact people's attitude towards a brand.

As mentioned earlier, there are many understandings of what corporate
branded space may be and many different types of corporate branded spaces can
be identified although there is no clear differentiation among the single types.
But, independently from the respective type of corporate branded space, the four
dimensions 'architectural dimension', 'program dimension/utilization concept',
'economic dimension' and 'organizational dimension' (see Figure 2) always
exist for built corporate branded spaces and mutually influence each other in
various ways:

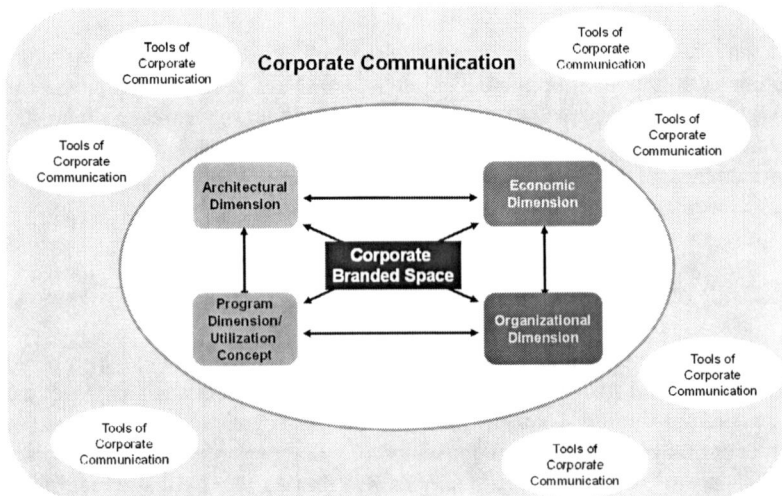

Figure 2:   Dimensions of Corporate Branded Spaces from a Brand Owner's
               Perspective. (Author)

The architecture and layout of the venues are of particular interest not only due
to the immediate visibility and recognition value. They directly impact the
utilization of the space and the program which is staged in the venue as well as
the organizational structures (ownership and management) and, therefore, finally
the economic dimension (operating costs and revenues). Insofar that building

10   http://saintpetersbasilica.org/, 12.08.2012.

architecture has an impact on operating costs of the venue as depending on building structures and room layout of the branded space operating costs such as cleaning, utilities, staff costs, etc., operating costs may turn out higher or lower. Considering that operations are usually not profitable enough to refinance the building costs of a corporate branded space, the question of evaluation of brand experiences and the effects on brand equity is more vital though hard to measure (concerning the challenge to measure brand experiences see Brakus et al. 2009).

Again, we state that corporate branded spaces are not only real spaces but also symbolic spaces. Space may be seen from many different perspectives and, therefore, not only considered to be built environment but also an intangible result of social interactions and relations. In the literature, this phenomenon is referred to as part of the 'spatial turn' (see Löw 2008, or the German publication of Bachmann-Medick 2009: 284) Space is derived from the interests and activities of individuals or groups so that the 'built space' is supplemented by a symbolic space, a socially and culturally impacted perception and construction of reality which is an interesting and beneficial approach when dealing with the perception and impact of corporate branded spaces. Accordingly, and this should always be considered when planning and developing a new corporate branded space in practice, such a venue is not only a built physical and tangible space but also a social, mental and intangible one. As a consequence, more subtle and intangible aspects such as the concept line and program of branded spaces, which have a big impact on the perception of these spaces, are crucial for success. Architecture, brand and program/utilization of the corporate branded space form the basis for a memorable experience of the visitors/users and, therefore, are a key to differentiate a brand from its competitors.

Interestingly, some corporations such as BMW or Prada seem to consciously select a famous architect in order to benefit from this architectural brand and accordingly invest hundreds of millions of euros or dollars into their brandlands. However, others work together with rather unknown architects, maybe in order to avoid the danger that the product's brand might be overshadowed by the architecture.

As already stated, corporate branded spaces in general and brandlands in particular as types of 'built corporate communication' and space for brand-related experiences assume different functions for the corporation such as the creation and cultivation of the brand's image and strengthening of the brand's identity, an increase in customer loyalty or simply being a communication platform for a brand's customers. In order to continuously hold these functions and motivate visitors to come again, the story line, program and single experience elements of a brandland have to be permanently updated. A corporate branded space's utilization concept and program elements should be concentrated on experiences, interaction, a high contact intensity and (emotional) attraction. Accordingly, corporate branded spaces concepts include as many multi-dimensional experiences as possible and provide a multi-sensory event (acoustic, visual, haptic, olfactory). Individuality, originality and immediacy are typical principles of a corporate branded space's story line even though there are a broad variety of programs.

There are various interrelationships between the above discussed architectural dimension and the program of a corporate branded space, amongst other design elements, the selection of materials and interior decoration. Therefore, when planning such a special venue, the development of the utilization concept which connects room and functional layout, program and design elements, is a vital step in the process. Exemplarily referring to a brandland, the following program elements or areas of activities and functional areas are often to be found in the utilization concepts:

- interactive product experience areas, test and/or taste areas
- special children's area/offers for children
- a flexible event area
- convention space, meeting rooms or similar
- an area where the company's and brand's history might be experienced
- restaurants
- a merchandising area/shop
- various storage and 'backstage' areas that are not visible for visitors but vital for operations of such a complex facility

In order to make that a little more graspable, an example of a food & beverage industry-related brandland which includes all traditional elements of a corporate brandland is now briefly introduced: the World of Coca Cola, Pemberton Place, Atlanta, Georgia. It opened in May 2007 and has a total area of about 90,000 m², thereof a 60,000 m² visitor area. The program consists of an exposition showing the company's story in the 'Coca-Cola Loft' and displaying a collection of old advertisements and artifacts. There is even an area telling about the beverage's relation to Pop Culture and co-operations with artists. The visitors may enter the so called 'Happiness Factory Theatre', where a musical journey takes visitors through a world inside a Coca-Cola vending machine, and may further go on to get to know the production process in a bottling line or the products themselves in a 'Taste it! Area' where 60 products may be sampled. Finally, the concept includes a merchandising area and a shop which is accessible without paying the usual entrance fee. According to their website, Coca Cola had five million visitors by the beginning of 2012.[11]

A consistent and vivid storyline is an important basis for continuous interest of people to visit the branded space. Generally, the more tangible, attractive and experiencable a brand and its products are, the more probable is sustainable success for a corporate brandland. However, a tangible and attractive product is no guarantee for success of a branded space as a failure example of the car manufacturing industry shows. Opel Live opened in 1999 on the occasion of the 100th birthday of the Opel car manufacturing company in Rüsselsheim where the corporate headquarters are. Opel invested about € 60 million in this permanent marketing event and expected about 500,000 visitors per year. In fact, only approximately 150,000 people visited Opel Live in 2000. After further decline in visitors, the entertainment areas, a 3D-cinema and a driving simulator, closed down and only 20 out of 120 employees were working for Opel Live. Today, Opel Live includes only guided tours and an exhibition of vintage cars.[12] Although there is no official statement of the corporation why this branded space didn't succeed, it can be assumed that amongst others it failed due to an inconsistent story line and defects of planning.

As far as the organizational dimension is concerned, corporate branded spaces such as brandlands are usually owned by the brand-giving company and managed by the company itself or by a subsidiary. This aspect makes corporate brandlands different from for example branded event venues which are normally run by either a professional event venue operating company (e.g. SMG Group, Anschutz Entertainment Group, Arena One GmbH or similar) and/or a facility management company or by a public entity belonging to the respective city, region or federal state. This direct connection or integration of corporate brandlands and the brand-giving company sometimes also distinguishes brandlands from branded leisure parks which might carry the name of a brand but are managed by a professional private management company as is the case for with Legoland (Billund, Denmark; Gunzburg, Germany; Windsor, U.K., etc.) and the Merlin Entertainment Group.

An advantage of corporate branded spaces being directly managed by the brand-giving corporation or a subsidiary is the accordance of the branded space's strategic direction and operations with the overall corporate strategy of the brand or the parent corporation. It allows a holistic corporate communication and, therefore, contributes to a consistent and coherent corporate image and culture to be experienced by external and internal target groups.

---

11   http://www.worldofcoca-cola.com/, http://www.worldofcoca-cola.com/aboutus.htm, 17.08.2012.
12   http://www.spiegel.de/spiegel/print/d-18204173.html, 17.08.2012.

Finally and as stated above, the architectural, the program and the organizational dimension also influence the economic dimension of a corporate branded space. Considering the enormous investment costs which may easily amount to several hundred million euros, it is quite obvious that these investments can't be refinanced by operations. Examples are the construction and maintenance costs of BMW World, Munich and Autostadt, Wolfsburg, both in Germany. Furthermore, continuous investments in program updates, new offers for the visitors and also the maintenance of the buildings have to be taken into consideration when discussing the economic dimension of corporate brandlands. Accordingly, primary economics of those special venues are in most cases negative. However, it is still economically interesting for corporations to run a brandland due to the secondary economic benefits and impacts such as increase in popularity, an enhancement of their own image and an emotional relationship of the customers to the brand.

After this short overview of different dimensions all corporate branded spaces have some aspects in common, albeit in various manifestations. The following paragraphs will be dedicated to a short introduction of several different types (see Figure 3) of those special venues:

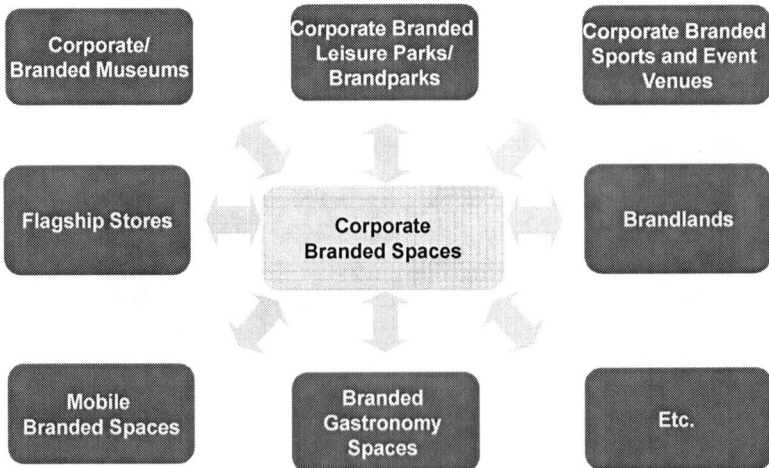

Figure 3:   Selected Types of Corporate Branded Spaces. (Author)

Corporate Branded Leisure Parks

As already explained in the historic overview of the development of corporate branded spaces, some examples of branded leisure parks show a long history and are established locations on today's market of leisure and entertainment facilities. At the beginning of the 20th century, we already found the first corporate leisure parks as branded spaces, such as Hersheypark in Pennsylvania which opened in 1907 next to Hershey Chocolate Factory. Originally, it was meant to be a development exclusively used by Hershey Chocolate Factory's employees, including sports facilities and carousels. Later, the park was opened to the public. Today, as a leisure park, it is an established 'branded space' in the United States, covering an area of more than 450,000 m². Some years later the Hershey's Zoo opened which is today known as Zoo America. In 1973, Hershey's Chocolate World was brought into being some steps away from the theme park. Today, different types of entertainment, numerous shows, chocolate-themed rides, a chocolate spa, shops, restaurants, etc. are offered to the visitors. A hotel, lodge and campground as well as a golf course, just to mention some further elements, are also part of Hershey's entertainment district. The venues are all operated by the Hershey Entertainment and Resorts Company which originate from Hershey Estates founded by Milton Hershey in 1927 in order to segregate the chocolate manufacturing business from the non-chocolate making enterprises.[13]

Comparable projects of branded leisure parks were developed in Europe where for example Legolands or the Ravensburger Spieleland try to attract customers. Whereas the Legolands with several locations in Denmark, England, USA and Germany have belonged to the British Merlin Entertainments Group since 2005[14], the Ravensburger Spieleland has been continuously owned and operated by the Ravensburger AG[15]. Therefore, in terms of ownership and management of those branded facilities, it has to be said that there are two main models in use; either the parent company is responsible for both or it is outsourced to professional leisure park operating companies. Whatever brand is branding the leisure park, an important characteristic of those types of corporate branded spaces is the focus on branded entertainment, interactive brand

---

13   http://www.hersheypa.com/press_room/press_kits.php,
      http://www.hersheyjobs.com/jobs/commercial.php, and
      http://www.amusementparkworld.com/index.php?option=com_content&view=article&catid=3
      4:pennsylvania&id=58:hersheypark&Itemid=374, all 12.08.2012.
14   http://www.legoland.de/en/About-LEGOLAND/LEGOLAND-Deutschland/, 13.08.2012.
15   http://www.spieleland.de/spielelandL/de/Unternehmen__3475392-3475407.html, 13.08.2012.

experiences and events, whereas, aspects such as corporate history of the brand (see also the section corporate museums) is usually, if at all, in the focus.

Corporate Branded Sports and Event Venues

Another type of corporate branded spaces, where the entertainment and event aspect is also a main factor although the facilities' program itself is less branded, is corporate branded event venues. They are insofar different from the other corporate branded spaces as they are usually not owned and/or operated by the branding corporation and their utilization concept or program is not connected with the brand. Generally, corporate branded event venues are more common in the Sports and Entertainment Events Industry than in the Cultural Events Industry or the Convention and Exhibition Industry, a phenomenon that may result from a major media presence of the first-mentioned.

In the sports events industry, facilities like stadiums or arenas were traditionally named after geographic regions, rivers, districts or merited sportsmen or other individuals. First, corporate naming rights were allocated to (multipurpose) sports facilities in the United States. It is said that the Buffalo Bills were the first to sell the right to name the facility to Rich Foods in 1973 when they paid a total of US$ 1.5 million over 25 years (for different types of corporate sponsorship in sports see e.g. Leeds and Allmen 2011: chapter 3, sports franchises as profit-maximizing firms). It is now a procedure which is common in many countries all over the world.

Corporations now pay enormous amounts of money for naming rights. According to Mediaventures and Leeds, Barclays Bank/Citigroup pays US$ 400 million for over a 20 year period to the Barclays Center in Brooklyn, New York, where the Mets play. Generally, naming rights are a common trend for mostly first and second league sports facilities in other countries such as the United Kingdom or Germany. But naming sports or other events venues might not be seen uncritically. Citigroup was under scrutiny because they received a $45 billion bailout from the government when they were paying $400 million spread out in payments of $20 million per year over the course of the next 20.[16]

In addition to the danger of the corporation of getting in financial troubles, there are many other open questions being important for the owning and managing company of such a branded event venue. Examples are: What happens with the branding and the naming rights if the team relegates in case that the

---

16   http://articles.cnn.com/2009-04-13/us/mets.ballpark_1_citi-field-mets-home-stadium-naming?_s=PM:US, 13.08.2012.

league is not a closed league? What happens if the team or the corporation is part of negative media coverage? Will this have an impact on the brand involved in the 'project' or on other brands and sponsors involved in the venue? Some of these issues are dealt with in the respective contracts; others may only be an element of a risk assessment strategy before making the decision and signing the contract.

Besides stadia, multipurpose arenas and halls, with or without permanent tenants, often have a corporate naming right. Again, the reason is usually the implicit use of the reporting on the facilities itself, but even more so on the reporting on the events that took place in the facilities. By being mentioned in the media, attractiveness to invest in naming rights increases. Whereas corporative naming rights are a marketing tool and, therefore, part of expenditure, for the venues it represents an additional source of income and can be seen as a financial tool. A challenge consists in changing the name of the event venue after several years. Once positioned on the market as a branded event facility, it's not easy to reposition the facility with a new name as several examples have shown, e.g. Bremer Stadthalle, Germany, later AWD Dome Bremen, today ÖVB Arena Bremen. Nevertheless, there are also examples of naming rights in the convention and exhibition industry such as the Frontier Airlines Convention Center in Milwaukee, Wisconsin, USA or the L-Bank-Forum of the Landesmesse Stuttgart, Germany.[17]

Brandlands

As pars pro toto for the category 'brandland', the following paragraph is dedicated to BMW World in Munich, Germany. The BMW World opened in 2007 and was designed by the architecture firm COOP Himmelb(l)au, getting in line with other innovative architectural projects of the BMW Group on its Munich headquarter location. BMW traditionally used corporate architecture beyond pure functionality. Already in 1973 the BMW administration headquarters moved into the current building-protected 'four cylinders' building designed by Karl Schwanzer. By its form the building underlines the relationship of the company to technological developments and engineering. Besides exhibitions of new or special car models, motorcycles and engines, BMW World also provides insights into technical and design solutions, offers a 'Junior

---

17   http://www.cvent.com/rfp/milwaukee-hotels/frontier-airlines-center/venue-
       8d360166c5a34edeb1edb29c8e7baad4.aspx and
       http://www.bw-fairs.de/veranstaltungsplaner/messe-stuttgart/messegelaende/l-bank-forum-
       halle-1/, all 16.08.2012

Campus' for children and differentiated guided tour programs for different interest groups. A multi-purpose events area with capacities for about 800 participants is also available. BMW drivers may pick up their new cars in the BMW World and the venue is open for everybody to visit, including the merchandising shop and restaurants. In order to also attract tourists coming over when visiting the nearby Olympic Park or people just being curious about the BMW World architecture and the brand itself, BMW decided not to charge entrance fees for the visit itself (guided tours are not for free).[18] Through this concept BMW World addresses a wide range of visitors which yields a high visitor frequency although it is more difficult to develop a program suitable for the requirements of all visitors.

Compared to branded leisure parks, corporate brandlands show less elements of leisure parks such as roller coasters, themed rides or similar, but also provide active brand experiences to their visitors. They reflect the respective brand in different attractions and also often include product test areas, company's history related features and merchandising shops. Usually, brandlands are to be found rather in the manufacturing industry producing tangible goods than in services industries. First of all, car manufacturing companies, food & beverage corporations or also life-style-product manufacturing companies include a brandland in their marketing strategy.

Corporate Museums/Branded Museums

Corporate museums are a quite established, almost traditional type of corporate branded spaces even though it wasn't the original aim to provide interactive brand experiences. Some museums, e.g. car manufacturing companies, have their origins decades back. The first Mercedes-Benz Museum was already opened to the public in 1936 and directly linked to document collections of the company. In 1957 the archive and the museum were combined and moved to a new building still on the plant site in Untertürkheim since 1960. Later, in view of the 100th anniversary of the company, the museum was rebuilt again. Today, the Mercedes-Benz Museum is part of the Mercedes-Benz World, operated by the Mercedes-Benz Museum GmbH, a subsidiary of the Daimler AG, and provides more interactive brand experiences than merely insights into the company's history.[19] Another example of the car manufacturing industry is the Porsche

18   http://www.bmw-welt.com/web_rb/bmw-welt/en/index.html, 12.08.2012.
19   http://barrierefrei.mercedes-benz-classic.com/en/news/news_details.php?oid=187 and
      http://www.mercedes-benz-

Museum which originally opened in 1976 on the former engine manufacturing plant in Zuffenhausen, Germany which was replaced by a new museum on the same location in 2009.[20]

A notable change took place in the conception of corporate museums in terms of the story line and presentation of the respective corporate history. More and more interactive elements were included in the expositions; corporate history should become tangible. Related to the general trend of increasing interactivity and entertainment elements in museums' conceptualization and management (Lord and Lord 2009), corporate museums today have many elements with brandlands in common. Besides interactive and often multi-sensory exhibition areas, they also provide meeting rooms or event space, restaurants, and shops as well as offer special programs for children, school classes or other specific target groups such as members of the company's loyalty programs. Today, there are both corporate museums only 'telling the (hi)story' of one single brand such as the Mercedes Benz Museum near Stuttgart in Germany or museums telling the story of a whole product category or several brands such as the Schokoladen-museum Köln, Germany[21].

Flagship Stores

Flagship stores or generally branded retail venues' stage products in a unique environment and represent an integrated branding concept. The customer shall multi-sensorially experience the products at the point-of-sale which is often designed with due regard to principles of neuromarketing. Same as in the case of brandlands, architecture and design are key features and distinctive characteristics for flagship stores. In some cases, for example as Prada did with Rem Koolhaas' flagship store in New York, USA, and Herzog and de Meuron's Epicenter in Tokyo, Japan[22], brands engage some of the world's most famous architects in order to stage their products in a unique built environment which is reflected in the high investment costs for those projects.[23]

Compared to branded leisure parks, branded event venues or brandlands, flagship stores primarily focus on directly selling the products even though they also aim to reinforce the brand image (Sayre 2008: 351).In the case of branded

---

classic.com/content/classic/mpc/mpc_classic_website/en/mpc_home/mbc/home/museum/merc edes-benz-museum/about/das_mercedes-benz.html, all 17.08.2012.

20   http://www.porsche.com/international/aboutporsche/porschemuseum/idea/, 12.08.2012.
21   http://www.chocolatemuseum-cologne.com/, 16.08.2012.
22   http://www.galinsky.com/buildings/pradatokyo/index.htm, 17.08.2012.
23   For the example of Prada in New York http://www.galinsky.com/buildings/prada/, 17.08.2012.

retail venues it is more important to provide special shopping experiences than to provide branded entertainment experiences or similar events. Areas where the products' manufacturing process or the corporate history is shown are usually not included (for flagship stores in general see Kent and Brown 2009 or Messedat 2007).

Branded Gastronomy Spaces

Branded Gastronomy Spaces, themed restaurants or cafés such as Starbucks, McDonalds, Burger King or KFC, which have become a brand themselves throughout time, represent a form of branded space which has been established on the market for quite a long time. They usually work on a franchise system but have to follow a very strict branding system defined by the owners. Compared to other corporate branded spaces, they are usually branded by their own brand even though there might be co-operations taking place with other companies or brands.

Today, there are also gastronomy spaces which are branded by companies that are usually not linked to gastronomy such as the Emporio Armani Caffès in Munich or Milan. However for all branded gastronomy spaces, there is the challenge of remaining credible and consistent in terms of the brand itself, its image and the branding activities and to make customers repeat their restaurant visits (Sayre 2008: 348-349).

'Mobile' Branded Spaces

Besides the above-mentioned types of branded spaces, we even find more 'exotic' forms such as 'mobile branded spaces' in transportation industries. Examples are several aircrafts of TuiFly which are painted according to sweets of Haribo Corporation and named 'GoldbAIR' or 'HaribAIR'. Further co-operations included or still include amongst others the car manufacturing industry by flying an aircraft named 'SharanAIR' (Volkswagen) or the food industry by having an 'Übärflieger' in its fleet painted like a can of condense milk of the Bärenmarke company.[24]

Comparable to branded sports and event venues, also for those 'mobile' branded spaces, a central challenge exists in the diverse brands represented in one physical space and in the necessity to coordinate the different brands'

---

24   http://www.tuifly.com/theme/show, 07.07.2012.

images by avoiding any possible damage to the other (e.g. the branding company and the airline).

Looking at the different types of branded spaces, we may state that branded spaces usually focus on b-to-c customers rather than on b-to-b customers. Despite their differences, they all aim at creating, maintaining and strengthening a certain brand image by continuously being present in the minds of their target groups. There are only very few examples of branded spaces for business customers such as the Boeing's Customer Experience Centre in Renton, Washington. This is directly situated near the customer training center and the Boeing's 737 manufacturing plant and offers amongst others product mockups, the 'live-experience' of airplane interiors and a Customer Solutions Studio showing business solutions throughout the product life cycle.[25]

Today, corporate branded spaces strongly focus on their own respective brand although there are some rare exceptions such as the Autostadt Wolfsburg or the Schokoladenmuseum Köln. These exceptions focus on a product category such as cars or chocolate in general. Most of all in a situation of continuously increasing global competition, corporate branded spaces may, to a large extent, contribute to the differentiation of brands by offering memorable brand experiences (Kilian 2009) and, therefore, creating and maintaining brand images. The often enormous financial investments may also be explained against this background.

Summary and Outlook

There is a wide range of corporate branded spaces. All have special characteristics, various stakeholders and different customer requirements and expectations to fulfill. Commonalities, however, are to concentrate people's attention on the respective brand and to embed a brand's image in the memory of people by offering multi-sensory brand experiences.

As marketing communication tools, many types of corporate branded spaces were later developed as exhibition booths or temporary marketing events and are an important element of the marketing strategies of corporations today. The enormous financial investments in corporate branded spaces underline their importance in the marketing mix of corporations. Companies derive benefit from brandlands, interactive corporate museums or corporate experience centers by reaching target groups which could not be easily reached with traditional marketing activities because corporate branded spaces as interactive, multi-

---

25   http://www.boeing.com/news/frontiers/archive/2006/march/i_ca2.html, 08.06.2012.

sensory built corporate communication well match the expectations of customers in times of the experience economy Furthermore, these corporate experience centers may sustainably link people to the brand.

Generally, careful planning is vital for the success of a corporate branded space. As in the case of traditional event or sports facilities and also of corporate branded spaces, a feasibility study should be carried out in order to confirm feasibility, to get valid and reliable indicators about the future success of the brandland and to know about the cost-effectiveness of the project. Such a feasibility study should at least include a market, demand and competition analysis, a locational analysis as basis for the locational choice, the development of a general utilization and room concept, an economic feasibility study or profitability analysis and a risk analysis in terms of planning, basic assumptions of forecasts, scheduling, financing, costs, permissions, etc.

It is crucial that corporate branded spaces are integrated in the overall marketing strategy of a corporation and that they are in line with traditional marketing activities like advertisement, sponsoring, exhibition booths, etc. When planning those special properties, architects, designers, technical planners and marketing experts should closely work together and carefully evaluate and consider the requirements of the various stakeholders.

However, the challenge remains to keep the program and experience offers attractive to customers and visitors in the long run. It is about considering the life-cycle of the venue and continuously reinvest into the building structures in order to remain attractive as well as considering the 'life-cycle' of the program. As a consequence, program updates and re-launches have to be taken into consideration forecasted as well as future operating, engineering and maintenance costs.

It can be assumed that the trend for corporations to own and run branded spaces or to brand other spaces with their names will continue. As exemplified by the increase of naming rights for sports and event venues but also universities or even aircrafts as mobile branded spaces show, companies clearly realize the benefits of those special venues. A quite recent development is the involvement of virtual spaces which brings along new perspectives and dimensions of corporate branded spaces specifically for branded retail experiences (Houliez 2010). It remains to be seen in which way virtual branded spaces in the future will influence 'built' branded infrastructure, mostly in view of branded retail spaces such as flagship stores or concept stores.

References

Ashworth, G. and Kavaratzis, M. (2010) (eds.): Towards effective place brand management: Branding European cities and regions. Cheltenham: Edward Elgar Publishing.

Bachmann-Medick, D. (2009): Cultural Turns: Neuorientierungen in den Kulturwissenschaften. Reinbek: Rowohlt Taschenbuch Verlag.

Brakus, J.J., Schmitt, B.H and Zarantonello, L. (2009): Brand experience: What is it? How is it measured? Does it affect loyalty? In: Journal of Marketing, 73(3), 52-68.

Buddensieg, T. and Rogge, H. (1993): Industriekultur: Peter Behrens und die AEG 1907-1914. Berlin: Gebr. Mann Verlag.

Gobers, R. and Go, F.M. (2009): Place branding: Glocal, virtual and physical identities, constructed, imagined and experienced. Basingstoke: Palgrave Macmillan.

Heller, A. (1998): Meteorit im RWE-Park: Eine Verwirklichung. Wien: Brandstätter.

Hospers, G.-I. (2006): Borders, bridges and branding: The transformation of the Øresund region into an imagined space. In: European Planning Studies, 14(8), 1015-1033.

Houliez, C. (2010): Branding places or branding spatial practices? Retail spaces in the age of mixed realities. In: Place Branding & Public Diplomacy, 6(2), 87-96.

Keller, K.L. (1993): Conceptualizing, measuring, and managing customer-based brand equity. In: Journal of Marketing, 57(1), 1-22.

Kent, T. and Brown, R. (2009) (eds.): Flagship marketing: Concepts and places. London: Routledge Advances in Management and Business Studies.

Kilian, K. (2009): Experiential marketing and memorable brand experiences: A conceptual framework. In: Lindgreen, A., Vanhamme, J. and Beverland, M. (eds.): Memorable customer experiences: A research anthology. Gover: Farnham, 87-99.

Klingmann, A. (2007): Brandscapes: Architecture in the experience economy. Cambridge: The MIT Press.

Leeds, M. and Allmen, P. von (2011): The economics of sports: 4th edition. Upper Saddle River: Pearson Prentice Hall.

Löw, M. (2008): The constitution of space: The structuration of spaces through the simultaneity of effect and perception. In: European Journal of Social Theory, 11(1), 25-49.

Lord, G.D. and Lord, B. (2009): The manual of museum management. Lanham, MD: Altamira Press.

Lovelock, C.H. and Wirtz, J. (2011): Services marketing: People, technology, strategy, 7th edition. Upper Saddle River: Pearson Prentice Hall.

Lucarelli, A. and Berg, P.-O. (2011): City branding: A state-of-the-art review of the research domain. In: Journal of Place Management and Development, 4(1), 9-27.

Messedat, J. (2005): Corporate architecture: Entwicklung, Konzepte, Strategien. Ludwigsburg: Av edition.

Messedat, J. (2007): Best designed flagship stores: Shops, showrooms, brandcenters. Ludwigsburg: Av edition.

Olmo, C. (1994): Il Lingotto 1915-1939: L'architettura, l'immagine, il lavoro. Torino: Umberto Allemandi & Co.

Pine II, J. and Gilmore, J.H. (1998): Welcome to the Experience Economy. In: Harvard Business Review, 76(4), 97-105.

Podesta, S. and Addis, M. (2007): Converging industries through experience. In: Caru, A. and Cova, B. (eds.): Consuming experience. London: Routledge, 139-153.

Ponsonby-McCabe, S. and Boyle, E. (2006): Understanding brands as experiential spaces: Axiological implications for marketing strategists. In: Journal of Strategic Marketing, 14(2), 175-189.

Sayre, S. (2008): Entertainment marketing & communication: Selling branded performance, people, and places. Upper Saddle River: Pearson Prentice Hall.

Schulze, G. (2005): Die Erlebnisgesellschaft: Kultursoziologie der Gegenwart, 2nd edition. Frankfurt am Main: Campus Verlag.

Brand Value in Real Estate:
The Financial Contribution of Property Brands

Bernd Ankenbrand / Sven Mussler / Timo Mussler

In most industries the significant contribution of brands to the value of consumer businesses has been recognized for years, decades or even centuries. In real estate business, however, the value of branding has been explored only recently. A few studies dealing with real estate brands focus on corporate brands of companies or organisations operating in the real estate industry. They do not, however, deal with brands of single real estate properties. We see this as one major gap in brand research in the real estate business. A second gap in our opinion is the lack of research related to the financial value of brands in this industry. It is our intention to shed light on these two 'black spots' and to start developing an industry perspective based on primary and secondary research as well as to further develop preliminary hypotheses for future research.

We start with a brief overview of the functions and relevance of brands across industries before we analyse the evolvement of single properties brands in particular. We deal with the question how single property brands support the creation of real estate value and how this value can be determined in euros and cents.

Status of Research on Brands in the Real Estate Industry

The relevance of brands has been explored and measured in many industries and market sectors. This holds true primarily in consumer businesses (Fischer et al. 2010) but also in B2B businesses (Khermouch 2001, Meyer and Perry 2010). In real estate, however, only few studies dealing with brands have been conducted and published so far due to the fact that branding in the real estate industry is not a predominant strategy, yet. Allemann (2009: 2) states that "real estate branding is still largely unknown and commonly used as a synonym for location or real estate marketing".

In 2009 Harald Steiner and Jürgen Fink published a 'real estate brand study' claiming to be the first to examine brands in the German real estate industry (Steiner and Fink 2009). Their explicit intention was to bring together know-how from the real estate experts and branding experts to increase both the understanding and visibility of brands in the real estate industry. Further, a "real estate brand award" (EUGIMB 2009) has been established that highlights 'best practices' in the various real estate sectors based on empirical brand performance data. Both the real estate brand study and real estate brand award were repeated in 2010 (Figure 1) and 2012 (not yet published).

Architects	Helmut John
Asset Management	Corpus Sireo
Banks	SEB
Facility Management	Hochtief Solutions
Funds/Investors	HIH Hamburgische Immobilien Handlung
Real Estate Agents	Jones Lang LaSalle
Online Portals	ImmobilienScout24
Project Developers	ECE Projektmanagement
Real Estate Project Managers/Consultants	Ernst & Young Real Estate
Property Management	Jones Lang LaSalle
Portals	Berlin Partner

Figure 1:   German Real Estate Brand Award 2010. (EUGIMB 2010)

Although the authors claim that no such study has been conducted before, two blind spots remain. Firstly, this real estate brand study examines corporate brands of real estate companies or organisations. They do not deal with 'product brands', i.e. single real estate properties. Secondly, this study does not deal with the financial value of brands. However, we think it is crucial to demonstrate that brand strategy can make a significant contribution to a company's profits, cash flows, and overall business enterprise value.

Objective and Structure of Our Study

The objective of our study is to investigate the creation and determination of brand value of single real estate properties, buildings or group of buildings which in all cases means a branding of spaces. When a brand is supposed to add value to a property, it is elementary to demonstrate transparently how the various stakeholders perceive this brand and how they benefit from what the brand has to offer over and above an otherwise 'plain' property. For this purpose, our study is structured as follows. Firstly, we elaborate on the functions and relevance of brands in general by building on the vast literature available and on established practices in businesses. In addition, we conduct expert interviews to establish a practitioners' perspective and to overcome the shortfall of research done in the real estate industry so far. A first set of interviews has been conducted with representatives of companies in the following sectors:

- architects
- brand consultants
- developers
- asset managers
- online portals
- banks
- funds
- real estate agents

Secondly, we analyse the evolvement of single properties brands. In particular, we deal with the question how single property brands facilitate the creation of real estate value, i.e. how brands support their managers to connect with the various stakeholders of a property, such as investors, brokers, or end-users, and how brands enable to establish long-term relationships with them. As part of this, we reflect why single property brands evolved much later than e.g. consumer goods brands. Thirdly, we establish the basis for financial brand valuations of single real estate properties.

Functions and Relevance of Brands

The importance of intangible assets in general and brands or trademarks in particular have been the subject of numerous empirical investigations conducted by both academic researchers (Fischer et al. 2010) and business practitioners (Maul et al. 2004). Two main observations in this context are the following:

(1) Intangible assets are the most powerful drivers of business enterprise value (Ranker et al. 2001).
(2) The importance of these assets increased significantly over the last few years. Studies conducted, for example by PricewaterhouseCoopers, demonstrate how the impact of brands has risen from 1999 till 2005.

The contribution of a brand to company success depends, amongst other factors, significantly on product characteristics, customers' buying behaviour and further industry dynamics. Several surveys, including three longitudinal studies by McKinsey Inc. and the University of Passau in 2002, 2006 and 2010, examine the relevance of brands in 30 product and service categories over years (Meyer and Perry 2010). These studies are based on the observation that the relevance of brands embraces three functions (Meyer and Perry 2010):

- *Information efficiency* which are brands that facilitate orientation in overwhelming product offerings
- *Risk reduction* which are brands that build trust allowing to simplify buying decisions
- *Self-actualization* which are brands that support the self-fulfilment of customers

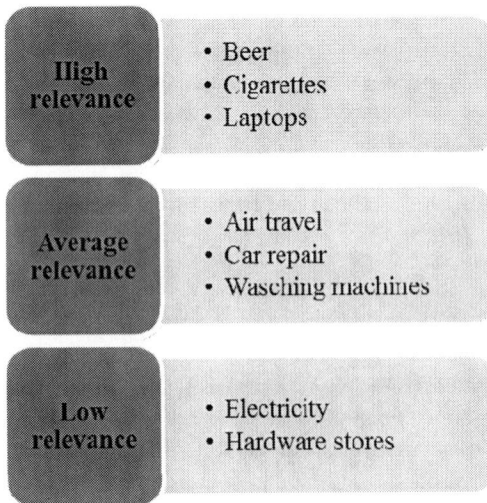

High relevance	• Beer • Cigarettes • Laptops
Average relevance	• Air travel • Car repair • Wasching machines
Low relevance	• Electricity • Hardware stores

Figure 2:   Relevance of Brands in Product and Service Categories. (Authors' own illustration based on Meyer and Perry 2010: 10)

Over the years these studies show steady and consistent results. As demonstrated by Meyer and Perry 2010 and shown in Figure 2, the information efficiency of brands is vital for most fast moving consumer goods ('FMCG') like beer or cigarettes, whereas, for durable consumer goods like laptops the risk reduction function is core. Life-style goods, like sunglasses, score significantly in the self-actualization factor. In summary, and by taking these three factors together, the overall brand relevance is high in product categories like beer or laptops. In categories like electricity and hardware stores, however, brand relevance is rather low which can be explained by the low level of tangible benefits offered by brands in these sectors and/or low customer involvement.

Evolvement of Single Property Brands

Brand strategy in the real estate industry has recently begun to turn from a field not yet dealt with (Allemann 2009) into a more relevant and visible one (Steiner and Fink 2009, EUGIMB 2010). Nowadays it is recognized more and more that the creation and management of brands has become a key success factor for companies in basically all real estate sectors (Henshon 2002).

The primary focus of our investigation of brand relevance in this industry lies on single real estate properties rather than on operating or strategic investment companies. Branding of single properties is a very complex process, given the fact that every property requires an individual approach which, ideally, should start no later than with the briefing of the architect at the very beginning of the planning phase (Mussler 2010). Further, the number of stakeholders and participants involved in the planning, development, and marketing processes adds to the complexity of brand building and development (Mussler 2011) which in turn stresses the importance of very focused and highly effective marketing and communication efforts.

One might ask, why bother at all about single property brands? In the course of the various expert interviews we have conducted in this context and based on related research (Anholt 2009), it has become more and more obvious that the nations, the cities, and even the buildings in which we choose to live and work and shop are increasingly benefiting from the classical functions of brands. With regard to information efficiencies, the positioning of office buildings or shopping sights as brands facilitates the information flow and communication with potential business partners and consumers. This provides orientation in an overwhelming product offering.

The relevance of brands can also be observed on city level. Frankfurt am Main is one great example for a city positioning itself as a centre for financial institutions (Frankfurt 2012). These approaches are known as 'city branding' and have been analysed and described extensively by Simon Anholt (2009) and, in Germany, e.g. by Mussler & Mussler (2011). Taking this concept further, brand on a property level also evolves. The MediaPark Köln (MediaPark Köln Entwicklungsgesellschaft mbH 2012) is one example for a group of buildings being successfully branded for the benefit of all stakeholders. The MediaPark has been positioned as „a new district to generate fresh impetus for the media city of Cologne, with offices, homes and culture." (MediaPark Köln Entwicklungsgesellschaft mbH 2012).

New real estate marketing services, known as single property sites, start to exploit this phenomenon (Single Property Sites 2012) by setting up internet sites exclusively devoted to the marketing of one single property. Professional real estate developers use this effect of information efficiency of brands as they increasingly start to brand facilities (Mussler 2011). For example the street named 'Zeil' in Frankfurt am Main is well known for its high street shopping offering and this street's name has recently been used for a local shopping center as a central component of its brand name, 'MyZeil', to position the center as "Frankfurt's premier shopping and leisure world" (DTZ Zadelhoff Tie Leung 2012).

In all these cases, single property brands help consumers and business partners to find orientation in overwhelming product offerings. In addition to the information efficiency, single property brands provide functions of risk reduction, too. They help to reduce risk by simplifying and justifying decisions with trusted brands. And finally, even elements of self-actualization related to real estate brands can be observed:

- The team operating the 'Malzfabrik' in Berlin, renting spaces to "visionaries, artists, snoopies, idealist and creative" (Malzfabrik 2012), created a single property brand positioned "as a vibrant island in an urban industrial zone that stimulates unconventional thinking." (Malzfabrik 2012). Working in the Malzfabrik is seen as a certain expression of self-actualization through one's own work.
- In the case of the shopping center illustrated above, "MyZeil" (DTZ Zadelhoff Tie Leung 2012), adding a pronoun like 'My' to the high street name 'Zeil' brings a personal connotation and emotional element to the shopping center brand.
- Real estate properties are seen more and more by private tenants and other end-users as a way to achieve self-fulfilment, rather than to benefit solely from the pure functional aspect of 'housing', like the "MarcoPoloTower" in Hamburg (DC Residential 2012). In this context, branding offers highly

relevant benefits by adding emotional aspects, such as life-style, to an otherwise 'plain' building.

These and many other examples illustrate that property branding may provide significant benefits. In all instances, it is an opportunity, even a pre-requisite, for 'product' differentiation. Whilst the main three factors for marketing and selling a specific property always were 'location, location, location', it has been accepted more and more that other factors, and branding being one of them, attach value to a premise, too. A full-spec marketing program, part of which is a brand's positioning, should focus on a wider set of factors, e.g. performance, services, and image (Viitanen 2004) to create advantages (Mussler 2010). Even if 'location' is, still and most likely remain to be, the primary driver of value in many cases, our research findings suggest that an increasing number of single properties successfully compete beyond this criterion.

Financial Valuation of Single Property Brands

The last part of our study is to demonstrate the underlying principles of and to establish a fundament for valuations of single property brands. In this context, we understand 'brand value' as a financial value which can be determined, and expressed, in euros and cents.

Although there are plenty of different ways to measure intangible asset value (Ankenbrand 2003, Anson 2005), the underlying principles are very similar in most cases. In so-called 'top-down'-approaches, the value of intangible assets is derived as a residual value, calculated as business enterprise value less market value of the fixed assets employed by a business (Anson 2005). The residual outcome of this analysis can be interpreted as the value of the intangible asset base of a company.

A more detailed perspective is required when valuing a single intangible asset such as a brand or naming right (Ankenbrand 2007) and various approaches and methods exist for this purpose (Salinas 2009). One method frequently applied by valuation practitioners is based on the incremental cash flows generated by a brand, discounted to a specific valuation date (Maul et al. 2004). In this context, brand value is generated by the following drivers:

- *Brand cash flows* which reflect the power of a branded business to turn growth opportunities into revenues, profit and cash flows
- *Brand contribution* which reflects the brands incremental contribution to business revenues, profits and cash flows

- *Brand-specific discount rate* which reflects an individual's brand systematic risk

Based on an Incremental DCF-Method, the value of a brand is captured by its ability to generate higher cash flows faster and less volatilely (Mussler 2010). Whilst this approach is based on generally accepted business valuation principles, i.e. on a discounted cash flows technique (Brealy and Myers 2000), the tricky part is to isolate the contribution of a brand as a single asset to the generation of cash flow (Sattler et al. 2003). Observations made in the course of various valuation studies suggest that the stronger the brand is in its competitive environment and the more relevant a brand is for a customer to make a purchase decision, the higher the brand's contribution is to profit, cash flow, and finally value (Maul et al. 2004). Understanding and measuring brand strength and brand relevance, consequently, is the path to determine brand value.

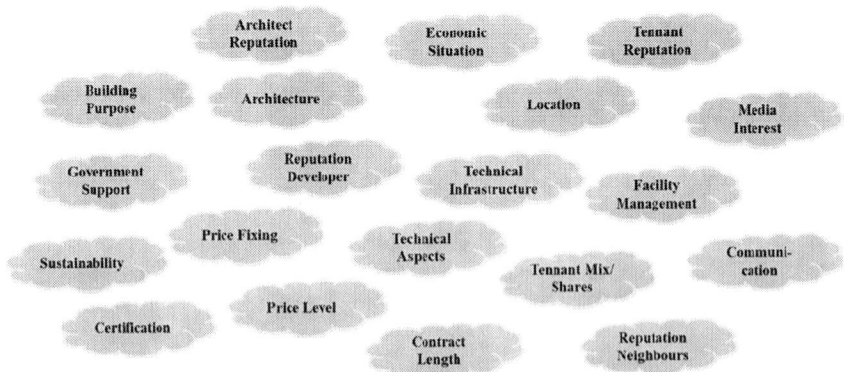

Figure 3:   Drivers of Real Estate Value (Exemplary Only!). (Authors)

One way to identify the relevance and strength of a specific single property brand is via an empirical driver analysis. An illustrative list of drivers which can be used for such an approach is shown in Figure 3. These and other factors represent what, from a customer's perspective, drives the perception of real estate properties and property brands and what finally drives the decision for and/or against a specific property. To understand the impact of a specific brand on property value, we need to assess the importance of these drivers, e.g. by stated or derived importance, and to evaluate how a brand performs on these drivers versus similar or alternative brands or buildings.

Only in those cases where a brand has the power to make a significant and positive impact on a customer's choice, can a positive brand impact on a property's cash flow and risk be assumed and transformed in a financial brand value. The main interim findings of our industry study related to property brands and brand value can be hypothesised as follows:

Firstly, property branding does not work in all cases. Whilst we observe great examples of successful property branding, we have seen at least as many examples where branding has not, or would not have, worked. It is our experience that only a strong brand positioning or brand profile with relevant brand attributes can make a significant and valuable difference (Mussler 2010).

Secondly, the effect and value of property branding strongly depends on the specifics and dynamics of a respective market segment. Brands work differently in a retail environment than for office spaces, and for hotel buildings differently than for private accommodations. Even within a specific segment, say office buildings, the dynamics differ and depend on a number of factors, such as the type of business. Like in every other product category, understanding the specific needs of a target group is the most important step to develop a unique and relevant brand positioning and product offering.

Thirdly, the way single property brands create value differs from case to case. This is primarily due to the fact that property branding is a very individual process and attached to a very individual product in contrast to, say, FMCG sectors with a higher degree of product homogenisation within a category. Consequently, brand relevance needs to be determined on brand rather than on a category level.

Conclusion

In the course of our study, one key observation has been made. Branding of single properties can be, but not necessarily is, a value adding strategy which enables real estate owners to generate superior financial returns over and above returns of an otherwise 'plain' building. However, a successful branding strategy requires a strong and relevant brand positioning, together with highly effective communication efforts as the immediate benefit of brands in this sector is not always visible.

References

Anholt, S. (2009): Places. New York: Palgrave Macmillan.

Ankenbrand, B. (2003): Methoden zur Konstruktion ökonomischer Realitäten: Die Identifizierung und Bewertung immaterieller Vermögenswerte. Witten: Universität Witten/Herdecke.

Ankenbrand, B. (2007): Die Verbriefung und Bewertung von Namensrechten mittels Informationsderivatebörsen. Köln: Eul-Verlag.

Allemann, R. (2009): When living space becomes a brand. Zurich: Branders Group AG.

Anson, W. (2005): Intellectual property valuation: A primer for identifying and determining value. Chicago: American Bar Association.

Brealey, R. and Myers, S. (2000): Principles of corporate finance. New York: McGraw-Hill.

DC Residential (2012): Lifestyle. http://www.marcopolotower.com/, 02.02.2012.

DTZ Zadelhoff Tie Leung (2012): MyZeil. http://www.myzeil.de/start.html?L=1, 01.02.2012.

EUGIMB (2009): Real estate brand award 2009. Berlin: Premise Group.

EUGIMG (2010): Real estate brand book Germany 2010. Berlin: Europäische Gesellschaft für Immobilienmarkenbeobachtung.

Fischer, M., Völckner, F. and Sattler, H. (2010): How important are brands? A cross-category, cross-country study. In: Journal of Marketing Research, 47(October), 823-839.

Henshon, A.T. (2002): An analysis on branding within the real estate industry. Boston: MIT Press.

Khermouch, G. (2001): The best global brands: BusinessWeek and Interbrand tell you what they're worth. In: BusinessWeek, August 5.

Lev, B. (2001): Intangibles: Management, measurement, and reporting. Washington, D.C.: Brookings Institution Press.

Malzfabrik (2012): The philosophy of the Malzfabrik. http://www.malzfabrik.de/en/malzfabrik/philosophie, 02.02.2012.

Maul, K., Mussler, S. and Hupp, O. (2004): Advanced brand valuation. Düsseldorf: Verlagsgruppe Handelsblatt.

Maul, K. and Sattler, H. (2001): Praxis von Markenbewertung und Markenmanagement in deutschen Unternehmen. Frankfurt am Main: Fachverlag Moderne Wirtschaft.

MediaPark Köln Entwicklungsgesellschaft mbH (2012): English short version. http://www.mediapark.de, 02.02.2012.

Meyer T. and Perry, J. (2010): Der Marken-Tachometer. In: McKinsey Akzente, 3, 8-14.

Mussler, D. (2010): Imageaufbau im Immobilienmarkt. In: New Business, Regionale Tageszeitung, September, 107-111.

Mussler, S. (2010): Wertschöpfungsprozesse für faszinierende Immobilien. In: New Business, Regionale Tageszeitung, September, 112-114.

Mussler, T. (2011): Qualitätsversprechen. In: Immobilienmanager, 6, 66-68.

Mussler, S. and Mussler, T. (2011): Die Metropolregion Rhein-Necker: Eine sportliche Aufgabe. In: Jahrbuch Sponsoring 2011, 160-164.

PricewaterhouseCoopers (2006): Praxis von Markenbewertung und Markenmanagement in deutschen Unternehmen: Neue Befragung 2005. Frankfurt am Main: PricewaterhouseCoopers AG.

PricewaterhouseCoopers (2012): Markenstudie 2012. Frankfurt am Main: PricewaterhouseCoopers AG.

Ranker, D., Wohlgemuth, F. and Zwirner, C. (2001): Die Bedeutung immaterieller Vermögenswerte bei Unternehmen des Neuen Marktes und daraus resultierende Implikationen für eine kapitalmarktorientierte Berichterstattung. In: Zeitschrift für kapitalmarktorientierte Rechnungslegung, 6, 269-279.

Reilly, R. and Schweihs, R. (1998): Valuing intangible assets. New York: McGraw-Hill.

Salinas, G. (2009): The international brand valuation manual: A complete overview and analysis of brand valuation techniques, methodologies and applications. West Sussex: John Wiley & Sons.

Sattler, H., Högl. S. and Hupp, O. (2003): Evaluation of the financial value of brands. In: ESOMAR, Excellence in International Research, 4, 75-96.

Single Property Sites (2012): Single property sites Inc. http://www.singlepropertysites.com/, 02.02.2012.

Steiner, H. and Fink, J. (2009): Die wertvollsten Immobilienmarken. Berlin: ProBusiness Verlag.

Viitanen, K. (2004): Brand in real estate business: Concept, idea, value? FIG Working Week, 22-27.05.2004, Athens, Greece.

Naming Rights for Sports Stadiums: Sponsor versus Club – Who Makes the Proper Brand?

Thomas Bezold

This paper describes the applications, benefits and risks of using naming rights at sports stadiums for branding purposes. Naming rights offer a broad range of marketing activities. For the arena operator, the selling of the naming right generates an additional source of income. In this context, our own research was undertaken to compare the naming right activities and contracted revenues in Germany, Europe and USA on the basis of selected examples of stadiums. Further, it shows the options of naming rights and discusses the main communicative functions to a sponsor and the branding possibilities. Finally, some light is shed on the critical question of the advertising effectiveness of this sponsorship tool and the questions who has more influence on the brand, the sponsor or the sport club as the main user of the stadium.

The allocation of naming rights in the sports sector has experienced a real boom in the last few years. While in the past sports facilities were traditionally named after regions, districts, rivers or merited individuals, today naming by a sponsor represents a business-oriented alternative (Sport+Markt 2011). Particularly the naming of football stadiums and large multipurpose arenas by sponsor companies against the background of new developments or conversions of German stadiums and declining public sponsorship of sport sites has led to a heightened allocation of naming rights. While an additional source of finance is made available for the proprietor or operating company of a sports facility in the first place with the mostly temporary sale of naming rights, the use of the naming rights for the naming sponsor is a promising instrument within their communication and branding activities. Here the biggest communicative use for a sponsor in a cleverly built-in integration of the naming rights is in a networked, strategically aligned business communication.

Origins of the Allocation of Naming Rights

Like many other trends in the commercialisation of sport, the allocation of naming rights has its historic roots in the US (Friedman 1999). The naming of halls of residences, libraries or charitable establishments in America, for instance through privately motivated, magnanimous contributions and financings, is basically accepted without question. The commercial allocation of naming rights also began there much earlier than in Germany or Europe (Ankenbrand 2007: 10-12). The metaphoric starter's gun fired with the buying of the baseball team Chicago Cubs by the bubble gum producer family Wrigley and the renaming of the arena into Wrigley Field in 1926 (Ashley and O'Hara 2001: 2). In the sphere of multipurpose arenas, the Key Arena in Seattle became the first large arena to market the naming right for $0.75 million/year with a validity period of 15 years in 1962 (McCarthy et al. 2000: 2). Meanwhile in America, the naming of sports facilities by a sponsor company was a part of the standard repertoire of sports facility marketing. It should be pointed out that in North America, contracts are valid for between 15 and 30 years on average and, therefore, it can be called a 'strategic communication (state) decision' which is connected to long-term financial obligations. Figure 1 summarises current, selected naming rights deals in America.

Stadium Name	Sponsor	Home Teams	Avg. $ / Year	Expires
Mercedes-Benz Superdome	Mercedes-Benz	New Orleans Saints	$12.5 million	2021
HSBC Arena	HSBC Bank	Buffalo Sabres	$800,000	2026
General Motors Place	General Motors	Vancouver Canucks	$844,366	2015
America West Arena	America West	Phoenix Suns, Coyotes, Mercury	$866,667	2019
Corel Center	Corel	Ottawa Senators	$878,142	2016
Compaq Center	Compaq Computer	Houston Rockets, Comets,	$900,000	2003
Cinergy Field	Cinergy	Cincinnati Reds	$1 million	2002
Ford Field	Ford Motor Co.	Detroit Lions	$1 million	2042
Delta Center	Delta Airlines	Utah Jazz, Starzz	$1.3 million	2011
Continental Airlines Arena	Continental Airlines	New Jersey Nets, Devils	$1.4 million	2011
Wachovia Center	Wachovia Bank	Philadelphia 76ers, Flyers	$1.4 million	2023
Air Canada Centre	Air Canada	Toronto Maple Leafs, Raptors	$1.5 million	2019

Stadium Name	Sponsor	Home Teams	Avg. $ / Year	Expires
Conseco Fieldhouse	Conseco	Indiana Pacers, Fever	$2 million	2019
Fleetcenter	Fleet Bank	Boston Celtics, Bruins	$2 million	2010
American Airlines Arena	American Airlines	Miami Heat	$2.1 million	2019
Bank One Ballpark	Bank One	Arizona Diamondbacks	$2.2 million	2028
Comerica Park	Comerica	Detroit Tigers	$2.2 million	2030
Citizens Bank Park	Citizens Bank	Philadelphia Phillies	$2.3 million	2028
Ameriquest Field	Ameriquest Capital Corp.	Texas Rangers	$2.5 million	2034
Great American Ball Park	Great American Insur.	Cincinnati Reds	$2.5 million	2033
Edward Jones Dome	Edward Jones	St. Louis Rams	$2.65 million	2013
Heinz Field	H.J. Heinz	Pittsburgh Steelers	$2.9 million	2021
HP Pavilion	Hewlett-Packard	San Jose Sharks	$3.1 million	2016
Gaylord Entertainment Center	Gaylord Entertainment	Nashville Predators	$4 million	2018
FedEx Forum	Federal Express	Memphis Grizzlies	$4.5 million	2023
Invesco Field at Mile High	Invesco Funds	Denver Broncos	$6 million	2021
American Airlines Center	American Airlines	Dallas Mavericks, Stars	$6.5 million	2031
Farmer's Field	Farmer's Insurance	Var. Los Angelos teams	$23.5 million	2044
Bank of America Stadium	Bank of America	Carolina Panthers	$7 million	2024
FedEx Field	Federal Express	Washington Redskins	$7.6 million	2025
Gillette Stadium	Gillette	New England Patriots	$8 million	2017

Figure 1:   Topic Naming Rights Deals in America. (Independent Research by Author)

Options and Roles of Allocating Names

Essentially anyone who holds a right, regardless of whether they are a proprietor, leaseholder, promoter or organiser, is free to allocate a commercial naming right for their stadium, event, tournament or league. In reality however, through frequency of use, the following forms have become accepted, namely the option to market the name of:

- arenas and stadiums
- teams (cycling/motor sports)
- events (golf/tennis)
- clubs (basketball)
- series (alpine ski World Cup)
- leagues (football in Austria, basketball in Germany) or
- track sections (motor racing)

Below, the two main roles of naming rights, which are connected to the sale or use of the naming right, will be discussed in detail. The temporary sale of the naming right particularly represents an additional financial instrument for the namesake, while for the naming sponsor it is a tool for their communication and marketing measures.

For proprietors of arenas and stadiums, for promoters of sporting events in organisational or commercial sponsorship, for clubs or teams, with the mostly temporary sale of the name, the opening up of financial means is top priority (Bezold 2005). However, this does not inevitably have to be the only reason. At best, a long-term naming rights deal also opens up strategic partnerships which provide desired access to resources on the procurement market or in distribution if the products or services are important for the naming right sale or to the target groups approached. Examples of this would be financial services or drinks suppliers, which if applicable, involve favourable logistical conditions or purchasing conditions for the arena operator.

One of the first examples occurred in 2001 with the renaming of the time-honoured Volksparkstadion in Hamburg to AOL Arena stirred up the industry and public interest in Germany. Meanwhile, many arenas and stadiums have changed names. The trend also applies to many other European leagues, but the contracted revenues of German football stadiums are the highest in Europe as shown in Figure 2.

DIE TOP-10-NAMINGRIGHTS AN EUROPÄISCHEN FUSSBALLSTADIEN*

Platz	Stadion	Kapazität	Land	Hometeam Fußballclub(s)	Summe Naming-Right (in Mio. Euro, p. a.)	Laufzeit
1	Allianz Arena	69 900	Deutschland	FC Bayern München TSV 1860 München (Mieter)	6,0	2005-2021
2	Veltins-Arena	61 673	Deutschland	FC Schalke 04	5,5	2005-2015
3	Imtech Arena	61 000	Deutschland	Hamburger SV	4,2	2010-2016
4	Signal Iduna Park	80 708	Deutschland	Borussia Dortmund	4,0	2005-2016
5	Emirates Stadium	60 500	England	Arsenal FC	3,7	2006-2021
6	Commerzbank-Arena	51 500	Deutschland	Eintracht Frankfurt	3,0	2005-2015
7	Volkswagen Arena	30 000	Deutschland	VfL Wolfsburg	2,5	unbefristet seit 2002
8	BayArena	30 210	Deutschland	Bayer 04 Leverkusen	3,1	unbefristet seit 1997
9	AWD-Arena	49 500	Deutschland	Hannover 96	2,2	2002-2012
10	RheinenergieStadion	50 000	Deutschland	1. FC Köln	2,1	2002-2014

AUSGEWÄHLTE NAMING-RIGHTS AN EUROPÄISCHEN FUSSBALLSTADIEN*

Platz	Stadion	Kapazität	Land	Hometeam Fußballclub(s)	Summe Naming-Right (in Mio. Euro, p. a.)	Laufzeit
....	PGE Arena	43 608 (im Bau)	Polen	Lechia Gdańsk	1,7	2010-2014
....	Ricoh Arena	32 609	England	FC Coventry	1,47	2006-2016
....	Turk Telecom Arena	52 600	Türkei	Galatasaray Istanbul	1,25	2007-2017
....	estadio Reyno de Navarra	19 800	Spanien	CA Osasuna	1,125	2005-2009
....	Swedbank Arena	50 000 (im Bau)	Schweden	National	1,043	2009-2025
....	MMArena	25 000	Frankreich	Le Mans UC 72	1,0	2009-2019
....	swissporarena	18 000 (im Bau)	Schweiz	FC Luzern	0,7	2010-2020
....	Liberty Stadium	20 500	Wales	Swansea City Association Football Club	0,6	2005-2010
....	Hypo Group Alpe Adria	12 000	Österreich	SK Austria Kärnten	0,5	2007-2012

* Die Fußballstadien sind nach der Höhe der jährlich bezahlten Lizenzsumme sortiert. Aufgelistet wurden die zehn wertvollsten Namensrechte im europäischen Fußball sowie eine Auswahl europäischer Fußballarenen anderer Nationen.

Figure 2:   Top Naming Rights of Stadiums in Europe, Season 2010/2011. (Rehm 2011: 55)

Naming Rights as a Marketing and Branding Instrument

Various possibilities within the communication and marketing activities for companies, which first of all enquire about purchasing the naming right, open up with the conclusion of a naming right deal. Sponsors benefit from being able to integrate five areas which are shown in Figure 3.

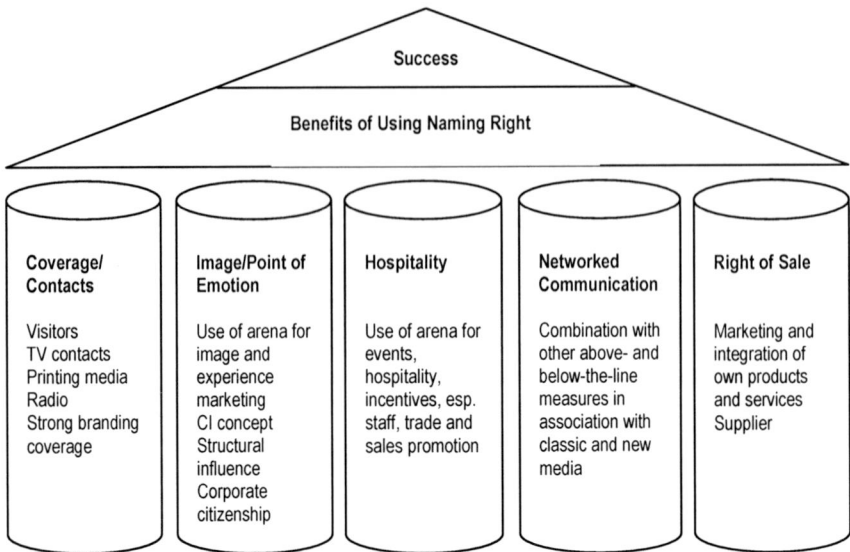

Coverage/ Contacts	Image/Point of Emotion	Hospitality	Networked Communication	Right of Sale
Visitors TV contacts Printing media Radio Strong branding coverage	Use of arena for image and experience marketing CI concept Structural influence Corporate citizenship	Use of arena for events, hospitality, incentives, esp. staff, trade and sales promotion	Combination with other above- and below-the-line measures in association with classic and new media	Marketing and integration of own products and services Supplier

Figure 3:   Benefits for the Namesake. (Author)

Alongside the traditional advertising objectives, such as increasing the level of recognition and image design, a naming right particularly serves as a suitable platform to combine sport with the company-specific associations. The assumed high costs for the temporary acquisition of the naming right and the additional costs to implement and use the other tools of the communication policies are accordingly seen in conjunction with numbers of contacts through the medial and multiplicative reproduction of the name as well as various options to combine other marketing measures.

Forming Contacts and Coverage

The great advantage of the 'naming right' tool, in comparison to other sponsoring measures such as perimeter advertising or shirt advertising, lies in the various multiplier effects of this form of advertising. By using the naming right, diverse contacts are made through the different media like TV, print, radio, online, outdoor adverting and stadium surroundings. Often mentions in the editorial environment are effective, whereby the advertising objective is refined and defensive behaviours such as reactance and zapping are virtually excluded.

Arena as a 'Point of Emotion'

By cleverly integrating the naming right into the company communication, the brand can be experienced in the arena and its surroundings. This occurs through structural influences on architectural elements for instance or by designing the stadium in a colour scheme to match the namesake's corporate design. Extra presentation features in and around the arena as well as matching lighting also reinforce the brand appearance. At most, it comes down to image transfer effects with popular sports between sports shows, arena management and the namesake. Moreover, with the current naming rights deals, sports facilities significantly prefer to list in which of the towns associated with the namesake they want to have their site (AWD-Arena in Hannover, Allianz-Arena in Munich, Volkswagen-Arena in Wolfsburg, BayArena in Leverkusen). In this way, the companies also demonstrate regional commitment which could be characterised as a specific form of corporate citizenship.

Hospitality

With the transfer of the name, many sponsors reserve relevant ticket deals, business seats and VIP lounges at the same time. This way further hospitality possibilities open up for customer acquisition and care. Various measures to manage customer relations can be transferred and used here. Ticket quotas and VIP boxes can also be used accordingly for internal marketing and for staff and trade promotions. There are more/better chances to use naming rights in b2b than in b2c campaigns.

Sales Rights

With many stadium projects, it is possible for the named sponsor to assure brand exclusivity within the naming right contract. In addition, a relevant supplier's right for certain products and/or services can also be agreed upon, whereby, the sponsor acquires the option to demonstrate the capability and quality of the product. Furthermore, football sales promotions and incentives would think of related in-house and external target groups, for whom the experience world of a stadium is particularly well-suited.

Networked Communication and Branding

A named sponsor provides the greatest use by cleverly networking the naming right into the various other features of the communication policy and branding (Bezold 2005). Here not just other sponsoring measures such as perimeter advertising, loud speaker announcements or hospitality features should be considered, but also networking with the classic media advertising such as TV spots, print and radio should take place. Internal and external marketing processes or lotteries can also be merged with the naming right. This advertising tool only becomes fully effective by incorporating and integrating the naming right in a textual-conceptual manner into other campaigns.

Branding Effectiveness: Some Empirical Findings

Although the metaphoric starter's gun fired in 2001 appears to give the AOL-Arena 11 years of experience, the branding effectiveness study of naming rights in Germany is still in its infancy because one must take into account the few experiences with naming right deals. Basically, however, the same instruments can draw on the classic advertising effectiveness study and be adapted to the 'naming right' application field. Recording recall values in the supported or unsupported form or calculating thousands of contact prices are also suitable for naming rights. Nevertheless, the fact should always be taken into consideration that the medial effect on the naming cumulates on different levels. The classic advertising value analysis appears to be particularly suitable because it is possible to include the individual media categories in the total sum of the advertising value. Through this, the result can also be used to assess to what extent the costs of acquiring the naming right are justified. On the other hand, this method can also determine a price for new naming rights. Very limited empirical data is published and available on the market. Within an independent telephone study conducted in the U.K. and USA by Performance Research (2007), less than one-fourth (23%) of U.K. respondents were able to correctly recall sports stadiums named after a company, brand or product. Bolton's Reebok stadium was recalled most frequently (54%), followed by Huddersfield's McAlpine stadium (48%). Another interesting question was if sponsors benefit from stadium naming. One-fourth (25%) of fans in the U.K. indicated that stadium sponsorship 'has or would increase purchase consideration' of that brand or product. Moreover, roughly one-half of the fans reported a 'more positive' opinion of a company sponsoring a sports stadium and 25% reported that a sports stadium named after a sponsoring company holds positive connotations, implying the team must be good. However, before sponsors consider signing a naming right deal, there are some aspects of which to be cautious. Although nearly one-half (47%) of U.K. respondents reported they were 'very' or 'moderately' in favour of a new sports arena named after a corporate sponsor, fewer than one-third of U.K. fans indicated they would be 'very' or 'moderately' in favour of changing the name of an existing stadium. Moreover, one in five U.K. sports fans reported just because a company was a sponsor did not make it right for them to change the name of the stadium and, unlike fans in the U.S., the majority (88%) of fans in the U.K. reported stadium naming would be of no benefit to them, indicating that stadium sponsorship was unlikely to result in lower ticket prices. Due to the empirical findings, the perception of the sponsor's brand seems to be more cognitive and less emotional. The perception of the team's/club's brand seems to be strongly emotional and only to a certain degree cognitive/rational. Therefore, naming rights are much more dominated by the image and brand of the home team/clubs rather than by their namesakes.

According to Mark Knight, Project Manager of Performance Research Europe, a company which undertakes sponsorship naming of a stadium without considering the needs of the club or fans is guilty of 'brandalism' of the worse kind and is only going to harm their brand image. A stadium can be a national icon or community focal point but an unnecessary name change may be seen as little more than a cold-hearted attempt to buy their way into a sport they ultimately don't understand (Performance Research 2007).

Generally fans in Germany have a very pragmatic understanding of accepting new sponsoring tools like naming rights as an additional source of income for the football club although there are cases of opposition. There is the case of the Bundesliga club 1 FC Nürnberg in which a great level of resistance was observed. The fans of the club were against the renaming of the beloved 'Frankenstadion', what 'used to be' a local icon and regional identification factor, into 'Easy Credit-Stadion' of a private bank. At a more ideological level, fan representatives complained that the deal was nothing else than a last step into the 'total commercialization' and the loss of club and fan identity. The management of the club stated that all relevant supporters of the club were involved in and agreed with the deal and the opposition was only pushed by the local media, who made a negative story out of it. However, fans' opinions should be taken seriously (Chadwick 2005). On the other hand, people have to see that fans always want to have and to see the best competitive team playing on the pitch. This pressure forces club management to explore new resources of incomes and naming rights is one way. In this greater context the often very emotional and sometimes very polemic discussion of football fans has to be seen as well.

Conclusion

The future market is limited for attractive naming rights in the area of football stadiums because only a limited number of attractive sports sites are suitable in the professional leagues of 1st and 2nd division clubs. However, in the future, it will also be attractive for smaller stadiums to use this tool because extra income can be generated through the temporary allocation of naming rights, where, apart from marketing efforts, no important costs are faced (semi-professional leagues and midsize events). Furthermore, a naming right contract can form the basis of a strategic partnership which can involve further synergy effects in procurement, logistics and sales distribution for both partners. A high demand for coordination could have a negative effect through a granted industry or product exclusivity and, connected to this, an industry exclusion of potential advertising partners. For enquirers of naming rights, this advertising tool enables highly-connected coverage and offers various branding possibilities within the integrated communication. In order to optimize the sponsor´s branding success, naming rights need to be activated and complemented with additional advertising and sponsoring tools inside and outside of the arena.

Particular attention is to be placed on the legal form of contract in order to avoid problematic areas from the first such as advertising freedom for certain events, industry exclusivity, pre-emption rights, supplier rights or aspects of facility management (Klingmüller 2002, 2006). Particularly in Germany, due to lack of experience with naming rights and cautious treatment, contracts are agreed upon with rather short periods of validity from approximately five years on average. If the contract is not extended, then a new named sponsor must be found. With re-labelling, however, serious delaying is necessary which at worst prevent a new named sponsor from being found and require when concluding the contract a sensitive treatment of the problem. Here renaming should ideally be combined with structural renovations or a re-opening in order to clearly signal to the public the beginning of a 'new era'. Also PR measures and accompanying information activities should be used in the phase. New names are essentially unproblematic. With re-naming, the 'old' namesake can possibly even benefit from the reverberation effect known from consumer research. The two former sentences are not discussed in the body of the paper and there is no documentation to support this conclusion. A crucial point for all participants is to secure a successful arena (marketing) management and a more technically-oriented professional facility management (Siebold 2004). So that the named sponsor experiences the desired positive effects, the different main and secondary users must also ensure positive headlines. Yet this cannot be directly guaranteed in the long-term in the domain of sport. In this respect, even the communicative success of a naming right is ultimately dependent on the sporting (and financial) success of the main user. Diverse marketing of an arena can lessen this dependency but never quite remove it. Operationally, a professional facility management should at all times guarantee the outer appearance, functionality, hygiene, catering, maintenance and repair as well as visitor safety. Proper facility management is a basic condition for branding success. Therefore, all necessary regulations, duties and competences should already have been contractually established very early (Wittneben 2006).

References

Ankenbrand, B. (2007): Die Verbriefung und Bewertung von Namensrechten mittels Informationsderivatebörsen. Köln: Lohmar.
Ashley, G. and O'Hara, M. (2001): Valuing naming rights. Ohama: University of Nebraska at Ohama.
Bezold, T. (2005): Namingrights als Finanzierungs- und Marketinginstrument. In: Horch, H.-D., Hovemann, G., Kaiser, S. and Viebahn, K. (eds.): Perspektiven des Sportmarketing: Besonderheiten, Herausforderungen, Tendenzen. Köln: Inst. für Sportökonomie und Sportmanagement, 7-28.
Chadwick, S. (2005): Addressing English football's stadium naming rights dilemma: Towards a model of good practice. In: Collins, M.F. (ed.): Book of abstracts of the 13th EASM European sport management congress in partnership with 75th Institute of Sport and Recreation Management Annual Conference 'The Power of Sport'. Newcastle: Bowden Publishing, 218-223.
Friedmann, A. (1999): Naming right deals: Professional sport facilities. Chicago: Princeton Hall.
Humberg, A. (2005): Sportstättensponsoring: Die Namensrechte bei Sportstätten. In: Juristische Rundschau, 3, 89-91.
Klingmüller, A. (2002): Namensrechte bei Sportstätten: Der Namensrechtsvertrag. In: SpuRt, 2, 59-61.
Klingmüller, A. (2006): Namensrechte von Sportstätten. In: Sponsors, 7, 48-49.
McCarthy, F., Larry, M. and Richard, I. (2000): An examination of the rationale and motives for corporate purchase of stadia and arena naming rights. In: Cyber Journal of Sports Marketing, 4(2/3).
Performance Research (2007): Naming rights, naming wrongs. http://www.performanceresearch.com/naming-rights.htm, 28.8.2011.
Rehm, H. (2011): Deutschaland ist Europameister. In: Sponsors 1, 54-55.
Siebold, M. (2004): Stadion/Arena: Geborene Rechte. In: Sponsors 6, 46-47.
Sport+Markt (2011) (ed.): Naming rights report 2011. Köln: Sport+Markt Verlag.
Wittneben, M. (2006): Naming-Rights-Verträge: Die Vergabe von Namensrechten im Sportbereich, GRUR. München: Beck, 814-818.

Senses and Sensualities

The Branded Experience: Decoding the Spatial Configuration of Flagship Stores

Garyfalia Palaiologou / Alan Penn

This paper is an effort to understand the role of branded architecture as a potential manifesto of organisational identity in the globalisation of economy. The aim is to bring to the fore the ways architectural space can define the composition of branded narrations and influence customer behaviour within branded spaces. The significance of architecture in creating branded experiences will be approached through the study of two flagship stores with both located in central London: the Niketown in Oxford Circus and the Apple Store in Regent Street.

The analysis of the two buildings focuses on three parameters: firstly on the spatial configuration and the emerging cultural phenomena, secondly on the customer-product interface, and thirdly, on the observation of customers' behaviour inside the store. The methodological approach includes the use of analytical tools of 'Space Syntax'. According to Space Syntax Theory, the organisation of space implies a primary distribution of users and their movement patterns. The study reveals how the spatial configuration affects the potential ways in which customers experience retail spaces. It is argued that both discussed flagship stores present such configurational properties that enhance the creation of cultural solidarities responsive to Nike and Apple's marketing profiles. More specifically, the Niketown building is argued to be a *conservative* and *moving* spatial model that constructs *transpatial* references to Nike's identity, while Apple Store is considered a *generative* and *static* model that supports the creation of *spatial* bonds between customers and brand identity.

Introduction

In contemporary retail processes and globalisation of economy, branded architecture is being used as a spatial manifesto of organisational identity; and as such a manifestation, branded architecture makes possible the existence of a brand's *imaginary community*. As Bauman argued, imaginary communities exist "through their manifestations: through occasional spectacular outbursts of togetherness or corporate presentation sessions" (1992: xix). A world is being constructed around the product and there is an evident effort by retail industries to achieve the materialisation of this world through the architecture of the selling point. Consequently, marketing policies started to employ the architecture of flagship stores as an additional advertising tool. Flagship stores are becoming the physical expressions of the product's cultural domain. Customers are invited to experience contextual notions of lifestyle and identity that are embedded within the store's physical boundaries. This marketing process, where buildings become products themselves, reveals the complexity of the mechanisms that are used nowadays to indulge consumers. Brands do not just sell products. Indeed, they sell identities and experiences of imaginary lives.

In this paper, the role of architecture as a marketing process will be approached in relation to the non-discursive properties of retail space. Hence, based on Hillier's propositions (1996: 27), the syntactic characteristics of the *spatial configuration* will be discussed in order to understand the way "buildings can transmit common cultural tendencies through spatial form". Spatial configuration, a notion introduced by Space Syntax theory, represents spatial patterns as highly relational systems and in constant liaison with the social patterns they support (Hillier and Vaughan 2007). Considering spatial systems in a configurational way takes into account both relations between the components of the system and between the parts and the whole (Hillier 1996: 24, Hillier and Penn 1991: 30). This type of analysis refers to the non-discursive properties of space and addresses the culturally determined patterns that are "embedded in material and spatial 'objectivity' of buildings" (Hillier 1996: 27).

The implications of this non-discursive transmission of cultural notions between retail buildings and consumers through branded architecture will be discussed based on the example of two flagship stores both located in central London: the Niketown in Oxford Circus and the Apple Store in Regent Street. The study presents the stores' policy of serving the customer, of deliberately orienting or disorienting him and examines the role of the spatial configuration in relation to the aforementioned intentions. It is suggested that the spatial layout of a retail store defines a prior distribution of movement flows in the building by implementing the most probable interior routes for visitors. In other words, it defines the way customers explore and discover space. Moreover, it is argued that architecture can embed in these possible routes culturally defined information regarding the brand, whilst controlling the way and the probable sequence that these branded notions are going to be communicated to the customer in order for him to construct *branded narrations*.

Retail Architecture: The Syntax and Cultural Context of Retail Space

Anthropologists have pointed out the fundamental role of cultural notions for consumption processes which is that objects present communicative properties by drawing references to social life, to *meaning* and *symbolism* (McCracken 1988: 58). Accordingly, the same communicative properties regarding social references are used also for the construction as well as constant renegotiation and transformation of individual and communal cultural models (McCracken 1988: xiv). As Arendt states (1956: 133), consumption has become a process that stretches beyond the actual necessities of an individual, creating on the contrary a subjective need for the 'superfluities of life'. Such subjective needs are cultivated within the stream of both established and contemporary cultural models. Specifically, cultural meaning is carried from the 'culturally constituted world' to the product, and the world that surrounds the product, then to the consumer and subsequently into his life (McCracken 1988). In other words, it could be said that through cultural meaning the process of consumption is transformed into an experience. Thus, brands do not advertise only the properties of a product, but emphasise the purchase and possession rituals as well (Du Gay 1997: 8, McCracken 1988: xii, 85). Namely, brands construct and sell as well the experience of consumption performed within the physical and contextual domain of their *branded worlds*.

This 'experiential place-making' (Kulkarni and Joseph-Lester 2004: 34) refers to the spatial materialisation of a product's cultural world. In order to understand the architectural mechanisms behind the spatial composition of a branded experience, it is important to understand the properties of architecture as a 'morphic language'. Hillier and Hanson (1984: 49) explain that architecture is being realised in the experiential world. Architecture can thus retrieve from its syntax or introduce in it various 'cultural intermediaries'. According to Du Gay (1997: 5) cultural intermediaries are shapes, forms, images, media, entertainment installations and art installations. Moreover, the authors suggest that architecture frames through spatial configuration the potential ways these spatial mediums can be conceived by the user, both in physical and cultural terms.

Penn, Martinez and Lemlij (2007: 15), in a discussion regarding the individual agents-building interface and the 'emergent cultural structures' that can be developed within the domain of this interface, introduce a consideration of spatial configuration as an "active stratum" (2007: 15). The authors explain that architecture can address two types of an individual's cognitive responses to the physical environment. These are the *physical* and the *social* responses. Firstly, the *physical* behaviour derives from the sense of vision and gives rise to *natural movement*. The theory of natural movement (Hillier et al. 1993) explains how the spatial configuration can shape movement patterns by defining possible distributions and encounters of physical users who are at the same time social users as well. This suggestion implies a prior relationship between spatial patterns and basic social phenomena of co-presence and consequently of potential interaction of social users. Secondly, when referring mainly to a cultural rather than a basic social level of cognition, an individual's *social* responses derive from visual culture as a transmitter of socially defined information.

Based on the aforementioned theoretical framework of considerations regarding the building-visitor interface, this paper examines the way organisational spaces construct *cultural narratives* where the consumer is being located in order to experience organisational cultures (Du Gay 1997: 253). More particularly, the aim is to understand the way architecture can promote, through spatial configuration, branded experiences of organisational identity and customer service in flagship stores. In other words, the discussion in this paper concentrates on the ways architecture shapes and implements the consumption experience primarily in the level of *physical* cognition, while at the same time architecture also enriches this experience with cultural references that address secondly the *social* cognitive level.

Case Studies and Methodology

In order to study those structural properties of architecture in terms of the branded experience, the case studies of the Niketown in Oxford Circus and the Apple Store in Regent Street were selected. These retail spaces were selected based on multiple criteria concerning both the characteristics of the brands themselves and the properties of the stores. The two buildings appeared to present interestingly different qualities regarding their spatial configuration in terms of mobility and of emergence of phenomena like co-presence, and also in relation to how space supports in each case the brand's suggested model of customer-product and customer-staff interfaces. It was evident that Niketown aimed in turning the consumption process into a *moving experience* of sequential revelation of the interior as a carrier of products and of brand's athletic notions. Customers' flow seemed the key idea of the spatial configuration. On the other hand, Apple Store appeared as a more *static model* of retail space that emphasised the customer-product interface and the experience of hi-technology through this customer-product interaction. In this flagship store, co-presence seemed the key idea of spatial configuration.

The methodological approach combines the use of analytical measures and tools introduced by Space Syntax research (Visibility Graph Analysis with DepthMap Software, Turner 2001) with ethnographic observations regarding the customer's profile and physical behaviour within these retail spaces (customers' route tracing and static snapshots, Sailer and Penn 2009). The analysis will focus on decoding the role of three aspects of each retail store in constructing Nike and Apple's *branded narrations*. Firstly, the *spatial configuration* of the interior layout is analysed in terms of its correspondence to its function as a commercial building and of the customer movement patterns that each layout generates. Secondly, the *product display* will be discussed in relation to each brand's strategic product placement policies within the spatial layout. Finally, both retail spaces will be considered in terms of the cultural and organisational references they support. More particularly, the analysis will discuss the way each spatial layout communicates the brand's cultural profiles and structures the brand's interaction with customers, whilst considering its policy concerning customer service.

In the following paragraphs Nike and Apple's branded worlds will be presented from the viewpoint of the visitors of the two flagship stores. After presenting the concept behind the architecture of the layout for these two contemporary 'boutiques', comparison of the structured retail models spatially and contextually will be formed. It is interesting to note that, in retail architecture, the boutique of the 1960's can be considered as the historical origins of flagship stores (Pimlott 2007: 1-8). The following comparative discussion shows the complexity and efficiency of contemporary marketing processes in addressing the deeper and more unconscious levels of customers' experiential behaviour. Moreover, the role of architecture in communicating these marketing processes and in relating the brand-product-customer cultural domains is revealed.

Two Brands; Two Narrations for the Customer

Niketown: The 'Town'

In its entire flagship stores around the world Nike aims in creating a collective experience that recalls athletic spirit and spectacle. Gordon Thompson, the vice president of Nike's Design Team, states in Architectural Record (March 1997: 103): "It's something like going to a sports event." In other words, the brand's policy in terms of retail environment is quite explicit: Nike's cultural solidarity tries to be established through customers' experience of its branded spaces (*experiential 'space'-making*). The Nike central London flagship store is located in the junction of Regent and Oxford Street in a two-storey high historical building. By using "architecture as a communication device" and "architectural gestures as promotion" (Dorris 1997: 103) the building was structured configurationally, architecturally and morphologically, the 1991 configuration, in a way that it would produce experiential references to city structures and the urban buzz. Such morphological elements for the different sport sections were the pavilion façades, the brick covered surfaces and the use of the format of London's street signs for sections' logos (Figure 1).

Figure 1:   Niketown 1991 Interior. The photo shows the city-like materials, shapes and layout of the interior design. (http://www.bdp.com/ Projects/By-Name/M-O/NikeTown/, 10.05.2012)

In contrast to common commercial environments, the open-plan space was not maximised in order to highlight the product. Here, the product display came gradually as an introduction to the brand's world where installations that resemble city patterns carried the merchandise. The measure of *visual step depth* shows the way visitors are introduced into retail space. Turner (2003: 662) explains that, in Visibility Graph Analysis (VGA) using Depthmap software, visual step depth is considered "a measure of the outgoing visual area on any path from a particular location". In Niketown, the entrance is visually open to the exterior so as to pull inside the urban flow in a square-like open plan space (Figure 2). From there and while moving to the interior, the visitor's visual field becomes smaller and reveals gradually the building and the products. The *isovist area* represents the visitor's visual field from a point within the spatial configuration (Turner et al. 2001: 107).

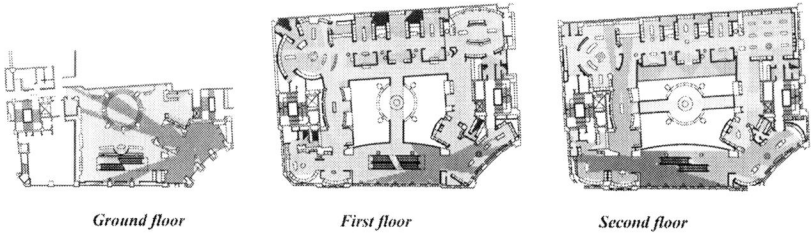

Ground floor   First floor   Second floor

Figure 2: VGA for Niketown 1991 Interior. The diagram shows visual step depth from the store entrance and from the escalator landing points of each floor. (Authors)

A characteristic of Nike retail spaces is the frequent change of interior design, layout and furnishing. This consists of a mechanism for embedding each time in retail space the contemporary marketing priorities. For instance, in the 2009 version of the store, which is the year when the study was made, the main theme of the interior design was Britain's football tradition. There was also an emphasis on personalised shopping and on customers' ability to order their uniquely designed shoes. The aim is to consider the product as an inextricable part of brand's world in order to intensify the cultural and transpatial bonds between the customer and the brand. Nike structures the policy of its retail space based on the idea that when discerning and strongly structuring the interior, *transpatial solidarities* are supported (Hillier and Hanson 1984: 145). Such solidarities can overcome the boundaries of space and, therefore, expand the brand domain to the more virtual fields of the customer's life. Gordon Thompson explains: "We need Niketown stores to carry the Nike story. If the customer buys a product at the Niketown store or goes down the street to buy it at footlocker, either way, we win." (Dorris 1997: 103).

In both 1991 and 2009 versions of the Niketown interior, the way customers experience the spatial-visual-informational continuum is highly structured and thus highly deterministic in terms of the emerged movement patterns. The linear aspects of the configuration such as the long corridors, along with the existence of only one entrance and exit to each product section, support ordered and sequential customer movement flows. Customers follow a route in which different thematic sections are being exhibited one by one. Consequently, a great amount of visual information is provided in an organised way which resembles some kind of spectacle. Moreover, the building shows unintelligible patterns

(Figure 3) in terms of 'locally perceptible information' regarding the whole configuration (Penn et al. 2007). Thus it disorients the visitor through informational 'noise' and customers feel lost in the brand's world. It appears, though, that this is Nike's intention to create emotions of constant change. Resembling somehow to a town, it appears as if the visitor moves in an outdoor environment which does not repeat itself.

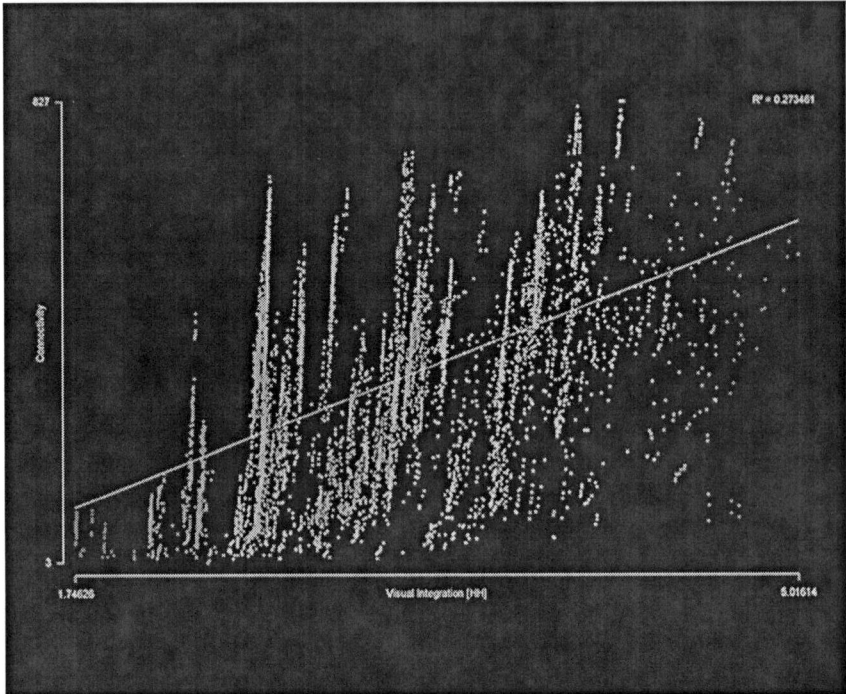

Figure 3:   Intelligibility Measure for Niketown 1991 Interior. The scatter plot presents on the vertical axis the values for spaces' *connectivity* and on the horizontal axis the values for *visual integration*. (Authors)

This implicit ordering of the way the space is experienced is the indicator of the type of model that this retail environment constitutes in terms of 'social programming' (Hillier 1996) and corporate organisation. Niketown is a *long model* and a deep configuration; therefore, events within this spatial system are being reproduced through time. In other words, the spatio-temporal phenomena developed in this store are mainly predetermined and they do not emerge as new probabilities. The fact that the spatial experience is structured through certain possible route sequences implies the degree of conceptual intervention in the space-time events. Accordingly, in Nike's flagship store there is a high level of control in the customer encounter rate and its sequence. The co-operation between the spatial patterns and product placement guides men and women, and accordingly boys and girls as well, to follow opposite routes and, consequently, to encounter one another as moving around and thus reminding one somehow of urban scenes (Figure 4, 5 and 6). The configuration increases the possibilities that visitors will move around the whole store. Selected and targeted shopping also exists although the customer passes through sections that do not deliberately interest him (Figure 6).

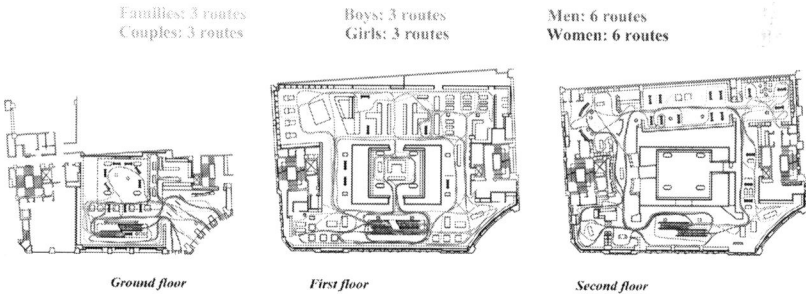

| Families: 3 routes | Boys: 3 routes | Men: 6 routes |
| Couples: 3 routes | Girls: 3 routes | Women: 6 routes |

Ground floor   *First floor*   *Second floor*

Figure 4:   Ethnographic Observations in Niketown 2009 Interior. The figure shows customers' route tracing, starting from the store entrance and from the escalator landing of each floor. (Authors)

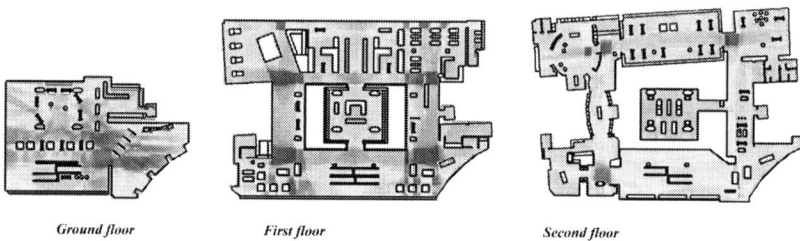

Ground floor   *First floor*   *Second floor*

Figure 5:   VGA for Niketown 2009 Interior. The diagrams show visual integration for accessibility level (furnishing considered). The deeper colouring represents the higher probabilities for movement distribution in the layout. (Authors)

Men: 6 routes

Women: 6 routes

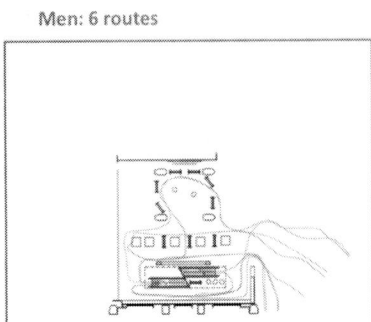
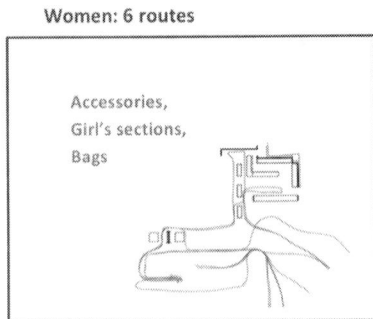

GROUND FLOOR

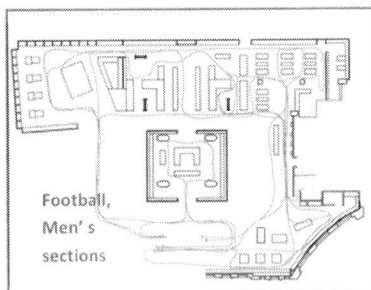
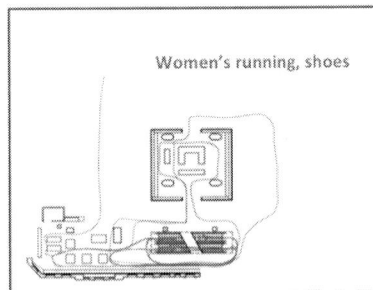

FIRST FLOOR

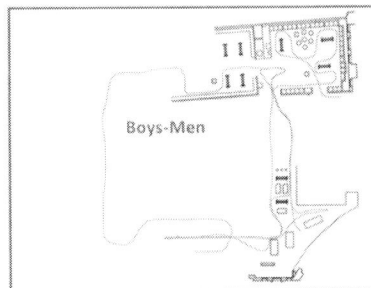
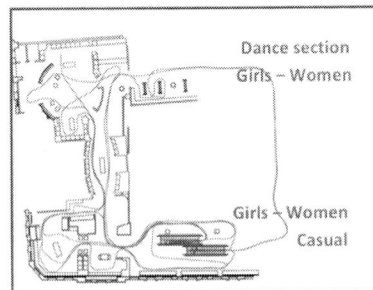

SECOND FLOOR

Figure 6:   Ethnographic Observations in Niketown 2009 Interior. The figure shows route tracing for different customer categories and the relevant product sections they encountered. (Authors)

Moreover, the rules embedded in the spatial configuration structure and support mainly relationships of a formal character between the users which are the customers and staff members. Each one's domain is well defined because customers move mainly in the linear parts of the configuration, the strangers' domain, while they enter as visitors the various product sections where members of the staff are located which is the inhabitants' domain. These formal relationships are expressed through brand policies concerning the customer-staff interface. In Niketown the developed customer-staff interface is similar to the 'inhabitant-stranger' model (Hillier and Hanson 1984: 146). In this way the customers are kept at distance from staff members who attain a different status-power as inhabitants of the retail space. It could be said that the spatial affirmation of their role re-affirms also in a way Nike's institutional structures. High levels of visual control (Figure 7) at corridors and of visual clustering of the segregated rooms/sections, which host different groups of products referring to different groups of customers, create an inhabitant-orientated spatial organisation where corridors behave like city streets (Hillier and Hanson 1984: 122). Visual control is "a local measure of the degree of choice of movement for each space in relation to its immediate neighbour" (Hillier et al. 1987: 273).

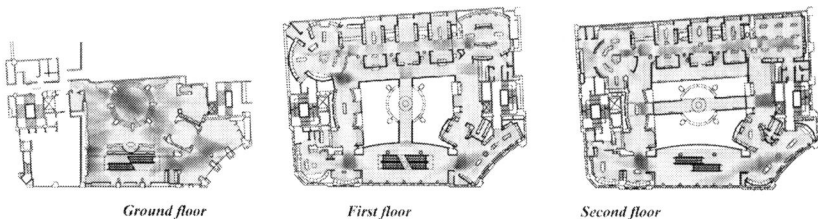

Ground floor   *First floor*   *Second floor*

Figure 7:   VGA for Niketown 1991 Interior. The diagrams represent the
                measure of visual control. The values are higher for corridor
                junctions and central areas in the layout. (Authors)

The aforementioned observations regarding Nike's retail environment could be summarised into two key characteristics: Niketown is a *conservative* model (Hillier 1996) in terms of its social functioning which means that it mainly supports and is shaped by social meaning invested in its retail space, that is in turn explored by customers in a deterministic and highly controlled way. In other words, the cultural narratives are already embedded in and supported by the spatial organisation of the interior layout. Secondly, Niketown is a *moving model* in terms of its spatially experiential aspects enhancing movement rather than phenomena of co-presence and occupancy, namely of interaction.

In the following paragraphs the retail space of Apple Store is presented. It configures quite contradictive results that are yet again correspondent to this brand's marketing intentions.

Apple Store: The 'Interactive' Store

Apple Store is a quite opposing model of retail space in terms of spatial and commercial aspirations. The brand's significant investment on its retail environments started when, in 2000, Ron Johnson took over as a vice-president of Apple's Retail team. He organised a sales strategy based on a clearly new retail fit that emphasised Apple's products. Accordingly, products stand out in space as important objects by being displayed in an exhibition-like open-plan layout. However, at the same time this display does not present museum-like formalities. Instead products are reachable by the customer and ready to be used. As Apple states regarding its selling points, the main characteristic of the brand's retail spaces are the 'hands-in-use'. With the new retail spaces, Apple's sales increased about 6% and the particular sales of iMac purchased in Apple stores have risen up to 50% (ifoAppleStore, http://www.ifoapplestore.com/ the_stores.html, 10.05.2012).

The product display is not the only thing that Apple emphasises. The branded experience offered to the customer is mostly about the developed in-store relationships and the provided service within the retail environment. The intention is to create "a club, maybe, in the sense that owning a Mac means joining something ... So we quickly moved from a buying experience to an ownership experience – Genius Bars, theatres, and face-to-face help and friendly people" (ifoAppleStore, http://www.ifoapplestore.com/the_stores.html, 10.05.2012). A symbolic cultural world is synthesised with aesthetics of interior design that recall the brand's minimal and high-tech design of products which are large display windows in the façade, bright and open interiors, simple materials such as only glass, steel, wood as well as logos in large posters on walls that constitute such architectural choices.

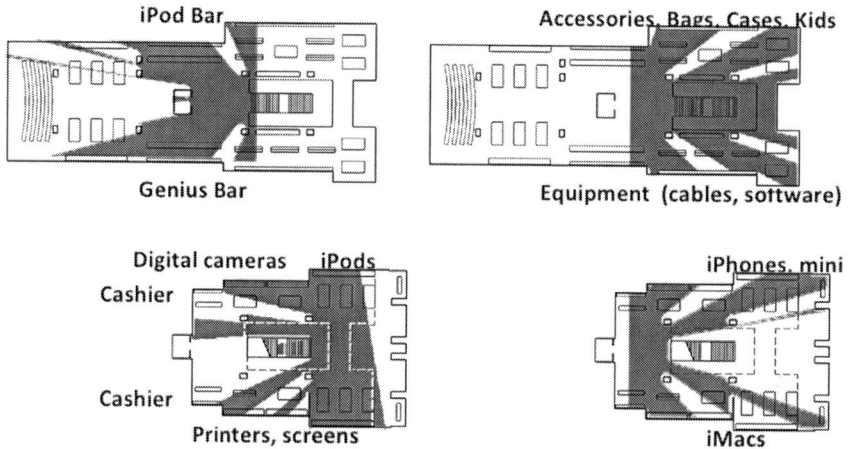

Figure 8:   Apple Store 2009 Interior Design. The figure represents targeted 2D planar views (*half-isovists*) of the potential visual field from four different points in relation to product placement. (Authors)

Consequently, the marketing intentions are summarised in the concept of highlighting the product and at the same time of establishing a spatial bond with customers through the cultural activities that take place inside the boundaries of its world (*experiential 'place'-making*). Here, the bonds created with the spatial aspects of the configuration are stronger in comparison to the ones of Niketown. The interior of the Apple Store is highly accessible from the outside regarding both the ground and the upper floor. The ground floor is accessed through a large entrance area facing directly to the escalator that leads to the upper store level. This weak boundary to the exterior is accompanied by a weak interior open-plan spatial organisation that presents high visibility levels. The aim is to create a spatial, rather than virtual, interdependence between the brand and the flagship store. In other words, to configure a *spatial solidarity* that is based on "contiguity and encounter" (Hillier and Hanson 1984: 145). In such solidarities, the configuration supports the emergence of cultural-social phenomena within the space. In this case, convexity rules over linearity thus allowing the occupancy to develop during time and generating high levels of co-presence (Figure 9 and 10). Moreover, visibility and permeability are highly free from obstacles and, therefore, allow the selection of multiple route choices and raise the probabilities for encounters (Figure 11).

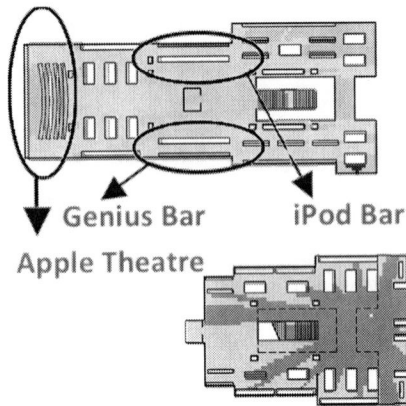

Figure 9:   VGA for Apple Store 2009 Interior. This shows visual step depth
from the store entrance and the staircase on the floor. (Authors)

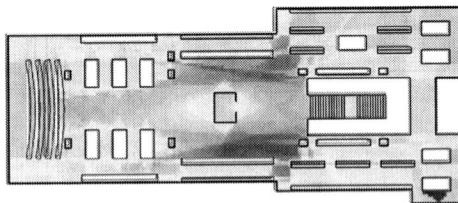

First floor

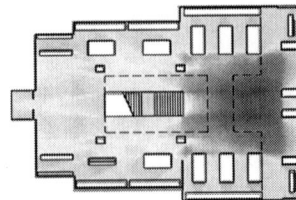

Ground floor

Figure 10:   VGA for Apple Store 2009 Interior. Here, the visual integration
measure shows the high level of integration of the central space for
each floor. (Authors)

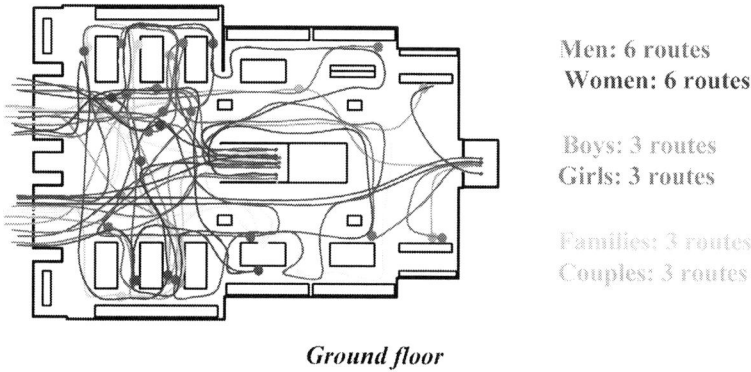

Men: 6 routes
Women: 6 routes

Boys: 3 routes
Girls: 3 routes

Families: 3 routes
Couples: 3 routes

Ground floor

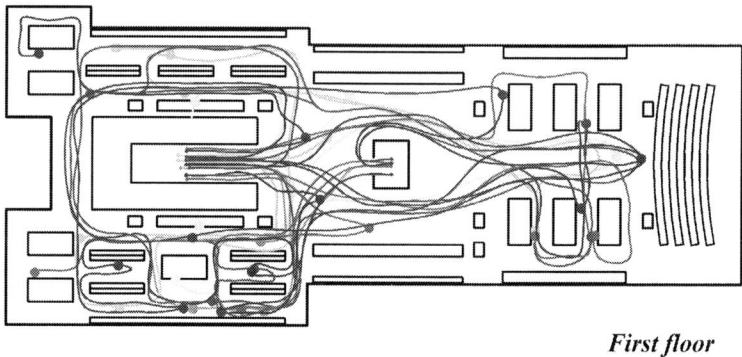

First floor

Figure 11:   Ethnographic Observations in Apple Store 2009 Interior. Graphs
show customers' route tracing, starting from the store entrance and
from the escalators on the first floor. (Authors)

As in Nike, there is an effort here also to form different product sections but in a
more *intelligible* way (Figure 12). The aim is to organise different activities
within the store where the customer will interact with different types of products
according to their technical characteristics. The educational activities are also
specified (Apple Theatre, Genius Bar), without however presenting clear and
strong boundaries from the rest of the layout. In this way an Apple expert is
always within reach and sight and services are also open on display whilst
remaining at the same time personalised. The customer is aware of the offered
help inside the store; personal treatment seems something usual that customers

150 Garyfalia Palaiologou / Alan Penn

observe at any time and from a close distance. This enhances a felling of familiarity with the place.

In Apple Store clusters are formed in a different way than the one presented in Niketown (Figure 13). Here, clusters are not only the sum of locations that are close to each other in terms of visual integration values. Instead, clusters in Apple are also located in proximity. In Nike visual integration did not mean proximity as well. Thus, clustering in Apple is obvious and clear. The spatial configuration contributes in an explicit and significant way to the division of products in groups that are consequently spatially categorised.

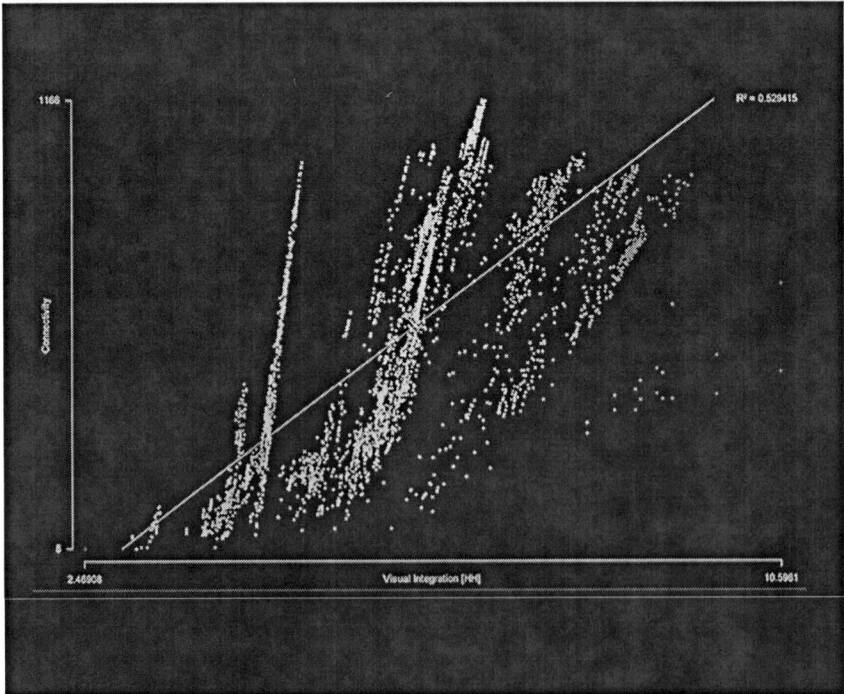

Figure 12:   Intelligibility Measure for Apple Store 2009 Interior. The scatter plot presents on the vertical axis the values for spaces' *connectivity* and on the horizontal axis the values for *visual integration.* (Authors)

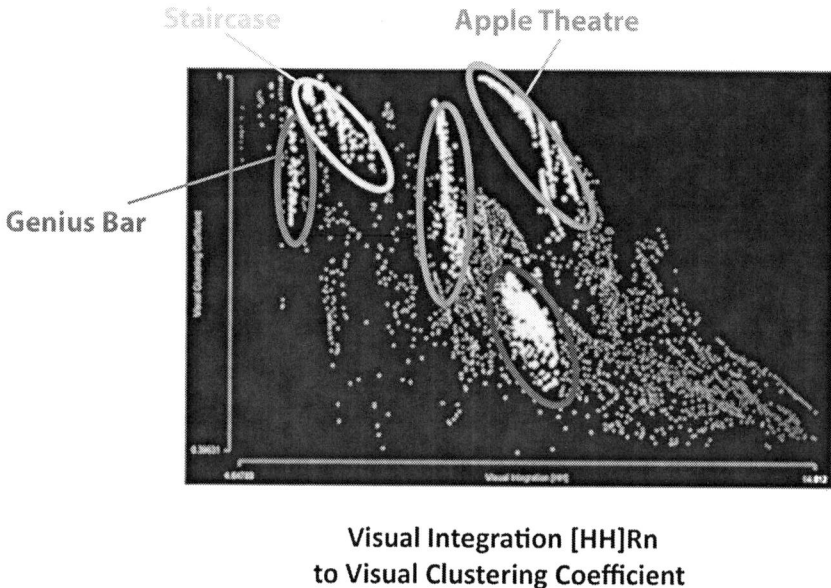

Visual Integration [HH]Rn
to Visual Clustering Coefficient

Figure 13:   Visual Cluster for Apple Store 2009 Interior. The scatter plot
shows visual clustering co-efficiency for spaces in the ground floor.
(Authors)

In terms of 'social programming' (Hillier 1996) and corporate organisation, this retail environment is characterised by the implicit informal and free way that customers experience space. The Apple Store is a shallow spatial configuration that presents characteristics of a *short model.* Namely, the spatiotemporal events are more likely to emerge through the store's configuration, as the ordering of the spatial patterns is weak. This means that the spatial layout does not interfere nor predefine the space-time events. The sequence of the spatiotemporal experience depends on the perceptual domain and the free will of the customer and no behaviour is implicitly forced by the spatial structure apart from the development of communal interaction. This can be seen in the patterns of the observed customers' route traces which confirm the irregularity of movement choices (Figure 11). In this way, spatial patterns give rise to informal socio-spatial relationships.

Additionally, informality characterises the customer-staff interface. Members of the staff are moving all the time among customers, therefore, being in proximity and participating in all activities performed inside the store. The customer-staff relationship is informal with no hierarchy or authority becoming perceived or even implied. In this way, Apple Store turns into a very familiar environment.

For these properties, Apple Store is considered a 'generative' model in terms of its social functioning (Hillier 1996) where spatial patterns shape social phenomena. In Apple's retail space cultural narratives are generated through probabilities emerging from the spatial layout. Moreover, regarding the spatial experience, Apple Store resembles a *static model* that emphasises co-presence and probabilities for interaction.

The 'Moving' Model; The 'Static' Model

This study was an effort to examine the contemporary retail space and the strategic brand notions that are embedded in the syntax of its spatial configuration, so as to be unconsciously transmitted to customers through its configurational level of interaction with space. In order to understand retail space in reference to these branded notions, two very different commercial environments were studied which were the Niketown in Oxford Circus and the Apple Store in Regent Street. The intention was to investigate the role of architecture, if there was any, in evoking the opposite feelings that these flagship stores seemed to create for the visitors.

The authors of *Disorientation and Spectacle in Retail Architecture* describe some of the ways that the consumer can be 'absorbed into architecture' passing from a process of "a retina experience to the one of embodiment" (Kulkarni and Joseph-Lester 2004: 5). This embodied experience is a strong means for organisations to communicate notions of culture and identity to consumers as well as constructing *transpatial bonds* with the visitor. The argument is based on the consideration that a lived experience becomes a memory and, therefore, it becomes a constant personal possession. Then as an accessible feeling, the consumer can recall the branded experience at any moment of his everyday life and not only at the limited time-space physical boundaries of the selling point. This is not only a creation of strategies of "displaced meaning" (McCracken 1988: 106). Indeed, it is also an effort to create transpatial unique communities in reference to a particular field of expertise and specialisation. Specialisation is considered a characteristic product of 'organic solidarities' and the 'division of labor' in modern societies as discussed by Durkheim (1933: 131). Accordingly, Nike and Apple's marketing policies presented the intention of configuring transpatial cultural bonds with their customers by generating from the spatial layout of their flagship stores references to their cultural domains.

The analysis for each store focused on three parameters: firstly, on the syntactic aspects of the *spatial configurational* and the supported/emerged socio-spatial phenomena; secondly, on the product placement and the mode of their display, namely on the *customer-product interface*; and thirdly, on the promoted organisational profile through the public face of each brand, namely on the way the *customer-staff interface* was configured. By combining data and results of analysis, the model of the customer experience offered at each store was discussed according to the spatial and cultural aspects of each retail configuration. The discussion was structured around conclusions regarding the functioning of the spatial layout and the embedded in it social programming which in this case reflects the corporate image.

As it has been clarified through the analysis, the priority for Nike is to create a strong bond between the customer and its characteristic branded notions through the architectural making of its branded world-*Town*. This was achieved by creating a moving experience of a constantly changing rich visual continuum that resembles city-like patterns. Niketown was argued to be a *conservative and moving* spatial model that aims in structuring a *transpatial solidarity*, while Apple Store was presented as a *generative and static* spatial model emphasising spatial references and supporting a *spatial solidarity* (Figure 14 and 15). In the case of Niketown, the brand narrates the commercial process to the customer in a 'predefined up to the extent way' performing, as it was argued, an *experiential space-making*. On the other hand, the Apple store performs as a setting where customers create their own narrations thus performing an *experiential place-making* that are, however, inextricably bound to the branded setting and in constant liaison with branded stimuli either products or staff members. Although pointing towards opposite directions, these brands' policies are in complete alliance with their identity and their advertised profile in relation to their field of expertise. Apple wants to infuse trust and originality to its spatial profile, while Nike seeks to create inspirations of spectacle, excitement and victory.

In both cases the purpose is achieved. For Nike, the interior design created an unintelligible spatial configurational which implies the brand's 'dominance'. On the other hand, Apple structured a more intelligible spatial layout that supports aspects of "autonomy" (Penn 2005: 39). It can be argued that both brands prove their expertise in creating well configured branded experiences and spatially 'tellable' branded stories (Penn et al. 2007).

Evening rush-hour (starting time, 17:00 pm)

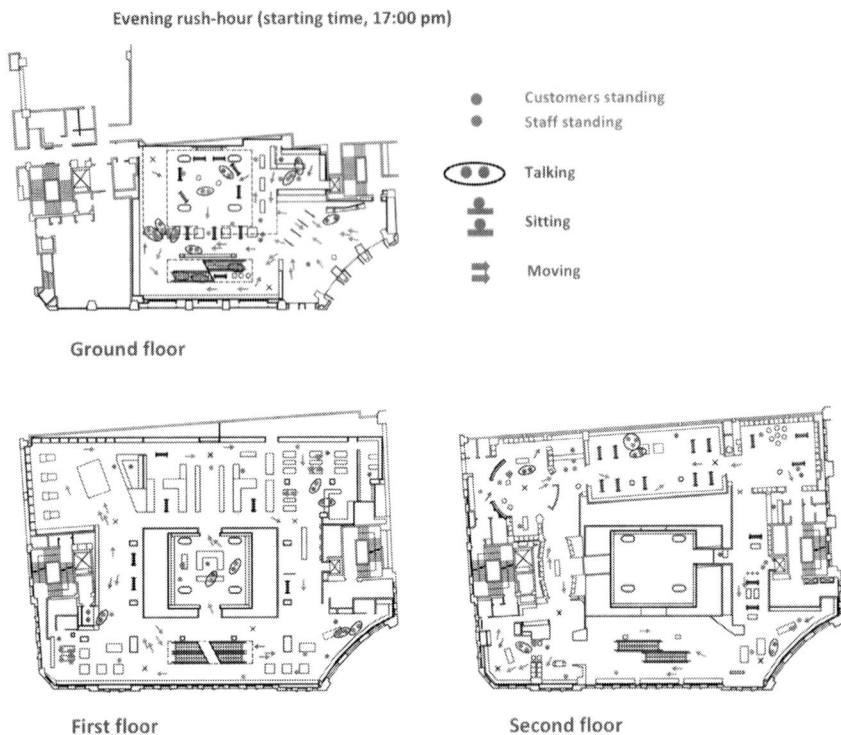

●   Customers standing
●   Staff standing

Talking

Sitting

Moving

Ground floor

First floor   Second floor

Figure 14:   Niketown, *the Moving Model*. Ethnographic observations show static snapshots that record the occupancy of space from spatial locations marked with 'x' in the plans for commercial rush-hour time. (Authors)

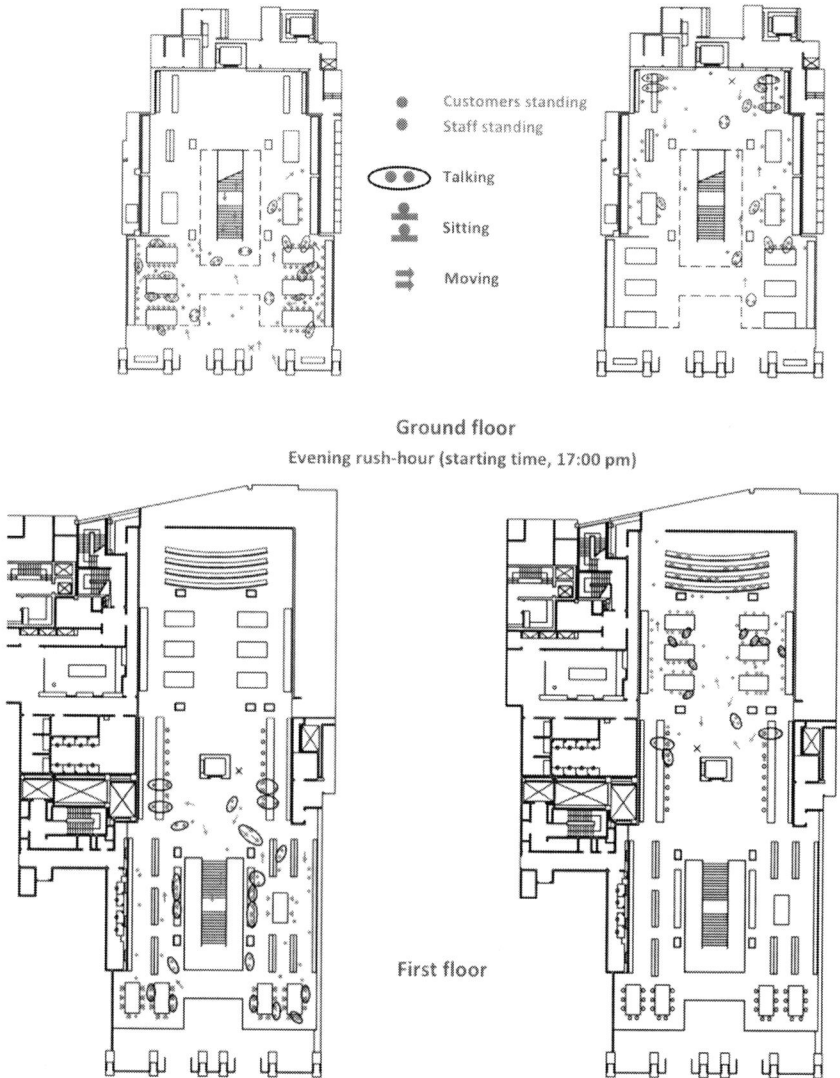

Legend:
- Customers standing
- Staff standing
- Talking
- Sitting
- Moving

Ground floor
Evening rush-hour (starting time, 17:00 pm)

First floor

Figure 15: Apple Store, *the Static Model.* Ethnographic observations show static snapshots that record the occupancy of space from spatial locations marked with 'x' in the plans for commercial rush-hour time. (Authors)

References

Arendt, H. (1956): The human condition. Chicago: University of Chicago Press.

Bauman, Z. (1992): Intimations of Postmodernity. London: Routledge.

Dorris, K.V. (1997): Nike Town New York City. In: Architectural Record, 185(3), 100.

Doxa, M. (2001): Morphologies of co-presence in interior public space in places of performance. In: Proceedings, 3rd International Space Syntax Symposium, Atlanta, USA.

Du Gay, P. (1997): Production of culture: Culture of production. London: Sage Publications, The Open University.

Hillier, B. (1996): Space is the machine. Cambridge: Cambridge University Press.

Hillier, B., Burdett, R., Peponis, J. and Penn, A. (1987): Creating life: Or, does architecture determine anything? In: Architecture & Comportment: Architecture and Behaviour, 3(3), 233-250.

Hillier, B. and Hanson, J. (1984): The social logic of space. Cambridge: Cambridge University Press.

Hillier, B., Penn, A., Hanson, J., Grajewski, T. and Xu, J. (1993): Natural movement or configuration and attraction in urban pedestrian movement. In: Environment and Planning B, 20(1), 29-66.

Hillier, B. and Vaughan, L. (2007): The city as one thing. In: Progress in Planning, 67(3), 205-230.

Kulkarni, N. and Joseph-Lester, J. (2004): Disorientation and spectacle in retail architecture. London: Artwords Press.

McCracken, G. (1988): Culture and consumption: New approaches to the symbolic character of consumer goods and activities. Bloomington: Indiana University Press.

Penn, A. (2005): The complexity of the elementary interface: Shopping space. In: Proceedings, 5th International Space Syntax Symposium, Delft, Holland.

Penn, A., Martinez, M. and Lemlij, M. (2007): Structure, agency and space in the emergence of organizational culture. In: Proceedings, 6th International Space Syntax Symposium, Istanbul, Turkey.

Pimlott, M. (2007): The boutique and the mass market. In: Vernet, D. and De Wit, L. (2007): Boutiques and other retail spaces: The architecture of seduction. New York: Routledge, 1-15.

Sailer, K. and Penn, A. (2009): Spatiality and transpatiality in workplace environments. In: Proceedings, 7th International Space Syntax Symposium, Stockholm, Sweden.

Turner, A. (2003): Analysing the visual dynamics of spatial morphology. In: Environment and Planning B, 30(5), 657-676.

Turner, A., Doxa, M., O'Sullivan, D. and Penn A. (2001): From isovists to visibility graphs: A methodology for the analysis of architectural space. In: Environment and Planning B: Planning and Design, 28(1), 103-121.

Applying Theory of Branding Synergy on Consumer Experience and Spatial Design: A Case Study

Erica Liu

This paper explores the possible application of branding theory in design practice with the objective of researching the methodology of knowledge transfer to the subject. The focus of the paper is on retail interior design. An experiment was conducted to create a synergy by combining two established brands, creating a unique experience and space. This involved a deep understanding of the brands and their customers, whilst also challenging convention and predictable solutions. The experiment involved choosing two well-known brands based on their brand personalities and possible outcomes. The two brands provide different customer experience, products, services, brand image and suggested lifestyles from each other. By exploring the possibilities of the joint venture, new ways of operation and potential new customer groups are established. A case study was used to demonstrate this experiment and the possible outcomes.

Branding as a design and marketing strategy has been widely used in the retail sector. An established brand suggests a certain lifestyle and an attitude. It teases customers with suggestions of certain ways of living and conveys lifestyles that customers may aspire to achieve. It also posts an attitude that may appeal to certain categories of customers. The process of designing and building a brand is a highly dedicated and intimate practice. Potential customer groups are targeted and analysed. Every single detail of the customers is studied repeatedly. Profiling customers helps a brand position itself in the market place accurately. To experience a brand, the entire cycle of, 'see it', 'like it', 'buy it', is no longer enough for today's retail practice. The customers' expectation is high and the competition is increasing. The longevity of a brand depends not on what products sell, but on how these products and services make the customers feel, and how the customers can relate to the brand.

A brand needs to be consistent in its presence; from its logo to its website, from its packaging to its display strategy in a store. The physical setting of a store is particularly interesting, for it is where the customers can interact with the brand in the most intimate way. However, is it all about selling? Not necessarily in the short run, but yes in the long run. A successful brand invents itself and has a unique identity, like a person, it has personality; it knows customers like a best friend. And customers identify themselves with the brand.

With this special relationship in mind, designers interpret a brand into a three dimensional space. The interior design of a shop is packed with sales strategy, relationship building and much more. As difficult as it seems, shop design for one brand is actually a straightforward exercise. The real challenge is when there are two brands in the same space and these brands try to act as if they are a single entity. To introduce this new entity to customers, it has proven more effective as a branding strategy to aim to create retail space that does not sell anything apart from an experience. A successful example is *Asian Paint* in India. Its showroom in Mumbai does not sell anything but simply provides an interactive experience between the customers and the brand. As a result, there was a 35% uplift in sales in nearby dealers stores; and over a 20% increase in sales conversion in 2010.[1]

When combining one brand with another, in some cases, designers need to identify if there is any mutual benefit which could enhance the brands' respective images and thus provide higher sales levels, or a new way of thinking and a new means of operation. In some cases, one brand may appear to be benefiting more than the other in the short run. In such a case, we need to find out if there is any common ground that the two brands can build upon which will provide benefit to both brands in the long run. This common ground could be a common brand philosophy or attitude. In such a case, one brand could be used as a platform to launch another brand into an entirely new scope of profession or audience. Through this exercise a new relationship was promoted between two brands. The outcomes were not necessarily aimed at selling any particular product, but promoting the two brands and the new brand relationship.

To provide further research into the potential synergy of merging two established brands, a core brand was chosen and carefully paired up with another totally different brand. A spatial design or spatial installation was obtained through the exercise. The thinking process will be explained and the results will be justified and illustrated in the paper. It should be noted that the experiment project was conducted in an educational environment and it has not been used or engaged in any commercial setting.

---

1   The numbers were provided by Mike Roberts, design director of FITCH Design Consultant who shared the Asian Paint case with the author.

Case Study 'Lego and Pantone': A Travelling Pavilion for Community Art and Space Experience[2]

Introduction

Lego is a timeless brand with its toy bricks sold all over the globe. The company is dedicated not only to classroom teaching and education, but also to 'lifelong play' for all ages to engage with 'the child within' and all stages of development (Cendrowicz 2008). The brand was chosen because it has successfully established a relationship with its customers across generations.

Pantone, similar to Lego, is a leading international brand. It is famous for its Colour Matching System. Its proprietary colour space has been widely used in printing and the manufacturing industries (Gable 2007). However unlike Lego, the customer base of Pantone is more of an elite sector, such as professionals in creative fields.

The two brands, Lego and Pantone, have already formed a basic relationship. Lego has used Pantone Colour Matching System to manufacture their bricklinks (Stephens 2008). A joint venture of the two brands could be a feasible progression of their existing business partnership.

The aims of the proposed project were:

1. To give the Pantone brand a personality and make it more accessible to the general public.
2. To expand the Lego brand into a different business field.
3. To engage the local community with interactive art activities and architectural spatial experience.
4. To synchronise among a series of pavilions in other major cities around the globe and thus bring different communities together.
5. To incorporate all communities into the brands' envelope.

---

2   The case study was designed by Luke Gillard who worked under the author's supervision.

Setting the Scene

After researching the background of the brands and obtaining a basic understanding of their existing brand ethos and target customer groups, we began to establish an ideal scenario with the best possible location and audience groups. For location, London Hyde Park was chosen because it is an open space in the centre of a world class city. With regard to the visitors, it is important to understand different visitors' requirements and anticipate the ways they may behave in the designed space. As such, a detailed visitors' profiling process is vital to the success of the project. Based on the existing customer groups of the two brands and the users of Hyde Park, we identified five audience groups who would be the end users of the pavilion. The five groups would be:

1. Families who would visit the pavilion on a day out. Average anticipated dwell time is 1.5 hours. The families are likely to take part in the art activities and experience the architecture as a whole.
2. Tourists who may stumble across the pavilion. Average anticipated dwell time is 20 minutes. The tourists may take a great interest in the project as a whole and bring the brands back to their respective countries.
3. Creative professionals such as designers and architects would visit the pavilion as an educational and professional pursuit. Average anticipated dwell time is 45 minutes to 1 hour. They would have higher expectations and take an interest in the structure and the space created.
4. Student groups and groups of friends would visit the pavilion as a scheduled event. Average anticipated dwell time is 2 hours. There would be a sense of competition and as such these groups are likely to get involved in all the activities.
5. Local park users who may or may not be aware of the project. Average anticipated dwell time is 5 to 10 minutes.

During the process of setting the scene with both users and location, we simultaneously brainstormed a list of fun activities that could be included in the project. The list was then filtered down to 5 activities:

1. Painting graffiti and artwork on the structure.
2. Using Lego bricks to create a new structure within the structure.
3. Interacting with pavilions in other cities via real time technology.
4. Experiencing the architectural space and the light and shadow that it creates throughout different times of the day.
5. Relaxing after all the above actions.

The Design and the Consistency of the Brands

The overall form of the design will be a cubic rectangular one because it has to be consistent with the most widely received shape of the Lego product, bricklinks, which are predominantly square and rectangular in shape. The spatial design of the pavilion was based on the flexibility and the modular system of Lego bricks. It should reflect the brick ratio but on an oversize enlarged scale. This design approach would suggest a new way of experiencing the Lego brand. Each component of the structure could be flat packed into four trucks for easy transportation and assemble. The end structure would be a two-storey high box structure. There would be supporting columns and partitioned walls on the ground floor with stairs and hydraulic platform access to the first floor. The first floor would be a covered structure with a small opaque glassed walled room sat within a big clear glassed walled room. The four walls of the small room could be built with Lego bricks by the visitors. This would symbolise building as at the 'heart of a community'. The corridor created in between the two rooms would have peep holes throughout the Lego walls to allow day light and allow artificial light out in the night. The holes also allowed visitors to peep into the small room and experience the central space through a series of designated viewpoints. Inside the small room, Barrisol material was used on the ceiling to create three cone shape canopies with openings on both ends. The narrow end that attached to the ceiling would host artificial lighting and a projector and the wider end would allow a visitor to stand in the middle and interact with images projected on the inside of the white canopy. Outside attached to the big room would be a spacious balcony with flexible outdoor furniture. (Figure 1 and 2).

To cater for the five activities above, the space is organized into three categories: messy zone, clean zone and chill zone. The messy zone was located on ground level for easy cleaning and maintenance. Visitors were provided with disposable protective clothing, pantone coloured paint and paint brushes. Most of the 'hands on' creative activities would take place in the open and covered spaces around and under the main structure. Visitors were encouraged to create their own wall art and graffiti in these spaces. And these wall arts would be washed away at the end of each day and allow new wall arts to be painted continuously throughout the installation period. The clean zone was a covered structure on first floor including both small and big rooms. Visitors would use the Lego bricks given to build the small room themselves. Inside the small room, visitors could go under and be surrounded by the hanging canopies to observe and to interact with images of other pavilions in other cities in real time. Finally, the chill zone was the outdoor balcony attached to the big room on first floor, providing a relaxation space to cool down after the actions in other zones.

Figure 1:   Techno Colour Pavilion Front View. (Author)

Figure 2:   Techno Colour Pavilion Back View. (Author)

The Marketing Strategy

To encourage interaction with the two brands, a wide audience needs to be captured throughout the city. The way that Lego bricks work involves putting together many small parts and building a bigger whole. Following this mode of operation, a series of small single cubicle unit structures were installed in key locations around the cities, such as Piccadilly Circus (Figure 3) and Covent Garden (Figure 4). The eye-catching structures would attract people passing by to explore and to collect a single pantone coloured Lego brick with information of the project and the location of the pavilion printed on it. They were encouraged to bring this small Lego brick to the pavilion and use it to build the central small room on the first floor. This activity physically draws people together and symbolises building a community through participation.

Figure 3:   Proposed Marketing Cube in Piccadilly Circus. (Author)

Figure 4:   Proposed Marketing Cube in Covent Garden. (Author)

Project Evaluation

This experiment project aimed to translate a consumer experience into a lasting relationship with two unique brands. While both brands have successfully established a connection with their customer, they were also able to cross over each other's boundaries through this joint venture project. Pantone was given a more accessible personality and engaged with the general public as well as professionals. Lego on the other hand was able to launch a more professional image which captivates the artistic installation and elite audience. Visitors experienced the two brands through architectural space, art activities and conversation.

To extend the longevity of the two brands, strategies were used to promote a "brand envelope" that "what's inside doesn't matter; it's what's around the envelope itself that matters. Consumers can step into the brand" (Palmer 2002). It is not about what products the companies make but how these products make the customer feel; this feeling would be translated to a perception of the brands. This experiment project enveloped two brands and sent them to next generations and to new geographical territories. The project has a vision of cross generation and cross-geographical boundary participation. A series of pavilions could be installed temporarily in different cities. Families and local communities were brought together in each city while different communities across the globe were brought together in real time synchronisation via interactive technology. At the end of the project, the pavilions would be flat packed and taken away; the brand's perception amongst communities however, would continue.

Conclusion

Through an understanding of how a brand behaves and connects to customers, this paper reported an experiment on combining two brands, which have two different behavioural patterns, and created a synergy that enables both brands to explore new markets. The interpretation of the brands in spatial design allows customers to relate to the brands on a personal level through experiencing the event and the space. This methodology could be applied to different fields such as hospitality and non-commercial areas of branding.

References

Cendrowicz, L. (2008): Lego legacy continues to be built. In: TIME magazine, January 28. http://www.time.com/time/world/article/0,8599,1707379,00.html, 04.02.2011.

Gable, G. (2007): Pantone 2.0: After 45 years, the sequel to PMS. In: Creativepro, September 5. http://www.creativepro.com/article/pantone-2-0-after-45-years-the-sequel-to-pms-, 05.02.2011.

Palmer, R. quoted in Roberson, B. (2002): Five best companies. In: Forbes, January 8. http://www.forbes.com/2002/08/01/0801marketers.html, 06.02.2011.

Stephens, C. (2008): Lego colour list. In: Isodomos, January 5. http://isodomos.com/Color-Tree/Lego-List.html, 05.02.2011.

Heimatklänge: The Conceptual Design of Branded Spaces by Means of Sonic Branding

Sonja Kastner

"If you don't have anything to say, sing it." David Ogilvy (Ogilvy 2007: 111)

I would like to begin with this quotation of the famous advertising expert and copywriter David Ogilvy to draw the readers´ attention to an aspect of branded spaces we normally perceive unconsciously. But sounds do have an immense impact on our perception and evaluation of brands, be it in a positive or in a negative way. What does sonic branding mean? Sonic branding is the design of a brand identity by means of sound. As a part of the corporate design, sonic brand-ing provides a brand with characteristic and distinctive sounds. Brand sounds deliver brand messages on an acoustic level just like a sonic logo or a brand song. In the following paragraphs I would like to pursue three main questions:

1. What does sonic branding mean?
2. What has this to do with branded spaces?
3. What are the biggest challenges in the design process?

There are elements of sonic branding which are created especially in order to give a specific character to spaces: the product in itself, a sonic logo, a jingle, a brand song, announcements, or ambient sound. These elements are described in a number of short case studies using brands like Nokia, Haribo or Rolls Royce.

What Does Sonic Branding Mean?

The German expression 'Heimatklänge' is constituted by the concepts of 'Hei-mat' and 'Klänge'. There is no equivalent in the English language for 'Heimat' except for native place or home. The German expression 'Heimat' refers to a place where one feels comfortable and at home. Heimat is a place where one returns gladly. In times of individualization and global mobility, the concept of Heimat plays an important role in our lives not only for the individual but also for brand companies. People are looking for intact, stable and trustful environments. The German philosopher Johann Gottfried Herder (1744-1803) commented on the concept of Heimat: "Heimat ist da, wo man sich nicht erklären muss."[1] Being asked what the concept of Heimat means to us personally, we may think of the voice of our mother, our way to school or how the soft hair of our cat felt.

'Klänge' means sounds. The sounds of our Heimat stay in our autobiographical memory for a long time. There are some other sounds that may remind us of our Heimat and make us feel well, for example, birdsong. It is one of the sounds people all over the world are likely to feel comfortable with. As a keynote sound birds chirping may not always be heard consciously, but it shapes the character of the perceived natural surroundings by most of the people (Treasure 2011: 98). The sound of birds has inspired many instruments and musical compositions.

Another example is bells because they serve for acoustic orientation just like a church tower serves as a visual orientation when we go for a walk in the village. Maybe it was under this impression that the Canadian sound artist Murray Schafer created the expression "soundmark" (Schafer 1993).

According to Schafer, this term just like a landmark is used to refer to a community sound which is either unique or has qualities which make it specially regarded or noticed by the people in that community. Soundmarks, therefore, are of cultural and historical significance and deserve preservation and protection. Whereas the church tower is a landmark of the environment, the bells are its soundmark.

Schafer also founded and developed the interdisciplinary area of sound studies, which examines both the production and consumption of sounds, music or silence. Sound studies nowadays have become a dynamic field (Pinch and Bijsterveld 2011: 7). A very famous example for bells is the Liberty Bell (Freiheitsglocke) in Berlin. The Liberty Bell in the tower of the former town hall of Berlin 'Rathaus Schöneberg' was first rung in 1950. After the Berlin blockade by the Soviets was brought down the bell was a donation of the people of the United States of America to the people of West Berlin. It is just like the Liberty Bell in Philadelphia, USA, an iconic symbol of independence and the freedom of the people. The Liberty Bell in Berlin can still be heard every day at noon.

Another example for the power of sound is music. Of all types of sound we find music the most fascinating. All of us know the melody of 'The James Bond Theme' in the first James Bond Film 'Dr. No' with Sean Connery and Ursula Andress and we are able to identify it after a split second. The song was written by Monty Norman and performed by Roland Shaw and his orchestra in 1962.

---

1   Heimat is a place, where we don´t have to explain ourselves. (Citation is accredited to Herder, translation by the author)

Since that time we listen to the theme and its variations in every James Bond film because it has become a brand theme. From the past examples we learned that sound affects us immensely and incorporates the following:

- Sound affects us cognitively; we remember voices or noise.
- Sound affects us emotionally; we feel well and even get euphoric while listening to our favourite tunes on the radio while driving. Or we listen to sad music in times when we are lovesick.
- Sound affects us physiologically; sound affects our heart rate, breathing rate, blood pressure, the ability to relax or falling into sleep. Disco beats let us walk or even run faster than classical music.

In the process of branding sounds also plays an important role. According to the 'branding square' there are four major elements of a brand: the brand name, as a visual brand the logo, the product and the packaging (Kastner 2010: 29).

BRAND NAME   LOGO

BRAND

PRODUCT   PACKAGING

Figure 1: Branding Square. (Kastner 2010: 29)

In sonic branding, the branding square has to be completed by brand sounds. The new brand pentagon includes the element 'brand sound'.

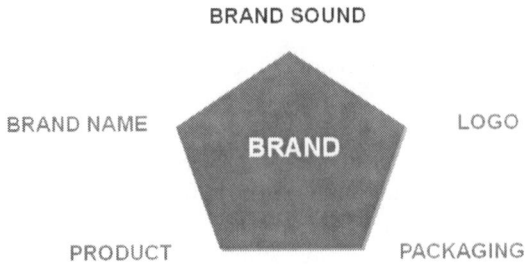

Figure 2:   The Brand Pentagon. (Author)

The brand pentagon can be illustrated using the brand Haribo. Haribo is a family-run company which was founded in 1920 in Bonn, Germany by Hans Riegel. Fruit gums, liquorice and foam-based sweets are the most important products. The brand name Haribo is an acronym for **HA**ns **RI**egel **Bonn**. The product is mainly fruit gums. The packaging as well as the jingle have now been part of the television and radio advertising for more than fifty years. Everybody probably knows the jingle and can repeat it easily. 'Haribo macht Kinder froh und Erwachs'ne ebenso.'[2] Whereas a jingle aims to be a mnemonic code, a sonic logo represents a collection of different associations (Jackson 2004: 9).

Figure 3:   Brand Elements of the German Brand Haribo. (Author)

---

2 Kids and grown-ups love it so the happy world of Haribo. (Translation by the Author)

Design and distribution of the most successful sonic logos have been for a long time rather different. The sonic logo of Nokia, for example, is mostly heard as a ring tone but is not a new composition. It is taken from a waltz composed by the Spanish composer Francisco Tárrega (1852-1909). The omnipresence of this ring tone is unique. Nokia's decision to choose this sound can be highlighted as a master achievement. Nearly one third of the 1,6 billion mobile phones sold in 2010 worldwide have this Nokia tune (Gartner 2012). We can easily imagine how often the Nokia tune makes advertising for Nokia without any extra spending on advertising.

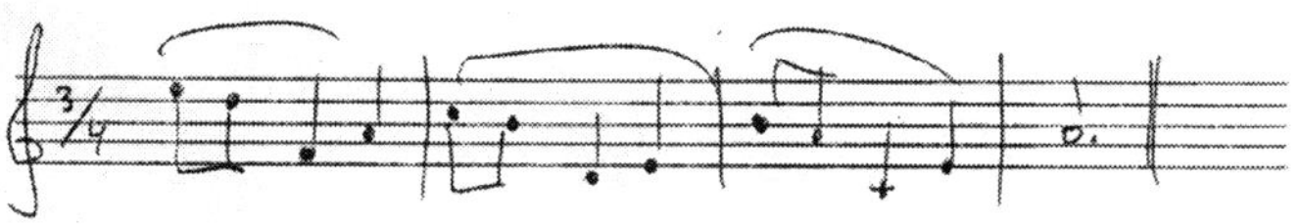

Figure 4:   Notation of the Nokia Sonic Logo. (Author)

Sounds and Branded Spaces

There are a number of sonic branding elements which can be created in order to give a specific character to spaces. Six major elements of a sonic brand are illustrated by the following examples:

- Sonic logo, e.g., Nokia
- Jingle, e.g., Haribo
- The product sound itself, e.g., Rolls Royce
- Brand song, e.g., Bacardi
- Ambient sound, e.g., Muzak
- Announcements and voice, e.g., Köln-Bonn Airport

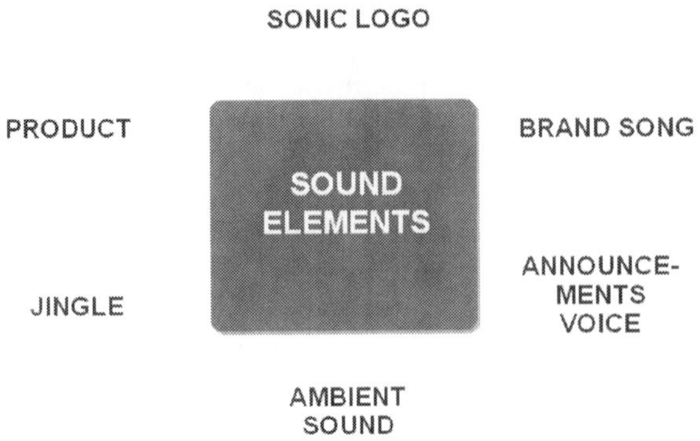

SONIC LOGO

PRODUCT   **SOUND ELEMENTS**   BRAND SONG

                                                    ANNOUNCE-
JINGLE   MENTS
                                                    VOICE

AMBIENT
SOUND

Figure 5:   Major Elements of Brand Sounds. (Kastner 2007: 64).

As we have already examined the brand sounds of Nokia and Haribo, we shall now continue with the brand Rolls Royce and the sound of the product itself. One of the most successful print ads of the last century picks out the product sound as a central issue. The ad was created by David Ogilvy. It refers to the product sounds or in this case actually the absence of any product sound. In 1958 he wrote the legendary headline for the brand Rolls Royce:

„At 60 miles an hour the loudest noise in this new Rolls-Royce comes from the electric clock." (Ogilvy 2007: 11)

The headline has a strong influence on the perception of driving noise for those who have it in mind. It shapes the imagination in a positive way. Although Ogilvy did not manipulate the sound in itself, the atmosphere of the interior space of a Rolls Royce appears, with this advertising in mind, rather silent and noble.

Let´s take a look at another more up to date example of product sound. In offices all around the world the characteristical fanfare of an Apple Macintosh computer can be heard all around when the computers are being started. An element which is obviously longer than just a few seconds is a brand song. Regarding tourism marketing, a nation has with ist anthem a „brand song" which is important for reference groups from abroad and domestic.

A well-known brand song is the song used by the spirits company Bacardi. The brand Bacardi is one of the most flourishing brands in the market for spirits. In many Bacardi television ads of the last decades the music is placed in the foreground. There is a simple story of some young and beautiful people who enter a Caribbean island with their boat and start to party. The song of the summer feeling and its variations is well known and cannot be separated from the Bacardi brand.

The next example is one of ambient sound. One species of ambient sound is called muzak which is a generic name for background music as played in lifts, lobbies, airports or bars. There is a lot of criticism about the muzak phenomenon as famous songs are deformed in a way we can hardly recognize them. Muzak is mostly perceived absentmindedly (Spitzer 2003: 125). Its principal aim to create a comforting atmosphere for all kinds of music preferences kills most of the characteristic sounds. Muzak is, therefore, not suitable to express a specific brand character in terms of sonic branding.

The next short case study is about Köln-Bonn airport. In public transport announcements human voice plays an important role. As a major part of communication, spoken language can be used to express both rational and emotional aspects of a brand (Felderer 2004: 19). Human voice is a major part of sonic branding because it always draws the attention to itself no matter what kind of noises can be perceived at the same time. Human voice, therefore, focuses the perception of the people who are listening, whereas noise or music retreat into the background. Human voice is a major expression of the individual and its personality. The following example shows how announcements in public transport can be designed in a very specific way.

In summer 2002 the management of Köln-Bonn Airport invited the Swiss design agency Intégral Rüdi Baur & Associates to take part in the design competition for their new corporate design. They created a Corporate Design for an airport. As "a territory, a transfer zone, a symbolic gateway to distant lands and a familiar face for homecoming, it should turn the airport into a pleasant place for changing means of transport. The visual identity set into place at Köln-Bonn aims at presenting a specific and recognizable airport but it is more than just a signature; it is part of the clear perception of something different, of simplicity and ease of use, by using a simple typeface and simple pictograms." (Köln-Bonn Airport 2003)

Figure 6:   CI Köln-Bonn Airport. (Köln-Bonn Airport 2003)

In matters of sound a sound logo and special welcome announcement were produced. The tone of the announcement sounds highly original, friendly, open and
is rather distinctive. It refers to the quotation "My name is Bond. James Bond":
„Willkommen in Bonn – Köln Bonn. Köln-Bonn Airport freut sich darauf, Sie
bald wieder zu sehen. See you soon." The welcome announcement in both German and English is spoken by Frank Glaubrecht, who is the German voice over
artist for James Bond actor Pierce Brosnan. From this case study about Köln-
Bonn Airport we learn that sonic branding is an element in the branding process
normally perceived unconsciously but which can be rather powerful. However
does this mean we have to design and play our sonic logo, our jingle, brand song
etc. everywhere and as often as possible?

Silence on the contrary is also a form of communication as we see in the
following example. In the 1980s the technology corporation IBM invented the
first silent typewriter. After years of noise in most of the offices, they thought it
may be a relief for most of the secretaries. The product however was a flop. The
secretaries felt unsafe with their typewriters because they thought the new silent
products did not work properly. The same would probably apply to vacuum
cleaners.

The example shows us that a brand or a product 'cannot not' sound. This finding derives from the famous Austrian communication scientist Paul Watzlawick who developed five axioms of communication. As first axiom he stated, "one cannot not communicate." (Watzlawick et al. 1967: 48). Due to his research, every behaviour is a kind of communication. As behaviour does not have a counterpart (there is no anti-behaviour), it is not possible not to communicate. Any perceivable behaviour, including the absence of action, may be interpreted with a special meaning.

Whereas Watzlawick said, "one cannot not communicate", we have to claim a brand cannot not sound. However, one must be careful because this does not mean that every product, every website, every showroom, every corporate reception or retail space has to have a specific brand sound. There is also silence which can be a major constituent for the design of brand sounds. At this point it is perhaps appropriate to refer to the topics of unwanted sounds, noise and acoustic environmental pollution. It is often claimed that it is easier to look the other way than to turn a deaf ear. The auditory perception is rather delicate and there can be enormous negative reactions due to repeated and repeated identical sounds. The Swiss designer Rüdi Baur described it accurately. According to him, products or brands start to prattle, 'lallen' in German. As a customer himself he thinks most brands act far too aggressive just by repeating and repeating the same tunes too often (Kastner 2007: 127). To summarize there are three major points that can be derived for a successful sound design for branded spaces:

1. Sound should be congruent to the brand.
   Sounds should be congruent to the product itself, its corporate visuals, its target groups and its communication aims. Sounds then may bypass cultural and language barriers and may help global brands to deliver their messages worldwide.
2. Sound should be matched with media.
   As a worst case scenario let us imagine a hardware store where we have to listen a hundred times to the same jingle. A jingle is of course appropriate at the end of a radio spot or an advertisement on television, but not in the shop itself where you will spend normally more than just a few minutes. Brand Sounds should vary from touch point to touch point and should be matched with media. In this case, it may help companies effectively to brand sound-enabled marketing interactions.
3. Sound should be useful and valuable for customers.
   It should create a positive atmosphere, should relax or stimulate. Sound should help with regards to orientation or navigation.

In Sonic Branding What Are the Biggest Challenges?

There are three major challenges in the design process of sonic branding:

1. Brand managers lack profound knowledge of sounds and sonic branding. Studies show that a major cause for conflicts between brand managers and agencies is that brand managers lack the knowledge to plan and implement brand sounds properly (Kastner 2007: 148). Brand managers should discuss the functions of a jingle, brand sound or ambient sound with the sound designer. They should decide which medium is suitable in which space or situation.

2. Advertising agencies´ approach to sonic branding is poorly structured or completely unstructured.
    Composers are often involved far too late in the design process. In this case, the client is not able to profit from the knowledge of the sound designer or composer. The composer often has no idea of the functional needs of the brand. As a consequence the sounds may appear inappropriate.

3. Uncertainty with brand sounds becomes apparent in a non-distinctive briefing.
    A non-distinctive briefing is the most permanent burden in the workflow between brand managers, composers and architects. A non-distinctive briefing often leads to many alternatives or styles. As a result, the decision process for the brand managers is complex and time consuming.

Regarding the design of spaces with sound, there are – apart from noise reduction – manifold possibilities to enhance the attentiveness or subjective well-being of customers or staff: lifts, toilets, restaurants, bars, offices, gyms, public transport etc. Sonic branding may act as a powerful aural locator. Sonic Branding can reassure people that they've come to the right place and are in good hands. The Swiss sound designer Lukas Bernays from Zurich found a good metaphor which explains easily the main challenge in sonic branding.

> "You have to go back to your childhood. Before you fall asleep, you listen to a tiny melody. This melody gives you the feeling of being home and being at ease with yourself. That's exactly what companies are looking for. You enter the shop and you know: this is my planet, that is where I feel comfortable." (Bernays in Kastner 2007: 123, translation by the Author)

References

Felderer, B. (2004): Die Stimme: Eine Ausstellung. In: Felderer, B. (ed.): Phonorama: Eine Kulturgeschichte der Stimme als Medium. Berlin: Matthes & Seitz Berlin, 7-21.

Gartner, Inc. (2012): Gartner says worldwide mobile device sales to end users reached 1.6 billion units in 2010. http://www.gartner.com/it/page.jsp?id=1543014, 09.01.2012.

Jackson, D. (2004): Sonic branding: An essential guide to the art and science of sonic branding. Houndmills: Palgrave Macmillan.

Kastner, S. (2007): Klang macht Marken: Sonic Branding als Designprozess. Wiesbaden: Gabler.

Kastner, S. (2010): Marken – Labels – Brands: Was leistet die Verpackung zur Markierung eines Produktes? In: Vaih-Baur, C. and Kastner, S. (eds.): Verpackungsmarketing: Fallbeispiele, Trends, Technologien. Wiesbaden: Deutscher Fachverlag, 27-42.

Köln-Bonn Airport (2003): CI-Buch Köln-Bonn Airport, Unpublished Booklet.

Ogilvy, D. (2007): Ogilvy on advertising. London: Carlton Books.

Pinch, T. and Bijsterveld, K. (2011): The Oxford handbook of sound studies. Oxford: Oxford University Press.

Schafer, M. (1993): The soundscape: Our sonic environment and the tuning of the world. Rochester: Inner Traditions.

Spitzer, M. (2003): Musik im Kopf: Hören, Musizieren, Verstehen und Erleben in neuronalen Netzwerken. Stuttgart: Schattauer.

Treasure, J. (2011): Sound business. Gloucestershire: Management Books 2000.

Watzlawick, P., Beavin, J.H. and Jackson, D.D. (1967): Pragmatics of human communication: A study of interactional patterns, pathologies, and paradoxes. New York: W.W. Norton.

Stories and Situations

South Tyrol: Destinations Can Be Brands Too

Christoph Engl

What Brands Can Do

Brands sell a certain attitude towards life.

It is indisputable. The decision to purchase a certain product is affected much more by emotions than it is by reason. This has become a truism amongst all companies producing brand quality consumer goods. Brands try to add an underlying philosophy or attitude to products. In this world where basic needs are satisfied, consumers buy to a great part the values connected with a product instead of buying the product itself. Ever since it became clear that the purchase of a new car does not serve the need of locomotion but the achievement of a social standard. AUDI has not sold cars but rather *'Vorsprung durch Technik'* (advancement through technology). BMW sells the lifestyle of 'sportive driving' and Geox 'breathes'. Brands serve the purpose of making customers feel loyal to their 'values'. The brand gives the customer confidence and the customer trusts the brand.

Brands are system providers.

In the past few years, producers of brand name products have constantly been diversifying their range of products and services. Companies that used to produce only brand name clothing are now offering all accessories for modern living, such as perfumes and handbags as part of their product range. The trust consumers used to have in one single product has now become trust in an entire brand. While it was possible in the past to buy skis from one brand and bindings from another, they now come together in a package from the same brand and include the option to buy colour matching ski boots and a ski suit made by the same brand as well. Giorgio Armani now sells watches, Mont Blanc sells belts and other leather goods, and Nike sells perfumes. Not all of these offers have been successful, but many of them have. Far beyond their core competencies, brands generate trust.

Not in every case the extension of product range under one label has been successful: Nivea tried to enter in the beauty market providing a modern designed range of NIVEA beauty products underestimating that consumers did not assign the competence in those fields to a label which became famous for being producer of healthy creams. The product range extension was managed for a long time quite excellently by NOKIA selling cellphones from 99 to 900 Euros under the same brand.

Brands do not participate in price wars.

One look at a modern shopping centre or supermarket will make you realize shop-in-shop systems guarantee that brands can present their entire product range inside a sales structure. In doing so, these systems valorize the structure itself. In these brand worlds, the importance of the price is ever declining. The aphorism 'experiences are not part of price wars', originally taught in the field of tourism, has applied itself to the brand worlds of the consumer goods industry much more quickly than it has to tourist offers. This happens because tourism industries quite often are an excellent field to discover trends and to be aware of how the behavior of consumers is changing. However, the time to implement these acknowledgements in concrete products takes too long.

The brand industry has come to understand that emotions, as long as they cover the core of people's basic needs at the moment, strongly increase the desire for a product and are, therefore, excluded from the modern consumer's price sensitivity. Of course, almost all brand name products are also available as so-called 'no-name products'. These products usually sell for lower prices only because they do not have a 'good name', i.e. a brand image. No-name products are forced into a cruel price war against other no-name competitors.

The Transformation from a Tourist Offer into a Brand Destination

Destination marketing is taking over from tourism marketing.

At first glance, all these theories do not seem to have much to do with a tourist destination. Normally, a tourist destination advertises its region and accommodations. Advertising agencies which specialise in tourism are expected to advertise the beautiful countryside with its many activities to holiday guests worldwide in order to fill up the available guest beds. In the past, this was achieved by distributing leaflets of which there are still far too many. Today, however, this is done via new media. The fact that all tourist destinations, tourist cities and tourist boards are still having their own logos designed and are using these logos to compete internationally is understandable, but outdated and not very productive. The majority of tourism logos has been developed for singular locations or villages which have grown touristy in quite different times and periods. It explains the unimaginable amount of different logos in the same geographical areas. From a consumer perspective, the big number of undifferentiated and difficult recognizable areas is unhelpful for creating a clear idea of what the key message or positioning of an area should be.

After all, the goal is to be clearly different from all other destinations and to convince consumers to choose this particular region for their holiday. One thing is certain. The common advertising strategies for tourist destinations would have led to guaranteed failure for brands. Just imagine a mobile phone company, a car manufacturer or a perfume brand sending out leaflets neatly listing all outlets for their products in order to entice customers.

So the question needs to be turned around by asking is it possible for South Tyrol as a tourist destination or region to establish itself as a brand following the same rules that have been successfully applied to the consumer goods industry? Is it possible for South Tyrol to become a well-known brand in Europe which can compete with other already established brands when it comes to popularity and attractiveness? This is precisely the question we at South Tyrol Marketing, together with our product partners, have been asking ourselves again and again over the past few years.

Destinations need a brand character.

The outcome of our deliberations was if South Tyrol does not manage to become an established destination brand, the region will lose market shares all across Europe. The effects of the change in consumers' needs only allow for one path. In the competition with other products, and holidays is a luxurious one, destinations have to respect the same rules in the decision process of customers as all the other consumer goods. Products without any added value or label supported character could be sold only and exclusively by best price. If destinations could be interchanged by customers easily because they offer same products and services, they will consequently run for the cheapest price offer.

A tourist destination that does not have brand character but has 29 million overnight stays and a bit less than 6 million visitors yearly (touristic data refers to the destination South Tyrol) will run the risk to lose important numbers of customers. It either has to give in to the price wars or it will have to sacrifice consumers to other competitors and, in that case, there would be no use in putting up a fight. It is obvious that a fight for the cheapest price is pointless because tourism is a service- and investment-intensive field and considering the emerging low-wage economies, no one in Europe can assume that this kind of fight would have any hope for success. On top of that, consumers are less and less interested in solely tourism-related offers and aspects, but increasingly interested in those aspects that make a region a tourist destination which are everyday customs, backgrounds, stories, and people.

Destination brands are not different from other brands because even a destination with its brand character has to concentrate on its points and services of excellence in one promise for the customer. Destination brands generate their efforts as well as they are able to evidence which values they stand for. Usually destinations are showing pictures and videos to convince customers to join them and do it from their own perspective. Long discussions have run for years and even for generations about which should be the right and most impressive pictures to show to potential clients. But the question in the center of all these discussions, 'Which are the right pictures to show?', is definitely the wrong one and, therefore, all answers are even unsatisfactory. The right questions in a more branding concentrated process should be: 'What picture should be generated in the mind of the customer within the communication process?' and 'Which feeling is communicated to his heart?'.

In the process of reflection, it has become clear to us that the message 'South Tyrol is one of the most beautiful landscapes in the world and offers outstanding recreational activities and accommodation' is not enough for most consumers. In the long run, this message does not stand a chance in keeping alive the demand for a region in consumers' minds and emotions. The demand for a product never arises in just one dimension because even the most beautiful country sides cannot fascinate a person for long if there is no other emotional aspect connected with them. This applies to the consumer goods industry in the same way as it does to tourist destinations. Roots become a driver for emotionality. There is an increasing longing for something that is rooted and, therefore, different from everything else; something that outlasts fashion and promotes authenticity.

System Provider South Tyrol – From Region to Product

South Tyrol is definitely worth a visit. However, it only becomes really desirable if there are other advantages associated with this region. South Tyrol has a list of local products which have the potential to become important advertising tools for the destination. South Tyrol produces Italy's best white wines and grows 10% of all apples produced in Europe. South Tyrol also has local products like South Tyrol bacon with its historical background of different methods of meat preservation in the North and the South which is closely connected with the region. South Tyrol borders the Alps and the Mediterranean. This geographic situation has considerable effects on everyday culture and customs. Just think about the eating habits which, to people outside of South Tyrol, have always seemed like a fascinating symbiosis of the Italian way of life and Alpine tradition.

In order for a tourist region to become a destination, it needs to have an integrated interplay of all these messages. South Tyrol Marketing has successfully joined all representatives of these different messages under one roof in the past few years, and has convinced all these key players to commit to a common vision for the destination. It was not easy to reach. The key of the whole process was the immediate and full involvement of decision makers in the branding process, done by working groups and seminar days. Since the process was started, all decisions were done with the consensus of sector responsible presidents or managers and due to this, the implementation process of the label afterwards was much easier to be organized. We have also synchronized the different communication campaigns in a way which enables an ever-changing image of a fascinating and desirable South Tyrol to manifest itself to the consumer (Figure 1 and 2).

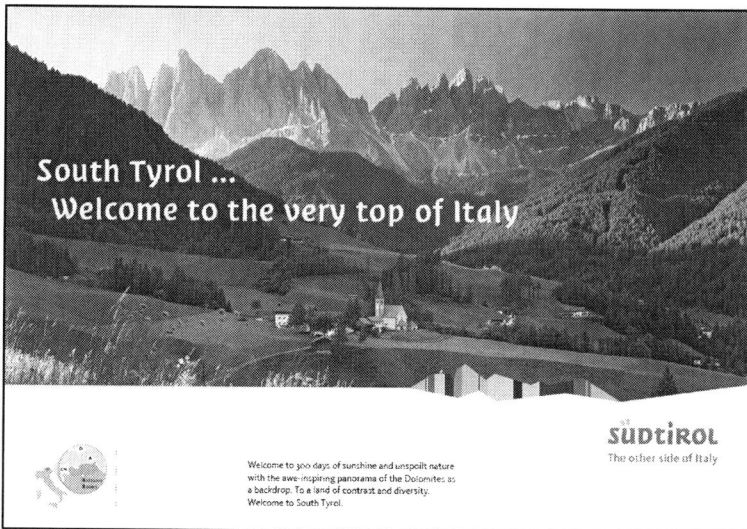

Figure 1:   Ad Example from Campaign. (Author)

Figure 2:   Ad Example from Campaign. (Author)

The goal is for South Tyrol to become a desirable brand, a brand system provider that opens up a world of adventure to the consumer and attracts visitors in many different ways. One day, it could be the landscape that fascinates the visitor; the next day, it could be the symbiosis of contrasting dishes in South Tyrol cuisine or the undisputed quality of South Tyrol wines; the next day, it could be everyday culture on mountain farms which produce milk of the best quality every day in the high altitudes of the Alps.

All of this combined forms the structure of a brand character destined for a brand presence in specific countries. South Tyrol tells captivating stories about the region, its people and its products with the aim of securing a place among the top 10 European destinations in people's and customers' minds. One of this stories kept from the historical context of the region could be told describing a famous traditional dish 'Schlutzkrapfen'. South Tyrolean farmers used an Italian ravioli style to create, with their own ingredients like spinach/chard and ricotta, typical alpine ones. It is a new dish in this region, refined on the plate with melted butter and Italian parmesan cheese. Mediterranean and alpine aspects were brought together in this dish forming proof of the umbrella brand asset. South Tyrol has also created a visual framework for this purpose which acts as an umbrella brand for all of the destination's assets (Figure 3).

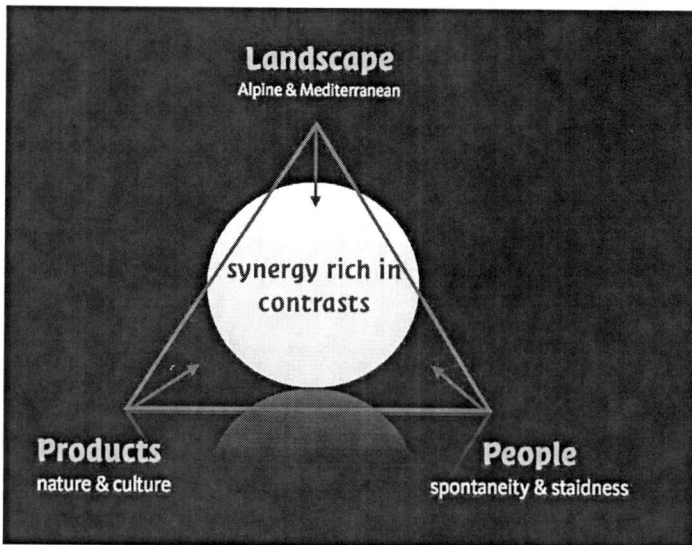

Figure 3:   The Visual Framework for South Tyrol. (Author)

The South Tyrol Umbrella Brand

Everyone under one Roof

Knowing that individual players on their own would have too little advertising power in the market to keep customers loyal to their product as well as knowing that the most important task of modern brand management is actually retaining people's loyalty to a vision and not to a product, South Tyrol Marketing has embarked on a path to a common vision and a common strategy. South Tyrol products are manufactured at many different types of 'sites' but with each wanting to enjoy a high degree of autonomy. For this reason, it was clear from the start that our project was not going to be the assimilation of our products, but simply the development of a common but strong framework – a brand. The word 'umbrella brand' and the image of 'everyone under one roof' describe our project very aptly. All partners come together under one roof while at the same time they continue to serve individually as the pillars that hold up the house.

It was not a logo or symbol that would put things on the right track, but simply the commitment of all partners to a common vision. Whether we are offering consumers a product for daily consumption, e.g., yoghurt from South Tyrol, or want to win them over for a week-long stay in the region, the question is what do we want our consumers to expect of South Tyrol as a destination brand. Slowly but surely, we became convinced that a dairy product can barely compete against the big players in the industry in the long run when it comes to price and quality. Only by emphasizing the product's origin could one generate the trust that would make the consumer buy a product at a higher price than other products which do not use origin as a selling point. For products aimed at tourists, it is true that the first thing that sparks a desire in people's minds is a region. It is only afterwards that a similarly strong desire for a hotel in the region arises. Basically, it can be put like this: The region valorizes the product and the product valorizes the region.

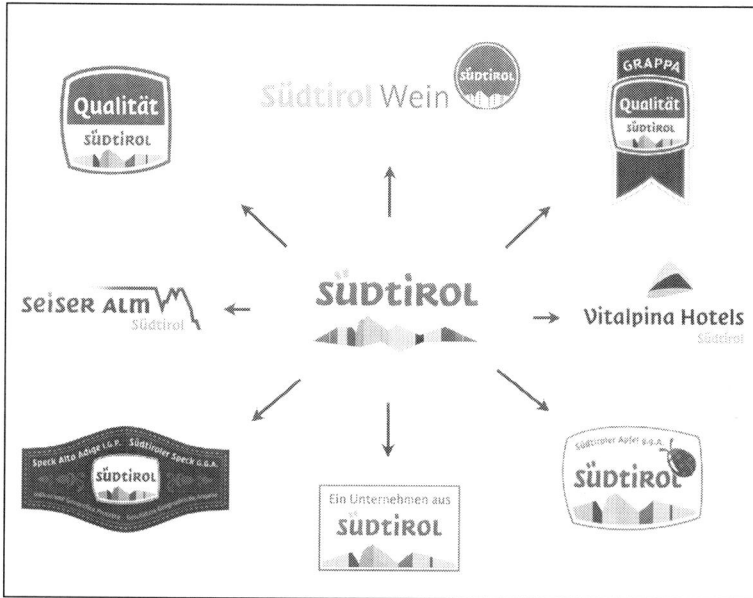

Figure 4:   Logos from South Tyrol. (Author)

Three rules on the Road to a Brand

So the task was clear. The more all the sectors of the umbrella brand South Tyrol invest in a common element of communication, the stronger the message becomes that works in consumers' minds and hearts. The brand slogan that all partners now subscribe to is this:

> "South Tyrol is a diverse symbiosis of the Alpine and the Mediterranean, of spontaneity and reliability, of nature and culture."

Everyone feels committed to this slogan and every product aims to fulfil this vision as closely as possible. Of course, this way of thinking has its consequences. Products and services in the whole destination have to be developed respecting and reframing the spirit of the brand slogan; some of existing products and events had to be reconsidered if compatible with the new vision. In the field of tourism, for instance, it is clear that a positioning as a 'party hot spot' that attracts the young, wild party crowd is not a viable option. In the area of agricultural produce, it means that advertising should be equally traditional and modern. All in all, it is a complicated project, but it is also a fascinating path which no other European tourist region has yet been able to embark on this comprehensively. In the meantime, even outside production and service companies that also want to benefit from the South Tyrol location have placed themselves under the umbrella brand. They use this brand in order to communicate to consumers that they are a company from South Tyrol and to take advantage of the positive spin-off effects of the umbrella brand for their positioning in the market. So a manufacturing enterprise located in South Tyrol offering its services in other Italian provinces, can definitely take advantage of using the communication tools of the umbrella brand to reach millions of Italian tourists.

The same could be said for retailers or producers of typical regional products or industries located in the region. All of them can take immediate advantage of the good positioning of the destination in the minds of customers in different countries. Any destination that wants to choose the path of consistent communication marketing with the aim of becoming a brand has to adhere to the rules of such a process and there are three basic rules.

First, you have to conduct market research. No product in the brand industry is introduced simply on the basis of trusting the producer's subjective feelings or past experience. In the past few years, we have conducted systematic research in the markets on the image of South Tyrol. We have asked consumers about our current positioning in the different markets and have started to find out about the current demand for South Tyrol as a destination. This market research has produced fascinating results which show that customers are just as aware of South Tyrol as the region of origin of certain products as they are of South Tyrol as a holiday destination. However, the market research also clearly indicates in which direction South Tyrol needs to move in its positioning. Customers identified clearly that they would like to find in the destination authenticity in products and offers because they like the contrasts of different cultures lived by local people day per day. Also, they would run for products linked to the territory because they are attracted by the South Tyrolean life style practiced by the inhabitants more than by museums or landscapes.

Second, you have to ensure that the brand is immediately recognizable at all times. This amounts to more than a common graphical logo, label or image. It is also the promise and this promise is contained in the words of the famous advertising slogan "when it says South Tyrol on it, there is South Tyrol in it". South Tyrol has to give guarantees to the customer fulfilling its promise with products and services in line with its own brand character. This is a need not only for the design of communication processes which have to be developed following clear regulations and rules, but it is even a need for offers and structures which have to be organized respecting the guidelines of the umbrella brand.

Finally, information is crucial because the dream determines the demand. In brand communication, the common task is to create the 'South Tyrol dream' in the minds and hearts of consumers. In order for this strategy to be successful, communication has to be enabled through those channels which are most likely to affect people's emotions. Soon we were convinced that this would not be possible in the main established markets for South Tyrol, which are Germany, Italy, Switzerland and Austria, without the use of the emotional medium 'television'. An appropriate PR strategy even increases the need to use television as a medium.

In communication issues a destination brand has to cover all channels with emotional efforts. Because the driver for decision to choose a destination is and will remain emotion for it, all information driven channels are less important than in other sectors of economy. The supply of relevant information, which follows the triggering of emotions, is carried out via print media and most importantly on the internet, where, once again, everything is concentrated on one platform designed specifically for the destination. South Tyrol as a destination is also present in Web 2.0. Our Facebook community is growing every month. Within 12 months 60,000 Facebook users became fans of the South Tyrol site and thousands became users of our video channels on You Tube, our pinterest, an online pinboard, our twitter account, our apps and our multimedia electronic magazine. In this field destination brands have big opportunities to be used as helpful and decisive instruments to create the right picture in the minds and hearts of customers.

The Power of a Brand

The South Tyrolean provincial government commissioned South Tyrol Marketing to form a cross-sector group to design a new umbrella brand for South Tyrol. The path we embarked on seems promising and after seven years we can already draw some results:

- Our common projects like common TV-campaigns, print and advertising campaigns in magazines, common fair structure, common database for pictures and movies etc. have produced synergetic effects as well as cost savings.
- The consumers' perception of the brand is very positive as has been proven by our market research. The tracking of label effects studies, done in three

most important markets, proved and underlined this important success. Recognition rates as well as positive connotation rates are high.

▪ South Tyrol has a common graphical appearance which ensures the recognition of products and tourist offers.

▪ South Tyrol bundles the partners' financial means in a way that enables broad-based media representation under the common 'South Tyrol umbrella brand'.

▪ South Tyrol frequently launches quality campaigns in order to maintain consumer's confidence in the South Tyrol brand.

This way, South Tyrol creates a demand which is constantly kept alive through products and tourist offers. It is becoming a destination with brand character. The coming years will show whether the conviction that South Tyrol has the potential of being converted from a touristic destination into a destination brand will be followed up by the appropriate steps for implementation.

Selling in the market is becoming ever more difficult whether one is trying to sell tourist offers or products for everyday use. This perception will be helpful in the attempt to convince all players in the market that one can no longer win alone. Tourism and regional products in the recognition of potential and real customers have to be considered as one unit, as one brand, as different parts of the same family. The region valorizes its products and the products valorize the region as a destination of origin. You buy 'South Tyrol' at the supermarket; you talk about South Tyrol as a region everyone should visit once in their lives. When you chat with your friends, you tell them how exciting your last stay in the region was and give them sought-after South Tyrol products as souvenirs from your last holiday. You are proud to read articles in the newspaper about this destination you have visited several times. If we can achieve something even remotely similar to the scenario described above, this former tourist region will have been headed in the right direction as a branded space.

A Guggenheim in Every City?

Antti Vihinen

"To take possession of space is the first act of living things, men and beasts, plants and clouds; it is a fundamental manifestation of equilibrium and of duration. The first proof of existence is the occupation of space." Le Corbusier (1962: 174)

During the last 10-15 years we have experienced a boom of cultural building projects in Northern Europe. In Oslo, Copenhagen and Reykjavik new opera houses and concert halls have been inaugurated and recently one in Helsinki in August 2011. The most spectacular and, indeed, the most expensive one, the Elbphilharmonie in Hamburg, is under construction. Comparing these projects we can find some similarities, even an often repeated pattern in their pre- and post-construction-phase. They all serve the same goal: destination image and branding of their cities. In almost all cases they also overspend their original budgets, sometimes with several hundred million euros. This seems to be the normal case with cultural buildings. Why?

All branded spaces are also stories. A brands story is essential for its success: managing a branded space is a story-telling-business. Stories are based on rhetoric. In the following I shall explain and analyze the rhetoric of cultural building projects.

Overture

On the 10th of June 2011, the Helsingin Sanomat, the biggest newspaper in Finland, wrote on its editorial page about a city council meeting in Helsinki. The politicians were exited, because representatives of the Guggenheim Foundation from New York had delivered their report to the city council. It was about the possibility of building a Guggenheim Art Museum in Helsinki. Only few critical voices declared suspicions on the project, everybody else was happy and in an enthusiastic mood. During the last decades Helsinki has been surrounded with spectacular new cultural building projects in the neighboring countries and cities but was finally about to get an internationally recognized brand into the city and become a member of the Guggenheim family. "We are back in business", the members of the city council proclaimed. Only one topic was not discussed on that evening: money and funding. It didn't seem to be important on a successful and cheerful meeting like this.[1]

Ever since the glorious and, indeed, successful Guggenheim Museum Project in Bilbao, this has been the dream of every city mayor; a complete change of image and infrastructure of the city with the help of a cultural site of international importance, and through this the change of an industrial city into a touristic attraction, the change of factory workers and miners into tourist guides or program planners. It is the fairy tale of modern destination management projects; with the Guggenheim Museum Bilbao even became a James Bond movie trailer city! Bilbao's success has led to an endless stream of political delegations from all over the world to this city in the north of Spain. They all want to learn from Bilbao, they all want to copy the Basque success story, they all want to have their own Gug.

I am afraid the city council meeting described above is something very typical for building projects like this, something all too familiar for most culture managers. In Helsinki we are experiencing the moment when culturally inspired rhetoric enter into to the world of politics. This is the second stage; there is one more to come. This article, rather an essay, analyzes the rhetoric of cultural city branding projects, the three essential rhetorical stages. It starts with a story, almost like a fairy-tale with a hero, with the good and bad, with a just cause and a false king, with a fair princess and her rescuing handsome prince. However, as a well-known branded space called Hollywood often puts it: This story is based on a true story, but all characters are fictional and their statements or opinions do not necessarily represent the views of the production company or the studio.

So let's start. Once upon a time there was a little town ...

Stage One: I've got this great idea!

Many cultural building projects start among arts communities like symphony orchestras, opera companies or art museum managers. It is often a heroic story of an energetic arts manager, who wants to have a hall for his orchestra, a better sounding stage for his opera, or uncompromising daylight circumstances for his exhibitions. Right from the start it is a battlefield. The hero of this part, this rhetorical stage of the story, tries to fight his way through a modern society of uneducated politicians, who can't tell the difference between Bach and Schönberg, through a hostile environment of city officials who would rather

---

1   Helsingin Sanomat June 10, 2011.

build a kindergarten instead of a cultural site, through a world of skepticism among sponsors, who don't care for culture really, but for their false, overrated and disgusting reputation as real inventors of the entire art and culture. No matter how much and how often our hero thinks he has just found the right words to convince the people making decisions for building projects like this, he always seems to fail in persuading his superiors. It is often a project of several years of tireless work. He (and very often she) tries to speak about cultural values of humankind, of the timelessness of Mozart and Beethoven, of the everlasting beauty of Verdi and Puccini arias, of the breathtaking and immaculate paintings of the city collection – all of them in the need of a new room, all of them desperately looking for a space to conquer, all of them looking for new audiences. All this seems to be in vain. Nobody gets excited, apart from some sponsors, and nobody pays him or her real attention. A change of tactics and a change of rhetoric are needed.

Our hero is well advised if he simply forgets his own and no doubt true love for music and arts. He will be much more successful if he starts to talk about the destination image of the city instead. He may refer to the modern gurus, such as Richard Florida, whose theories about the prosperous cities are based on successful destination management campaigns often introduced by a major cultural building site. The world is full of brilliant examples: Sydney Opera House, Berlin Philharmonie, Guggenheim Museum in New York, just to name a few. These monuments of arts and culture, their importance for their cities may well attract the fascination of the city council members or those in charge of shaping the image of the destination. This is the moment, when the building project starts to spark, and this is the moment when we enter a new rhetorical stage of the project.

Stage Two: In the loving memory of our Mayor!

The mayor of the city is excited. When the plan is presented to him, he already sees the headlines with the magnificent new hall in his city, perhaps even bearing his name. This iconic hall, masterpiece of architecture and arts, will make him an icon, too. It is a dream coming true for a small time politician like him! His orchestra manager has contacted the world famous architects: Renzo Piano, Frank Gehry, Henning Larsen, Jean Nouvel and the Swiss company Herzog and de Meuron. They all may be too busy in building equal projects throughout the world, but in the end they didn't turn him down. Finally a draft of a kind, first in the line of many, is produced by the famous company X. The mayor's excitement grows as the sketch of the building is presented to him. However, before he can introduce the plan to his fellow politicians and city officials, he must have a figure, a rough estimation, a budget. How much will all this cost? Furthermore: Who is going to pay all this? What else is needed to finalize the project?

Perhaps he is familiar with equal building projects of the past in the neighboring cities and countries, perhaps he can still remember the horrendous headlines of doubling or tripling the original budgets in the town next to his own. However, he is assured that this time it will all be different. No public funding is needed and the costs of the hall will be sensationally cheap, let's say some 40 million euros only. For this amount the city will have its iconic building and it will become an iconic destination envied by every other city in the country.

With these facts, or should I say so-called facts, the project is presented to the city council. The reaction is two-fold. On the one hand people do see the importance of destination management with the help of a project like this, but on the other hand the uncertainty of the final costs and preliminary budgets of the building, based on rudimentary calculations only, make the decision difficult. And there is another important point. Should the city build a temple for classical music, opera or fine arts for the rich people of the city, for their amusement only, for those who seem to have all the money of the world anyway, for those who could easily have the money to build a hall for themselves? A John Doe, an average working man, doesn't take his family to a Beethoven concert or Verdi opera. It is a tricky situation because a new election is just coming up and the politicians are always worried about their re-election. One must be very careful, one must take a good care of picking up the right words, whether for or against this project. A new rhetorical approach is needed.

We enter a new rhetorical stage. It is the moment when we begin to hear more and more statements about the indirect benefits that a city can get with a project like this. It is not the money or costs of the hall that count, it is the money we can get from tourism, from the hotels and restaurants and the glorious meetings and conferences that will also take place in the new hall. This means new jobs in the service providers sector for the city that has lost all its traditional industrial production for the Chinese. So, it is after all a social project, not a cultural one, it is all about well-being and future of the citizens, not about the amusement of the rich and beautiful. This is the vision of the politicians defending the project. They want to have a guarantee for the multipurpose use of the hall; i.e. not only upper class entertainment but conferences and popular music as well to fill the hall and, indeed, the hotels of the city and thus generating jobs for the service industry. They get this promise from the city mayor and from the reluctant orchestra manager.

There is one more thing that needs to be decided. Without a magnificent building site the world famous architects are unlikely willing to participate. Zoning is today perhaps the most important political decision making process of all city councils. For a project like this, the city wants to find the best' possible place, i.e. the best possible site. This is often in the city center or in another posh location, like the waterfront or a riverbank. For the building project this means almost inevitably more costs, because the best sites automatically double the costs. Moreover, riverbanks or waterfront sites very often cause problems for the construction and again raise the budget.

However, these questions, construction problems or budgets, seem to be in the distant future. Everybody is still too exited to think about them now.

Stage Three: The Black Swan[2]

When we enter the third rhetorical stage, we already find ourselves in a stage of confusion. This confusion is caused by the two earlier rhetorical stages and their different vocabulary. The confusion is amplified through the fact that the future perspectives and expectations of the arts community and political elite of the city differ from each other in a dramatic way. There may be a common goal, more tourism in the city and change of the city employment infrastructure, but the ways of achieving this mean for the arts community something else than for the politicians. Also the actual building process needs qualified people, i.e. constructors, architects etc., and these people bring with them the third rhetorical stage. It is the stage of experts and surprises. It is the moment when white swans turn into black swans, when the need of explaining takes place, when the unpleasant facts, until now hiding in the mud, come up and into the daylight.

The first shock caused by the experts is the money, of course. The rough sketches at the beginning of the process prove to be inaccurate for a proper estimation, and when the final drafts are brought in, the real price of the building begins to take shape. In some cases this price may exceed the original budget by 1000%. This is a tricky moment for the lord mayor, who so boldly gave the city council a promise, that no public funding would be needed. Whoever believed him or her at the beginning will be disappointed now, and whoever was critical will have his political field day. However, the best site of the city cannot be left unfinished and the project, now already for months the headline-story of the newspapers at least on the national level, is simply too important to be stopped with the humiliating perspective of a shameful retreat.

---

2   The Black Swan Theory was presented by Nassim Nicholas Taleb (2008).

A battle of money starts. The gap may be several 100 million euros. At first private funding and sponsors are called in, but even the most generous art lovers can seldom cover the whole deficit and save the project. Their sponsoring is often a symbolic act, a gesture of goodwill at the most, probably ending with the new hall bearing the benefactors or his company's name. However important these people and their involvement for the entire society may be, their money is not enough. More public funding is needed.

The political battle between the diminishing social budgets in the modern dire strait of demographic change and destination management delays the project. The opening ceremonies have to be postponed to the unknown future. Usually the public funding is finally granted. It is somewhat astonishing, but this almost always happens. Even in a situation of most desperate economical crisis these projects find their ways to successful happy ends. For example the Reykjavik Concert Hall, a one hundred million euro project at the harbor and center of the city, had its opening in 2011. It was completed during the most severe financial crises the country of Iceland has ever experienced, when the state was bankrupt.

However, when the reality of the budget is revealed the opposition is furious: Who is responsible for this catastrophe? The third rhetorical stage is full of accusations and harsh voices. The city may well start a process against the constructing company, first of the many to come. During this battle the new hall is being built and finally finished.

The experts deliver yet another surprise. Another line of experts is brought in. These people are the ones who will be in charge of running and maintaining the building. Once the real costs of the building are revealed, the costs of maintenance and use of the building are also revealed. The sum often exceeds even the wildest dreams of the city council. If an arts community, let's say a symphony orchestra, is going to use the building, it will need more public funding because the rent of the hall is simply too high and it can never collect the money by selling tickets only. Moreover, the maintenance costs are so high that program activities outside the arts community are needed. This means that pop, rock or entertainment music will enter the hall designed for classical music, as well as conferences and meetings entering the art collection premises. At this point the arts community begins a rhetorical battle against the management of the hall: "This is not why the building was built". Further: "This is not what we wanted and we are the ones who started it all. The society should cultivate the cultural values of the civilization and now these values are put into question by renting the hall for pop groups or meetings of the local heart surgeons."

However, the management of the hall is not interested in cultural values. Its plain duty is to keep the hall going. Whatever crowd fills the hall is all right.

This again leads to even more desperate attacks from the side of the arts community.

The rhetorical stage of experts is the stage of black swans, the stage of surprises and amazement. All swans are not white. Within the flock of white swans a black swan surprisingly appears. This rhetorical stage is filled with surprises, which repeat themselves in almost every project.

Rhetoric and Managing a Branded Space

This little story, a little fairy tale, may sound very familiar to you. Indeed, it is to a certain extent the true and sad story of the new glorious Elbphilharmonie in Hamburg, which is being built at this very moment. The story includes some elements of the new Music Hall project in Helsinki and the Radio Hall in Copenhagen, and some elements of the hall I was in charge of for more than ten years, the Sibelius Hall in Lahti, in Finland.

Most of the management level work of these projects includes the three rhetorical stages described above, and I dare say most of the management work of a hall like this is managing these three rhetorical stages. In a simplified manner, we can call the three rhetorical stages as following:

1.   Corporate Cultural Responsibility (Artists)
2.   Corporate Social Responsibility (Politicians)
3.   Corporate Financial Responsibility (Experts)

What makes managing a brand of a concert hall so difficult is that these three stages affect the activities and decision-making processes of a CEO. They are all part of the every day business of a concert hall management. All are equally strong, all full of surprises, and it is the management of these surprises and management of the rhetorical stages that a concert hall CEO must be able to do.

These people are difficult to find. In order to be a successful concert hall manager you must be able to speak or at least understand the rhetoric of the arts community surrounding you; moreover, you must be able to co-operate with the local politicians whose knowledge of arts or management is on a very modest level, to put it mildly; and even further you must be able to understand the rhetoric behind the economical reality. You must be able to manage the hall as a unified branded space combining all the three rhetorical stages and their hidden values. Very often the city council makes the mistake and engages somebody from the arts community or a local politician to do the job. In my opinion this is the worst possible solution, which, unfortunately, is often enough repeated with disastrous results.

Why does it happen again and again?

One may wonder why the contractors and cities of new concert halls or art museums always practically fail to complete the building within the original budget. There is a simple explanation for this. Of course it is difficult to foresee what happens when big buildings with spectacular architecture and complicated acoustical design begin to take shape. However, there is another logical reason for the budgeting problem. It is in the interest of the arts community and the political elite as well as the construction company to downplay the first budgets. Once a project like this gets started, it is practically never stopped unfinished. A project with unlimited government funding is a gold mine for a construction company, but it is a gold mine for the arts community, too. This is why the first budgets, often presented by the arts community or other semi experts, make the destination management project look cheap and tempting.

The fairy tale at the beginning of this essay may appear a little bit exaggerated. It also may give the impression of the good guys being the ones of the arts community defending the corporate cultural responsibility values and bad guys being, as always, the politicians and the management level of the project. However, it is not as simple as that. For the arts community it is vital, and indeed essential to have a project and hall like this. Being part of the cities best site, part of its most important and visible cultural activities guarantees the flow of subsidies. For example, the new Music Hall in Helsinki is situated right across the street to the Finnish Parliament. All major orchestras and music institutions of the country have declared the new hall as their 'home'. Having a 'home' on the best site of the country is the best possible way to guarantee the everlasting flow of government funding for the Helsinki orchestras. Whenever a Finnish member of the Parliament steps out of his 'home', the Parliament House, he will always inevitably see the Music Hall. It is his first vision of society when he leaves the decision-making platform just to go home. To leave the resident orchestras of this hall without subsidies, even to cut them down a little bit is practically impossible. The Helsinki orchestras are facing a future of multiplying their subsidies in the near future simply because without their program activities the new hall would remain empty. There is a lot of money and a lot of political prestige involved, which makes the process of branding a space with the help of culture so interesting. Branding a space means occupation of a space; concretely and also symbolically.

This is why the Helsinki orchestras and the music university Sibelius Academy wanted to have the new hall right in the city center at the most expensive site of the country, which is the heart of political life of Finland. The difficulties in building the acoustics and, indeed, completing the whole building were enormous. A train track had to be removed, the sea water level at the Töölö Bay caused several problems and an old architecturally important building had to be destroyed because of this project.

During the decision-making process, the rhetoric of the arts community in Helsinki achieved an astonishing level. It was a mixture of religious feelings and nationalistic aggressions, delivered in a touching 'unisono' of powerful lamentations that sounded almost like the Lacrimosa part of Mozarts Requiem. For example, one of the most famous Finnish conductors, Leif Segerstam declared that if the new hall were not going to be built and right there where the arts community wanted to have it, the 'Finlandia-Jesus' would not be born (Vihinen 2005: 225). He thus combined the nationalistic aura of the Finnish music culture, its hero Jean Sibelius who composed 'Finlandia' during the days of Russian oppression, and Christian religious feelings. On another occasion a member of the Radio Symphony Orchestra in Helsinki said that a possible rejection of the plan of the new hall would 'kill Mozart again'.

Reading between the lines, I think he was referring to one of the most persisting myths of classical music. It is the Amadeus Myth suggesting that the uneducated society and simpleminded political elite of Vienna turned their backs on Mozart and let him 'starve to death'. Tshaikovski already called Mozart the 'Christ of Music' because of the Amadeus Myth. Mozart, or rather Amadeus, seems to be a useful and often used rhetorical tool in defending the corporate cultural responsibility values of an arts community.

Conclusion

I'm afraid we cannot go on like this. The poor management of the building project in Hamburg as well as the constant overspending for opera houses and concert halls because of mismanagement lead us to an unbearable situation. In Hamburg the cultural life of the city is suffering because of the Elbphilharmonie and its horrendous costs. The Altona Museum has already been shut as well as parts of the fantastic Kunsthalle. In Copenhagen the Danish Broadcasting Company had to sack their entire sports department just to pay the skyrocketed costs of the new concert hall. The Guggenheim Foundation's preliminary report, commissioned by the City of Helsinki, costs as much as the annual budget of the whole country's art museums for buying new works of art for their collections.

Furthermore, in Helsinki the new Music Hall management is already renting the hall for entertainment music groups and conference organizers against the earlier promises of having the hall sanctified for classical music only. Even before the opening season started the Radio Symphony Orchestra of Helsinki applied for more funding from the state because the rent of the new hall is simply too high for the orchestra, as it is for all classical music ensembles.

Indeed, Hamburg seems to mark an end of an era. The city politicians cannot afford financial catastrophes like this in the future, even if the Elbphilharmonie should turn out to be a success for the destination image campaign of the city on the Elbe. The project in Hamburg today is more than 1000% more expensive than its original budget, which already caused a political defeat of one 'Bürgermeister', a significant political change at the Senat of Hamburg, and a beginning of a battle between the city and the contractors has already started. I'm afraid there are more to come.

What can be done in order to have new fantastic cultural sites in the city centers in the future? How should we change the destination management projects business environment and its practices of the cultural building projects? One of the most important remedies would be the involvement of true experts and consultants at the earliest possible stage of these projects. Their voices should be heard and considered seriously, their warnings taken into account openly with a transparency of modern democratic societies. This would be a major step toward a reliable business environment within the cultural construction world. Moreover, the senior management of cultural sites should be given to professional culture managers of today, not to artists without business background or working experience, nor to local politicians. After all, we all want to hear good music, see wonderful exhibitions and enjoy a great opera every now and then. Don't we?

References

Le Corbusier (1962): Architecture and the mathematical spirit. In: Le Lionnais, F. (ed.): Great currents of mathematical thought: Vol. II. Dover: Courier Dover Publications, 174-189.
Taleb, N.N. (2008): The Black Swan: The impact of the highly improbable. London: Penguin Books.
Vihinen, A. (2005): Musiikkia ja politiikkaa. Helsinki: LIKE.

AAALBANIA:
Possibilities and Limitations of Nation Branding Using the Example of Albania

Jörg Dauscher / Frank Otto Dietrich / Ralf Schmidt-Bleeker

When branding a region, building up an amalgam, a destination or a certain space of brand and location is the task at hand. The aim of doing so is to propagate closely defined conceptions of the respective location. Naturally these do not cover all the issues involved. While there is nothing more complex than a certain location, conventional branding rather works with reduction of complexity. The only way branding can deal with the abundance of meanings, references and interest out there is to narrow them down and make a choice. A location will either be communicated as a touristic gem, as promising high returns or as offering great education and formation. Conventional branding will inevitably fail to deal with the holistic demands of space marketing; there is no way it could communicate the identity of a certain location by methods of reducing complexity. The reason for this is simple. Conventional branding is still relying on simple messages.

Using the example of Albania this paper reveals the problems any attempt of space branding is about to encounter. Moreover the authors outline a practical alternative to simplistic brand management. Simple messages fail to grasp the spirit of a location and the identity of a country. They even fail to raise attention because antagonisms, suspense and conflicts are things that interest people. Therefore, disaccord and contrarieties are in trend but single-minded brand positioning cannot handle these. Static brand positioning does not really pay off in the long run because successful marketing depends on persistent agenda setting. This is where contemporary, more dynamic branding schemes come into play and choose narration as starting-point for marketing.

Albania as a Brand

The Republic of Albania is situated on the east coast of the Adriatic Sea and the northern part of the Ionian Sea, between Dubrovnik and Corfu, opposite of Bari and Brindisi. Although Albania is closely connected with the Italian ports by regular ferry service and can be reached by international air connections within a few hours, this country of great natural beauty and singular culture has remained largely unknown. Even today people are reluctant to visit a country that has so far hardly promoted itself and is still considered a dangerous territory for foreigners.

The main reason for this prejudice is the extremely bad press Albania has had to face since its departure from communism. The collective memory is determined by pictures of overloaded refugee boats, dirt and abject poverty, by civil war-like conditions and heavily armed guerrillas. Moreover, in public perception the young republic is readily lumped together with the Kosovo War and the Hamburg Mafia, although one has nothing to do with the other. To make matters worse, the memory of more than 40 years of Stalinist dictatorship, which led to the country being covered with 700,000 mushroom-shaped bunkers, lurks in the background. While one is inclined to think these are 'bygone times', a stigma can impose suffering for a long time because it was a case of successful, albeit negative, branding. Ferro concrete is durable and so is the public opinion.

Therefore, Albania should urgently be subjected to a re-launch. The small nation needs rebranding in order to attract tourists to the empty beaches of the Ionic Sea, to point out high-yielding possibilities to investors and to have better chances in Brussels. Let us assume a young Berlin agency (i.e. we) would be contracted for nation branding and immediately set out to find what makes Albania special.

Going to the Core

A prerequisite for defining the brand core is to find out what the essence of Albanian identity is. Why define the 'brand core'? The brand core is only one of the numerous marketing tools for tackling the phenomenon brand (Hellmann 2003). Successful brands have developed into highly complex reference systems with differentiated functions. According to marketing engineer Heribert Meffert a brand has to fulfil various functions for customers and companies: identification, orientation, confidence, competence, safety as well as image and prestige functions (Meffert et al. 2002: 9). In companies and organizations, marketing consequently results in a kind of special brand department which is responsible for organization and control of this reference system. Those methods in marketing practice, which are focused on reduction of complexity, have gained acceptance. The brand core is one of those constructs that reduce complex and variable meanings to a fixed market positioning. This in turn is conveyed to people by repetition in the hope that the message, not unlike a parasite, takes hold of the consumers' brains by redundancy and repetition.

So let us start looking for Albania's brand core. Field research, interviews, theme clusters and a relatively big budget allow for certain assets to be isolated and complexities to be 'broken down' to a few ingredients. After that the ingredients are thoroughly screened and finally boiled down and distilled.[1] This distillate is clear and almost colorless, of large range and effectiveness; Albania's distillate is the raki. If we wanted to reduce Albania to one single issue, we would have to raise our glasses and propose a toast because raki already contains everything that makes up Albanian pride and hospitality. Within a few hours after entering the country a foreigner is usually sat down at a plastic table and offered home-made raki from a plastic bottle. Since this is true for both tourists and entrepreneurs we would have different target groups on board already. Also, it is a proven fact that the population identifies with raki; even in the blocks of flats in Tirana you will find plastic buckets swarming with fruit flies in the corner.

The Client's Point of View

Chances are that the client would probably not play along. To simplify matters let us assume the client would be the Ministry of Economics. In that case, our request would certainly cause indignation as raki and home-distillation stand for the backward Albania. It's the modern Albania that is to be presented to the world such as the new sky-rise and office complexes in Tirana, the brand new airport and the comfortable hotels located directly on the beach. Our team would withdraw for consultation and soon after return to the negotiations with a new proposal. All building operations, whether in villages, on the beach or in the capital city, have one thing in common. It is a kind of optional architectural style that comes to a standstill whenever money runs short or when there aren't any investors. "Albania in the Making" would be a possible claim for an advertisement campaign in the international trade journals of the building sector, where half-finished, planned and expandable projects would be shown to illustrate the future-oriented Albania.

Sali Berisha, astonishingly still Albania's Prime Minister, commissioned over a hundred different building contractors with the expansion of the road from Durres to Shkodra a few months before his re-election just to have something to

---

1   "Trying to boil down the facets of a brand to a single essential, generally accepted characteristic is tantamount to reductio ad absurdum." (Liebl 2006a: 34)

show for himself. Each contractor was assigned his own road section. As could be expected, this rendered correspondingly diverse results. The tunnel of Kalimash, which was to link Albania with the Kosovo, was opened in great haste shortly before the elections in 2009 only to be closed due to 'maintenance work' after the elections. Shortly afterwards, parts of the tunnel collapsed (Balkan Web 2009). Therefore, our suggestion for a national core message would be: "It's impossible. But do-able."

Given that we had received the consent of the Ministry of Economics for one of our proposals and could start planning the campaign, the Ministry of Tourism would, by then at the latest, voice resistance because it has lately invested a little money, launched a website and commissioned a tourism campaign under the heading "Albania. A new Mediterranean Love" (National Tourism Agency 2011). The Ministry of Foreign Affairs would join the protests because, firstly, they back the campaign and, secondly, what on earth should suddenly be wrong with it? The issue of Albania's strategic realignment would inevitably end up on the desk of the Prime Minister who would get his hands on the project and commission his cousin's advertising agency with it because a small foreign ministry cannot possibly decide alone on fundamental national issues. After all, what is the head of the government for? A conflict with the President would follow who in turn would feel both responsible and excluded at the same time. The leader of the Socialist opposition and former mayor of Tirana, Edi Rama, would go his own way in the meantime and would, one day before Berisha goes public, present a concept for city marketing: "Tirana, the colourful heart of Albania".

What Went Wrong?

In the meantime, we would have headed home. Back in Berlin we would have to consider what had gone wrong. First of all we had a client who did not have the instruments of power to push through a nation branding campaign. However, is there actually an institution or authority that can order a strategic realignment of a state? Well, in the military sector this is done by the government and parliament. But what about the vast field of the identity of a state? Can a government decide on something like that at all? Nation branding and strategic realignment might be realised by means of a UN mandate or under the protection of Blue Helmets, but is there any other way? So the major problem is that there is no one who can order as well as realize a nation branding campaign. Wally

Olins, the 'Grand Seigneur' of branding, (Saffron, London)[2] describes the expectations of an agency that is supposed to conduct a nation branding campaign as follows, "If we do this [Nation Branding] we expect to get paid for it. We expect to have a client. We expect to talk to people, we expect to present things, we expect a reaction." And he closes with the rhetorical question, "Who do you want to deal with"? (Olins, W. 2007: *Chairman of Branding Agency Saffron*, interview by Dietrich, F., Lutea, M. and Kress, J., London, 22.08.2007).

The next problem is the procedure itself. A prerequisite for nation branding is that an entire state can be regarded as a complex enterprise, which is checked out for assets, whose self-conception is challenged, whose history is considered etc., etc. This is where the crux lies since one single brand core must be defined now. Why only one? According to the theory of conventional advertising, campaigns can be developed and communications tools defined, smoothly and consistently (Duckworth 1997: 158) based on it. Therefore, one would only need one single compelling idea, a simple message, and, if possible, also one single key visual. However, isn't Neuschwanstein Castle as one single key visual for Germany, for instance, a little bit simplistic?

Simply Impossible!

It must be permitted to ask why nation branding would aim at reconciling so many different things such as the secluded beaches of the Ionian Sea, the highlands of the Albanian Alps, the traffic chaos of Tirana, the lack of infrastructure, the cordiality and hospitality of the population, the opportunistic behaviour of the politicians, the problems and possibilities of an emerging nation into one simple thing. This is simply impossible. If it happens, nevertheless, it will soon get embarrassing. Telling people over and over again that it is all about passion in Spain might satisfy the need of the marketing industry for a simple message, but apart from that it is boring at best and confirms a silly prejudice at worst and nothing will be gained. Walking past a billboard by day that praises Spain as the country of passion will not cause anybody to go home at night and tell his/her partner about it and decide to go there, invest or study there. This will simply not happen, no matter how many contacts are established or how often a website is accessed. There is no point in increasing the frequency, booking

---

2   Wally Olins, brand strategist, agency founder and author, is considered to be pre-eminent in the field of advising on CI, branding and communication issues. He has advised international brands and organisations for many years and has a special interest in nation and region branding. With his London agency Saffron he has, amongst other things, worked on the creation of branding concepts for Spain, Portugal and Poland.

various channels and being 'liked' on Facebook. Simple messages don't tell because today brand communication differs a lot from the ideas of classical advertising. It is not only the increased number of communication channels, but also the fragmentation of the markets and the consumers which creates almost unsolvable problems for classical advertising agencies. The ideas of single-minded strategy and simple message simply cannot cope with the plurality of life worlds and communication channels. Therefore, the creative brief is no longer the most important tool of strategic branding.

Consider the story of the two Spanish artists who set out to take the matter into their own hands and paint at least some of the mouse-coloured bunkers with brilliant colours so that others would follow their example and colourful mushrooms would spread all over the country. Like Edi Rama who had the facades in Tirana painted because there were no funds for substantial changes (The New Yorker 2005), the two artists react to the 'grey depression' by using paint as the simplest of means to deal with the "Communist concrete" (YouTube 2010). Such a story would find an audience, simply because it does not conceal history and conflicts, but captures them and leaves them uncommented for the audience to take in; and also because it captures the heritage, the present and the future. Moreover, this story raises interest and, probably even more than that, empathy. This could never be achieved by a simple message. No matter which medium is used for this story, putting up posters of colourfully painted bunkers, shooting a short film or running a feature, such a measure would imply that it is necessary to talk about the complexity. The underlying idea would not be a one-eyed but a *narrative brief.*

In our understanding a narrative brief aims at making the whole tension field of the Albanian transformation efforts, including the conflicts, the asynchronies, the coexistence of old and new, and the pace of change that buries, ignores and eliminates many a thing, the subject of discussion instead of negating it. People go to the cinema in the evening because they are interested in conflicts and need opportunities to empathize with others, to share their excitement and joys. Diversity and otherness are not an obstacle, but actually fuel sympathy and interest.

Formulating a narrative brief is already a decisive creation process. Although it translates complex strategic considerations into a simple story, the story is not aimed at complexity reduction. Instead, it is a matter of building up complexity by using the conflict as a multivalent condition. As Alex Wipper-fürth, marketing avant-gardist and author, states in his book *Brand Hijack: Marketing without Marketing* (2005), exciting and successful brands are characterised precisely by this complexity. Therefore, complexity needs to be built up instead of reduced. For Wipperfürth this is an important strategic advantage, since complexity offers the chance to create excitement, arouse curiosity and finally inspire participation.[3]

Divergent Messages for a Divergent Audience

On the one hand nation branding as well as city or regional marketing aim to depict the identity of a geographical entity. On the other hand the target audience is highly divergent; some are interested in yields, others in the choice of the breakfast buffet. It would, of course, be conceivable to run several campaigns for different clients and target audiences, but that's not the intention of nation branding to, respectively, lower the bar but set it still high enough for local marketing. The intention is to communicate the image of the respective geographical entity in a controlled manner. This last sentence does however contain at least three errors.

Error number one is image. An image cannot be reinvented by branding agencies by means of reduction and cannot be expected to eventually get through by means of mechanical repetition. An image exists from the start and can be corrected and transformed by information and narration. Simple messages, however, are entirely inadequate for this because they are not credible at all.

Error number two is control. Classical marketing believes that value judgements can be generated by frequency and by reduction. Success is, and this is very telling indeed, determined quantitatively because so and so many people were reached via so and so many channels within so and so much time.

Error number three is communication. Sending verbal and graphic messages to people via diverse channels can hardly be considered to be communicative. People will not waste another word on this one-way, terse and simplistic kind of communication. Real communication begins when people's interest is aroused. This can only be achieved by suspense, conflict and diversity. Good stories are

---

3   "One of marketing's immutable laws has been to keep things simple. To keep them single-minded, focused. ... But every brand with a deeper meaning has a timeless story to tell, a hundred different ways of telling it, and millions of willing participants to enhance this story ... Hence the advantage ... lies in their complexity." (Wipperfürth 2005: 84) Classical strategic communication planning is often prone to overrating analytical and logical concepts and thus jeopardizing the actual vigour of the order communication. A conventional *creative brief* prematurely restricts, not yet elicited, spaces of possibility. This results in monothematic treatment and the platitudes we know from classical brand communication which doesn't allow for contradictions or vagueness. However, contradictory and conflict-laden issues are far more newsworthy and, thus, make it onto the public agenda more easily (Schulz 1994: 330). Also, the vagueness of a brand personality can awaken public opinion precisely because it is vague (Liebl 2006b).

'self-telling' because they are retold by people. They take on a life of their own and can no longer be controlled by classical branding.

Misconception Breeds Mistakes

These errors may be the logical consequence of a fundamental misunderstanding; that something like brand *management* is possible at all. A brand is not a dog that can be put on a leash by an agency and taken wherever it pleases them. It is not a chip that would have to be implemented with customers (Esch 2002).[4] Brands have got an identity even before the strategist starts working on them. They are living cultural assets either because they have existed for such a long time that the values they represent have further developed in stories and myths or because the people who represent them follow their very own values and convictions. It's hubristic to think that brands and their appearance could be defined and created in line with the market. The point is rather to develop them by building on what is already there and develop it instead of moulding the material according to one's will. Only then authenticity and credibility can be created.[5]

The claim that states can be branded only transfers the hubris of the agencies to a new structure which is bigger and more complex than a company that manufactures clothes and trainers. But even clothes and trainers have got, by virtue of the brand, developed a life of their own which cannot and must not be changed at will. "It's bigger than both of you!" one would like to call out to agencies and customers, whenever it's about Nike, Levis or Nivea, not to mention states! Wally Olins actually openly admits this. When asked how he thinks about the efforts to brand Lisbon as the IT capital of southern Europe he says, "It's bullshit. It's rubbish. Complete nonsense."And he adds, "Why should it be the IT capital? I mean there are plenty of places where the IT is much better

---

4   But it's been a long time since marketing was in the comfortable position of being able to dictate a product's meaning if it ever was (Sonnenburg 2009). The attribution of meaning to brands arises, then and possibly now, when the product or service is used, i.e. consumed. That is, consumers negotiate the meaning of brands by using them. This represents a second production step. The French Jesuit, sociologist, historian and cultural philosopher Michel De Certeau describes this production step as a kind of guerrilla strategy or the artfulness of the 'weaker' in a system of unequal power positions between producer and consumer (De Certeau 1988). The genesis of brand meaning should be understood as the strategic negotiation, as it were, of consumers. Consumption in this context means production.

5   The anthropologist and branding consultant Grant McCracken describes the central task of marketing as "meaning management" (McCracken 2005: 175-191). Mc Cracken believes that meaning represents the most important driver in marketing products and further that culture, as a superordinate component, generates this driver. Brands are built upon 'cultural meaning'. Brands gain their meanings from cultural meaning.

than in southern Europe, than it is in Lisbon, or Portugal." And the following statement makes us prick up our ears, "What I am saying is, that you need to get under the skin of a nation. I don't care if you call this branding or what you call it" (Olins 2007).

Under the Skin

So, according to Wally Olins we have to get under people's skin in order to be successful. This means that we must not remain on the surface of the matter but get to the bottom of it. It will be complicated at first to leave the world of external appearances and attend to the details because they are what really matters. We suspect that this one crucial detail, which encompasses all others, does not actually exist. It only exists in the laboratories of the marketing industry which is able to communicate anything but the reality of life. Reduction, unambiguity and the lowest common denominator are definitely not requirements for successful brand planning in the future. The way people interact, obtain information and deal with media is much too differentiated for that and ultimately no longer controllable. The times to invent unique positioning in order to showcase one's USPs have gone. The world of communication has become too complex for simple messages. What we need today is brand planning that can deal with complexity, integrates conflicts by not disregarding them, but by narrating them constructively which generates stories which are worth to be retold.

Meaning Means Complexity

But let us get back to our example 'Albania'. It has got a certain image whether the Albanian administration likes it or not. This image diverges from country to country; in Germany it is particularly bad. This is partly due to ignorance, partly to history. This fact should not be ignored, but instead be used as a basis to build on or 'to pick people up where they stand' as the phrase goes. This cannot be achieved by inventing a beautiful image and by defining brand cores and core messages, but rather by rendering an unadorned, authentic and diversifying account of Albania. The willingness to do so would be the beginning of a process called narrative brand planning.

At first this sounds more complicated than it really is because narrative brand planning breaks with the conventions of positioning marketing. Its goal is not to position brands clearly but to specifically tell about their complexities of meaning. This procedure does not focus on reduction or the compelling idea but on a list of relevant topics which have to be covered within the frame of a campaign. Narrative brand planning does not stage the brand but lets it speak for itself. Contrary to conventional story-telling, where any story is purely operatively built around the brand in the commercial break or online banner, the brand itself must be understood as the story: Don't tell a story! Be the story! The individual stories are no longer completed actions within singular communication measures but are, rather, part of a superordinate open action at brand level. After all, communication measures are meant to enrich or support the central story with facets, suspense and twists. This, in turn, creates exciting and, above all, credible stories which people enjoy retelling.

Taking the Task Stepwise

In order for market leaders to be able to offer and tell exciting and credible stories, a brand concept is needed. This brand concept must be oriented towards the functioning of good stories and provide strategic guidance for brand communication. Developing such a narrative brand concept, which subsequently will determine all further communication measures, is one of the goals of narrative brand planning. The development of a brand concept consists of the following process steps:

1) Collection of semantic data: Conducting interviews with consumers and internal interviews ('story listening')
2) Semantic reflection: Interpretation of brand meaning ('semantic space')
3) Semantic genesis: Strategies for influencing brand meaning ('narrative brand concepts')

A quick reminder is that the term *communication* means that something individual is shared with a general public, disclosed and made available to it (in Latin: *communicare*, to take part in sth., to let sb. take part in sth., to share sth., to communicate sth., to make sth. available to a community). To make something available means to refrain from control. However, the only way to refrain from control is to communicate the whole truth. This means not avoiding breaches, discrepancies and conflicts, but making them productive and bringing them under control by applying the constructive-narrative method. We call this method narrative brand planning. This essay is an example of a measure within this approach. On the first few pages we talked about Albania without trying to gloss anything over, touched various issues and listed diverging points in order to draw a much more complex picture of the small country and its transformation efforts than would have been possible or even conceivable within the frame of classical branding. In a brief, we abandoned branding in favour of narrative branding. We tried to arouse interest by revealing conflicts and tensions by narrative means. If we had only 'spewed out' simple messages and described how we had developed them, we could have been confident of gaining the technocrats' praise but not the readers' interest.

References

Balkanweb.com (2009): Rrëshen-Kalimash, ja prova e shembjes në tunel. http://www.balkanweb.com/homepage/rr%EBshen--kalimash,-ja-prova-e-shembjes-n%EB-tunel-2032.html, 19.01.2012.

Cramer, J. (2005): Painting the town: Letter from Europe. http://www.newyorker.com/archive/2005/06/27/050627fa_fact_kramer, 12.12.2011.

De Certeau, M. (1988): Kunst des Handelns. Berlin: Merve.

Duckworth, G. (1997): Creative briefing. In: Butterfield, L. (ed.): Excellence in advertising: The IPA guide to best practice. Burlington: Elsevier Butterworth-Heinemann, 147-169.

Esch, F.R. (2002): Strategie und Technik der Markenführung. München: Vahlen.

Hellmann, K.-U. (2003): Soziologie der Marke. Frankfurt am Main: Suhrkamp.

Liebl, F. (2006a): From branding goods to hacking brands: A beginner's guide to the brand universe. In: Heusser, H.-J. and Imesch, K. (eds.): Art & branding: Principles – interaction – perspectives. Zürich: Swiss Institute for Art Research, 25-42.

Liebl, F. (2006b): Unbekannte Theorie-Objekte der Trendforschung: Die Unschärfe als strategische Dimension der Markenpersönlichkeit, Antrittsvorlesung im Studiengang Gesellschafts- und Wirtschaftskommunikation der Berliner Universität der Künste Berlin, am 3. November 2006. http://www.iris-media.com/spip.php?article1626, 27.12.2011.

McCracken, G. (2005): Culture and consumption II: Markets, meaning and brand management. Bloomington: Indiana University Press.

Meffert, H., Burmann, C. and Koers, M. (2002): Markenmanagement: Grundfragen der identitätsorientierten Markenführung. Wiesbaden: Gabler.

National Tourism Agency (2011): Official Web site of Albanian tourism. http://www.akt.gov.al/index.php?lang=2, 15.01.2012.

Schulz, W. (1994): Nachricht. In: Noelle-Neumann, E., Schulz, W. and Wilke, J. (eds.): Das Fischer Lexikon: Publizistik, Massenkommunikation. Frankfurt am Main: Fischer, 216-240.

Sonnenburg, S. (2009) (ed.): Swarm Branding: Markenführung im Zeitalter von Web 2.0. Wiesbaden: VS Verlag.

Wipperfürth, A. (2005): Brand hijack: Marketing without marketing. New York: Penguin Books.

YouTube (2010): Albania: Not every day HD.wmv. http://www.youtube.com/watch?v=3IQKCyJNw-g, 01.12.2011.

Critiques and Consequences

Branded Space; Branded Consumers: Spaces for Consumption and the Uncomfortable Consequences of Complicit Communality

Steven Miles

The branding of spaces for consumption can only be fully understood in the context of a broader sociological process in which the very cities in which we live have themselves become branded entities. In this article I will consider the suggestion that the contemporary city is best understood as what is primarily a space for consumption. I will argue that the cultural sphere, and specifically galleries and museums, play a key role in the maintenance of cities as branded spaces, whilst pointing out that this process frames the everyday experience of the city as an experience filtered primarily through the processes that consumption implies. The concern here then is with the role of consumption in framing residents' everyday relationship with the city and how this relationship inevitably involves a degree of what might usefully be described as a 'moral compromise'. The suggestion is that in such circumstances the individual may give up some everyday freedoms in order to take advantage of the other that a consumer lifestyle implies.

Consumption and Identity

Consumption has had a profound impact upon the cultural landscape over a period of decades and if not centuries. However, it wasn't until the 1990s that a concerted discourse emerged in the social sciences around the role of consumption in the construction of social change (see Featherstone 1990). This discourse was at least partially tied up to notions of the post-modern and the suggestion that in a world of apparently limitless choice an individual's relationship to consumption was potentially as significant as his or her relationship to the means of production. Some commentators addressed this issue in the context of identity, arguing that consumption played an increasingly prominent role in who or what the individual is or aspires to be (e.g. Beck 1992).

Bourdieu's (1979) work on the cultural capital of consumption has of course been especially influential in the above regard in drawing attention to the role of cultural capital in creating differences between social groups; differences that were manifested through forms of consumption that either were or were not available to you depending largely on the nature of your educational experience. Equally significant in this regard is the work of Zygmunt Bauman (1998) who suggests that what emerged from the above process was a new kind of citizenship, where the extent to which you belong is defined by your ability or your lack of ability to consume. As Bauman (1998: 1) puts it in his discussion of the 'flawed consumer',

> "it is one thing to be poor in a society of producers and universal employment; it is quite a different thing to be poor in a society of consumers, in which life-projects are built around consumer choice rather than work, professional skills, or jobs. If 'being poor' once derived its meaning from the condition of being unemployed, today it draws its meaning primarily from the plight of a flawed consumer".

For Bauman a new 'self-culture' has apparently emerged in which the individual makes of his or her life what he or she wants to be as part of a broader lifestyle orientation. In addition, any consciousness of freedom is internalized; we become self-authored. As consumers we are effectively the products of a society that lauds the ethic of self-fulfillment and achievement. Unfortunately this kind of a society has its winners and its losers. In some senses the society it creates is an increasingly divided one. Your ability to belong is defined by your ability to consume, so without consumption you are effectively disenfranchised. And yet everywhere you go consumption rules. You may not be able to partake in this society fully, but you still have to live by its rules. As the geographer Robert David Sack (1998: 658) suggests,

> "the tensions in the structure of consumption point to a world that is becoming more homogenous overall, with fewer cultures, religions, languages, etc., but in which most individuals have far more variety at their fingertips. In other words, for the world, variety has diminished. For the individual, variety has increased".

Cities for Consumption

This apparent contradiction lies at the heart of what it means to experience city life in contemporary consumer society insofar as the contemporary city has apparently become defined through the cultural capital of consumption. However, the tools with which commentators have sought to understand such processes have tended to be rather blunt in nature. Such bluntness is the product of a set of circumstances in the political perspective of such commentators insofar as they are reluctant to be seen to criticise consumers for making conscious decisions about the role of consumption in their lives.

We can certainly identify a long and ongoing discussion around the construction of the neoliberal city within the social sciences. Authors such as Ward (2003) have described the changing nature of urban governance and the increasingly high profile that consumption has played in the emergence of the neoliberal city, to the extent that the consumption of the spectacle has apparently encroached into the very fabric of the public realm (see Gotham 2005). Authors such as Harvey (1989) have furthermore recognised that beyond the desire to improve conditions in specific territories, through housing and education for instance, there is a broader (more speculative) commitment to the image of place, which it is hoped, will have a trickle-down effect for the city as a whole. The contention of this chapter is that consumption lies at the heart of a strategy, in which the added value of a city competing in an increasingly global market becomes defined by its branding, by the cultural capital that consumption permits it. Moreover, I will argue that we should not assume that consumers are the powerless victims of this process. In other words, the residents of the contemporary consumer city are, at least to some degree, complicit in the emergence of a city that is defined through commodification.

The contemporary city is very much the product of the so-called experience economy (Pine and Gilmore 1989). Cities are no longer the fundamentally productive environments they were in the past and as such policy-makers have had to ascertain a viable economic alternative for the evolving city. The end-product of this process is a city that is designed to be an exciting place to live and visit, and above all, in which to consume, so that urban governance, as Harvey put it in 1989 is increasingly about how best to lure consumption flows into its space. This creates a divided city in which the symbolic enhancement of place is given disproportionate attention (Jessop and Sum 2000). From this point of view the new 'urban glamour zones' of the neoliberal city are the product of a highly selective and discriminating urban renaissance in which perception becomes more of a priority than the lived reality of city life (MacLeod 2002).

The contemporary city is thus constructed by city boosters, the product of a process in which several different visions of local culture are diluted into a single orthodox stereotyped vision that reflects the aspirations of a powerful elite (Broudehoux 2007). In effect, the contemporary city is constructed around what Corner (1994) describes as a 'consumptional identity'; a sort of urban impression management in which invocation of authenticity is the ultimate ambition (Prentice 2001). This precipitates an environment in which consumption, whether you can afford to engage actively in it or not, sits at the forefront of what is effectively a new kind of public realm (Goldberger 1996, Hayward 2004, Swyngedouw 1989). The move towards a neoliberal city represents a move away from urban planning that prioritises medium over message and image over substance (Harvey 1989: 13). The neoliberal city is grounded in a sense of place built around a conception of prosperity, rather than the more uncomfortable reality that lies beneath. It is in this context that Goldberger (1996: 27) laments the rise of the 'private city', a quasi-urban environment that does all it can to promote the energising, stimulating immediacy of city life whilst shutting out the less acceptable unequal face of the city of poverty and crime. Such a contention quite rightly draws attention to the potential social problems caused by the so-called neoliberal city. Consumption, in effect, becomes an agent of neo-liberalism; a key 'mediating phenomena' (Holland 1976) between the individual and the social structures in which he or she is implied, so that an individual's sense of citizenship can be said to have been reconfigured around their experience as consumer to the extent that social and civic disconnectedness is a product of the consumer society. This is an overwhelmingly negative picture and one that smacks of seduction. It implies a kind of empty soullessness in which the pervasiveness of the branded city becomes more important than everyday life in that city.

The kind of city described above is post-industrial and homogenized. We live in a global market in which cities are increasingly obliged to compete. As Zukin (1998) puts it, the more cities compete the more intense become the claims of uniqueness and yet the more standardised those cities become. This fosters a new kind of engagement with the public realm which constitutes what Mullins et al. (1999) have described as a 'third space' other than that of home and work that brings people together for sociability and other forms of social contact. This realm is primarily defined by retail or at least by the selling of the retail experience. But the problem here is that the retail experience has for many people become *the* urban experience. The broader impact of a market mentality and the increasingly speculative nature of the city creates a situation in which for developers, elected officials, financial institutions, and architectural designers the only possible response seems to be to merge public and private markets (Zukin 1993). As such, spaces for consumption such as hotels, department stores and museums have morphed into disorienting liminal and yet ideological spaces in which consumption of all kinds can take place (Zukin 1993) so that the city itself becomes branded as a symbolic entity whose messages are easily consumed. In a consumer society public space is increasingly tightly controlled and highly policed. Such space is often increasingly subject to private rules of access and as such symbolises the partial nature of the public sphere.

Galleries and Museums

In considering the above processes I want to suggest that museums and galleries play a key role as frontline vehicles for the promotion of the branded city. Commentators like Richard Florida (2002) talk about the role of creativity in constructing an economically vibrant city. But not far beneath the surface of the argument is the need to present a branded city in which opportunities to consume are maximised for the economic good and in which culture provides a means to a collective end.

Galleries and museums are often deemed to be of particular strategic import and provide a very visible means of maximising a city's geographical and historical location. Ward (2003) describes this as the construction of an 'animated' urban landscape. In other words, and from this point of view, as Landry (2006) puts it, galleries and museums become part of the city's 'sensory experience'. They are marketing statements first, entertainment centres second, and arguably cultural centres last of all. Or to put it another less generous way museums and galleries have become both the pawn and the porn of the post-industrial city. They are carefully exploited not only as branded spaces in their own right, but as spaces that symbolise a city committed to an outward looking future in which cultural consumption is a primary signifier of cultural capital and excellence. From another point of view this process effectively involves the exploitation of the cultural sphere as a form of urban pornography.

In many ways the reinvention of the post-industrial city is about presenting the city as a place in which the opportunities to consume culture in this way are prevalent so much so that any form of culture is deemed fair game in an effort to carve out some kind of a new economic future for the city. Thus according to Prentice (2001) the job of cultural tourism is not to present authenticity but to invoke it. Critics such as Richards and Wilson (2006: 1212) have thus argued that, "the effect is to produce a growing series of relatively sterile, inflexible cultural tourism spaces, dominated by passive consumption and the use of familiar historical references". The need to present the 'authentic' is of course not new for museums, but the pressures for museums to compete with other organisations presenting the authentic *is* new to the extent that, "museums are today immersed in a wider commodification of culture: the extensive proffering of place as a means of attaining the 'real'" (Prentice 2001: 7). Museums are often increasingly associated with the themed and the interactive or, in other words, with the immediate experience rather than with an in-depth interaction with meaning. This could be said to reflect the existence of a depthless society in which cultural tourism offers a means of searching for meaning in a society in which that meaning is arguably otherwise bereft. In effect, heritage sites, for example, act as an emotional stimulus for people's nostalgic cultural and in particular their thirst for heritage. Museums sell that pre-meditated experience to the consumer, they are, from this point of view, ideally situated institutions for the marketing of cultural capital (Wallace 2009).

For Podesta and Addis (2007) entertainment is a vehicle through which consumers' learning is maximised so that the consumer feels more involved in the 'product' that the museum provides. In this context McCracken (2005) suggests that a preferment model of the museum in which the role of the museum is to advance and civilise the individual through culture, has gradually been superseded, so that the visitor to the gallery and museum are no longer looking for experiences that pull them upward in the hierarchy, as may have been the case in the past, but rather outwards into a world of experience. Even where the interactive is not so evident museums operate as sites of heritage providing an emotional stimulus for people's nostalgic thirst for the past. They sell that experience and the apparent fulfillment of that emotion to the individual consumer, in the UK at least, as the product of government policy that has obliged museums to do all they can to seek 'diverse' audiences. In short, at least superficially, and as Kirshenblatt-Gimblett (1998) argues, museums appear no longer to be defined by their relationship to objects but rather by their relationship to their visitors or at least to their potential visitors.

Ideological Spaces?

The concern here is whether this process enables the consumer of the interpretive museum experience or inevitably results in the emptying out of place through the superficial consumption of the city. Spaces for touristic consumption are often subject to a highly staged experience or escape that privatises the nature of social experience and in doing so appears to reject the very social nature of that experience. As branded spaces, galleries and museums are complex and contradictory spaces being pulled in a variety of ideological directions. On the one hand they have effectively become politically obliged to be at the centre of social inclusion agenda, as defined by the UK government under Tony Blair's New Labour for example. On the other, they are bastions of cultural excellence and capital (Arnold 1965). In this context, the question is how far does the consumer ethic allow museums and galleries to square this circle? Galleries and museums are inevitably infused by notions of cultural capital and this is perhaps no better demonstrated than in the case of the starchitect phenomenon: a process whereby a world famous architect is commissioned to produce an iconic building that is branded by the name and reputation and thus the celebrity of the architect

– the cult of the architectural personality. Fein (2007) thus describes 'starchitects' such as Frank Gehry or Richard Meier and their work as 'brand-able'. They are branded for the benefit of global buyers of high-end luxury goods, in the form of very high-end envy-enducing real estate.

The Imperial War Museum of the North in Salford, England is a typical example of the starchitectural project because this is a museum that endeavours to recreate the unsettling experience of war through the 'personal' experience of an entirely disorienting building. Museums are public-private enterprises and often constitute part of a bigger picture of 'designscapes': an ensemble of buildings and cultural amenities that produces a consumer experience bigger than its concomitant parts (Julier 2005). In this case, the Daniel Libeskind designed museum sits on the other side of the river to the Lowry Centre designed by James Stirling and Michael Wilford. In juxtaposition the two cultural institutions create a critical mass of spectacular architectural consumption.

Complicit Communality

The end result of all this for the consumer is that museums and galleries appear to have what in effect are split personalities so that the branding of space as a symbol of cutting edge culture is less than partially successful. Branded spaces are sophisticated entities that appear to maximise an individual's control over the consuming experience (through his or her relationship to technology for example) whilst arguably simultaneously reducing his or her control over space and place in the more generic sense. Crucially however, a lack of control should not lead us to conclude that the individual consumer is powerless simply because he or she is escaping into the moment. Rather the consumer is engaged with a culture that privileges notions of choice and freedom, whilst framing those choices in very specific ways.

The point here of course is that however active the consumer may or may not be in this context there is no escaping the fact that such mindful experiences are made possible within the parameters laid down for the individual by the space for consumption in which he or she consumes (Miles 2010). In other words consumption ties us to the society in which we live through a sense of pseudo-belonging and citizenship and hence of 'complicit communality'. To put this another way, consumption effectively offers a sense of communality that is otherwise absent in western culture. The ways in which the consumer acts upon the sense of freedom that consumption engenders is not purely a demonstration of some kind of a dominant ideology. It could indeed be argued that consumers are willing to concede to this ideology for the immediacy of the freedoms that such an action would provide.

The above creates a problem for sociologists reluctant to appear to blame consumers for their own demise. The traditions of critical social science tend to be more adept at describing, indeed of condemning the deficiencies of the capitalist system than they are of understanding the complex interplay of structure and agency such a system can often imply, as if to do any differently would undermine their own political credentials. The recognition that consumers actively engage in the consumer experience and are able to put up with its limitations for the freedoms that experience provides is not a comfortable thought for an approach that is intent on blaming the system rather than the individuals who live through and interpret that system on an everyday basis. The process of complicit communality implies a connection with the public realm and establishes that connection through individual engagement so that the communal experience is defined by the ideology of consumption rather than according to any kind of a discernible community. This is not so much about sensory overload as about a context in which the individual garners control over the consumer images which he or she comes across in commodified space. The consumer uses branded space for his own ends, but there is apparently a price to be paid in the way in which the ideology of consumerism is reinforced along the way.

Conclusion

Perhaps the real challenge facing museums and galleries is actually to de-individualise the experience they offer; to aspire to a world in which the mere *sense* of communality, or of belonging, is simply not enough. Perhaps the narratives of space being deployed in museums are simply too individualised, they are arguably *too* visitor-centred so the only narrative that the visitor is left with is a narrative in which he or she sits at the centre of a much broader process of regeneration. Such narratives serve to promote the notion of the museum as nothing more than a space for consumption, as an empty symbol of the city, a symbol so ubiquitous that any effort by one city to brand itself becomes indistinguishable from any other.

The role of culture in promoting the city as a branded space is, as Richard Williams (2004) puts it, all about creating a visual tableaux to be touristically and vicariously consumed. From this point of view the city is rhetorical and picturesque. Thus, in discussing Liverpool's Albert Dock whose declined mercantile spaces have been regenerated into spaces for eating, drinking, and shopping as well as proving a home for the Tate Liverpool, Williams describes what is essentially a process of 'aestheticization'. In effect, the Albert Dock is rhetorical and indeed branded. It symbolises something important about Liverpool's mercantile past, about Liverpool as a brand, but it commodifies that brand in such a way to nullify any possibility of pleasure beyond that defined for the consumer and by consumption. This, for Williams is also a process of the picturesque, a response to an urban problem through the aestheticization of that problem.

Simmel's pupil Siegfried Kracauer (1995) observed the rise of 'surface culture' in all facets of the city, but particularly through the development of a shop window culture emerging over a hundred years ago now that enticed consumers into a world to which they had not previously been exposed, at least not in such a direct fashion. As a means of demonstrating the everyday ideological significance of everyday manifestations of the consumer ethic I quote Kracauer (1995: 75) directly,

> "the position that an epoch occupies in the historical process can be determined more strikingly from an analysis of its inconspicuous surface-level expressions than from that epoch's judgments about itself... The surface-level expressions... by virtue of their unconscious nature, provide unmediated access to the fundamental substance of the state of things".

Another way to put this in an urban context might be to say that the branding of cities is less about the construction of predictable environments and more about a profound effort to sweep away alternative ways of being in the city (Sorkin 1992). The machinations of individual city's and their marketing campaigns are incidental in an environment in which the consumer experience is all pervasive. For this reason the consumer city constitutes an extraordinarily limited public realm and yet one that from this perspective is not as depthless as orthodox analyses suggest.

Consumers unconsciously engage with a set of meanings that have in effect been allocated some of kind of privileged status. Visitors are not 'duped' by the excessive sense of escape offered by the branded city. Rather the consumer operationalises a degree of control that is not otherwise available to him or her and in doing so is complicit in a world of consumption in which he or she partakes so that consumption becomes a privileged site for citizenship. Branded space is from this point of view more than a commercial branding opportunity. It is a space, a physical and an emotional space that consumers engage with in a self-conscious fashion. This reflects a decline in the value placed on 'abstract principles of citizenship' in favour of a world in which poles of identity are more immediate and particularist in their form (Canclini 2001). A reinvention of citizenship in which politics is left behind in favour of the more immediate freedoms provided by the material world.

To belong to contemporary society and to demonstrate our belonging to that society is to be a consumer; the political arena is rendered inadequate, wieldy and inconsequential when measured against the dazzling, though partial freedoms offered by the consumer society. Perhaps public space has been parochialized and branded so that spaces for consumption are merely *occupied* rather than activated in any kind of animated fashion. The consumer has a degree of freedom, but the nature of that freedom is decided for him or her. From this point of view branded spaces symbolise a particular kind of citizenship and a partial sense of belonging in which the individual consumer gladly dances to the tune that the consumer society has chosen.

The potential for maximising economic value through branded spaces is apparently limitless, but such spaces do more than simply fabricate retail experiences. The frustration here is with a world in which the subtleties of the experience of branded space are not yet fully understood. Consumers are implicated in what could be described as a process of moral compromise, but the conceptual tools with which social scientists seek to understand such processes are equally as compromised. Consumers of branded spaces should not be condemned, nor can they be celebrated. These spaces actively redefine how it is consumers relate to the public realm. The ultimate concern here then is that while branded spaces have social power, they do not have social responsibility. The challenge now is to ensure that the methods used for developing a more sophisticated understanding of such complexities are both powerful and responsible.

References

Arnold, M. (1965): Culture and anarchy. Ann Arbor, MC: University of Michigan Press.
Auge, M. (1995): Non-places: Introduction to an anthropology of super-modernity. London: Verso.
Bauman, Z. (1998): Work, consumerism and the new poor. Buckingham: Open University Press.
Beck, U. (1992): Risk society: Towards a new modernity. London: Sage.
Bourdieu, P. (1979): Distinction: A social critique of the judgment of taste. London: Routledge, Kegan and Paul.
Brenner, N. and Theodore, N. (2002): Cities and the geographies of 'actually existing neoliberalism'. In: Antipode, 33(3), 349-379.
Broudehoux, A.-M. (2007): The making and selling of post-Mao Beijing. London: Routledge.

Campbell, C. (1989): The Romantic ethic and the spirit of modern consumerism. Cambridge: Wiley-Blackwell.

Canclini, N.G. (2001): Consumers and citizens: Globalization and multicultural conflicts. Minneapolis, MI: University of Minnesota Press.

Corner, J. (1994): Consumption editorial. In: Media, Culture and Society, 16, 371-374.

Featherstone, M. (1990): Consumer culture and Postmodernism. London: Sage.

Fein, S. (2007): Condo cool: Starchitect branding and the cost of 'effortless living' or another episode in the continuing quest for social status through design. http://internal.gsd.harvard.edu/research/publications/hdm/back/26_Fein.pdf, 24.02.2012.

Florida, R. (2002): The rise of the creative class. New York: Basic Books.

Fuller, G. and Harley, R. (2005): Aviopolis: A book about airports. London: Black Dog.

Goldberger, P. (1996): The rise of the private city. In: Vitullo, M.J. (ed.): Breaking away: The future of cities. New York: The Twentieth Century Fund, 135-148.

Gotham, K.F. (2005): Theorizing urban spectacles. In: City, 9(2), 225-246.

Harvey, D. (1989): From managerialism to entrepreneurialism: The transformation in urban governance in late capitalism. In: Geografiska Annaler: Series B, Human Geography 71(1), (The Roots of Geographical Change: 1973 to the Present), 3-17.

Hayward K. (2004): City limits: Crime, consumer culture and the urban experience. London: GlassHouse.

Holland, R. (1976): Self and social context. Cambridge: Macmillan.

Jessop, B. and Sum, N.-L. (2000): An entrepreneurial city in action: Hong Kong's emerging strategies in and for (inter)urban competition. In: Urban Studies, 37(12), 2287-2313.

Julier, G. (2005): Urban designscapes and the production of aesthetic consent. In: Urban Studies, 42(5-6), 869-887.

Kirshenblatt-Gimblett, B. (1998): Destination culture: Tourism, museums and heritage. London: University of California Press.

Kracauer, S. (1995): The mass ornament. Harvard: Harvard University Press.

Landry, C. (2006): The art of city making. London: Earthscan.

McCracken, G. (2005): Culture and consumption II: Markets, meanings and brand management. Bloomington: Indiana University Press.

MacLeod, G. (2002): From urban entrepreneurialism to a 'revanchist city'?: On the spatial injustices of Glasgow's Renaissance. In: Antipode, 34(3), 602-624.

Miles, S. (2010): Spaces for consumption: Pleasure and placelessness in the post-industrial city. London: Sage.

Mullins, P., Natalier, K., Smith, P. and Smeaton, B. (1999): Cities and consumption spaces. In: Urban Affairs Review, 35(1), 44-71.

Pine, J. and Gilmore, J. (1999): The experience economy. Boston: Harvard Business School.

Podesta, S. and Addis, M. (2007): Converging industries through experience. In: Caru, A. and Cova B. (eds.): Consuming experience. London: Routledge, 139-153.

Prentice, R. (2001): Experiential cultural tourism: Museums and the marketing of the new romanticism of evoked authenticity. In: Museum Management and Curatorship, 19(1), 5-26.

Richards, G. and Wilson, J. (2006): Developing creativity in tourist experiences: A solution to the serial reproduction of culture? In: Tourism Management, 27, 1209-1223.

Ritzer, G. (2005): Enchanting a disenchanted world. London: Pine Forge.

Sack, R.D. (1998): Place, modernity and the consumer's world. New York: John Hopkins University Press.

Sorkin, M. (1992): See you in Disneyland. In: Sorkin, M. (ed.): Variations on a theme park. New York: Hill and Wang, 205-232.

Swyndegouw, E.A. (1989): The heart of the place: The resurrection of locality in an age of hyperspace. In: Geografiska Annaler, 71 B, 31-42.

Wallace, M.A. (2009): Consumer research for museum marketers: Audience insights money can't buy. Lanham, MD: Alta Mira.

Ward, K. (2003): The limits to contemporary urban redevelopment: 'Doing' entrepreneurial urbanism in Birmingham, Leeds and Manchester. In: City, 7(2), 199-213.

Williams, R. (2004): The anxious city: English urbanism in the late twentieth century. London: Routledge.

Zukin, S. (1993): Landscapes of power: From Detroit to Disney World. London: University of California Press.

Zukin, S. (1998): Urban lifestyles: Diversity and standardisation in spaces of consumption. In: Urban Studies, 35(5/6), 825-840.

Cannibal Architecture Hates BANANAs: Post-Communist Rebranding of Historical Sites[1]

Florin Mureşanu / Monica Mureşanu

This paper analyses the urban phenomenon of the new infill buildings arising in key urban locations such as historic areas, the vicinity of established landmarks or purely out of regulation bending on protected sites. This is facing the associated critique coming from the revived public opinion and local communities with support from urban conservationist organizations and even sections of the media, oriented towards public awareness. In a post-Communistic environment, due to several decades of obstructed urban evolution, the process is confronted with a fundamental crisis such as the transition to democracy and capitalism. Therefore, regarding the urban development, there is an under-standable tendency to regain the lost time in a short period. But on the downside, the lack of synchronization between the faster capital flow of the open market and the slower adaptation of the urban society to changes leaves room for open urban conflicts.

The opposing sides face each other with contradictory arguments that would favor some of the city's transformation and some its conservation. Therefore, since there's no halfway in either direction, there's also no search for common ground. All that's left is a battle of wills which gives birth to undesirable compromises and no mutual satisfaction.

The paper will investigate the conditions that led to this particular situation, from a historic, economic and cultural point of view. It will also try to theorize on the typology of the resulted situation, based on the case of Bucharest, with the intent to demonstrate that even the long constructed identity of the cities can be subject to unwelcome rebranding if confronted with a steep change of their socio-economic structure.

1   Acknowledgements: The Romanian Academy, Cluj-Napoca Branch. This work was possible with the financial support of the Sectorial Operational Program for Human Resources Development 2007-2013, co-financed by the European Social Fund, under the project number POSDRU 89/1.5/S/60189 with the title 'Postdoctoral Programs for Sustainable Development in a Knowledge Based Society'.

Communist Urban Context Development and the Contemporary Aftermath

As an architect in a developing former Communist country you often wonder what is best for your city and that is the renewal or the conservation. At a certain point, you even get to question the authority and the morality of the structures that surrounds you and also, your role as a professional somewhere in the middle of the chain that links the strategy with the action. You most certainly at some point get caught between opposing forces facing each other with no common ground and no will to compromise. On the one hand you have the Goliath of site developers forcing the regulations and exploiting the legal gaps. These are backed up by funds, economic interests and administration corruption. On the other, the David of urban resistance represents the citizens and NGOs struggling to keep the communities untainted.

Socialist Romania experienced a period of great momentum for urban development, as it made the transition from a predominantly agricultural country to an industrial state. During this period the creation in the building sector suffered from repression and restrictions within the limits of a programmed architecture that consisted almost entirely of standardized medium height and tall housing units, industrial facilities and public buildings. Being focused almost exclusively on functionality, this led to the creation of whole generations of blasé architects, engaged in the routine of adapting typological projects to the particularities of each site. These, corroborated with the restriction of access to information and most especially the one coming from the capitalist countries, conditioned the Romanian architecture to undergo a static period concerning the modernity and innovation.

After the 1989 Revolution, architecture as well as other creative professions that were freed from the communist censorship, experienced rapid development and an unprecedented opening to the new. As a result, the style and language of the Western architecture were soon adopted it in the contemporary Romanian architectural expression. The massive infuse of technical and artistic information, unknown for a couple of decades, degenerated gradually into an indiscriminate use of the new architectural vocabulary. The effect is controversial even amongst professionals who are facing critique that spares no one involved in the building industry.

At first, there was a timid approach to the architectural innovation since in the first years of democracy there was the will although it required the power. As is with ever centralized economy relying heavily on standardization, Romania had a large prefab production for a whole range of constructions. These were not required anymore, partly because of the diminishing need for standardized buildings. Equally, the dwelling's association with the equalitarian Communist confinement in a highly ergonomic, but relatively small space, repeated all over the country, was reconsidered as lacking in character and in no way reflecting the personality, social class or education of the residents. Technically, there was no immediate need for new dwellings since the former public housing policy left a saturated market, but there was a particular demand that came from the newly enriched entrepreneurs for individual houses and bigger apartments. Moreover, the opening of borders made the travel abroad easier and the import of new ideas not only for the architects but also for the owners of capital. However, the development of the housing sector did not much affect the urban fabric. At most it spiced it up a bit with a variety of new forms and colors that added to the traditional gray concrete block.

Secondly, the bankruptcy of the construction industry happened in a series of events that would lead to the weakening of the entire heavy industry. After the 1992 *Rio Declaration on Environment and Development* there was a global trend in greening the production and diminishing the pollution by banning the overrated and inefficient 'old plants'. A lot of economic sectors went almost bankrupt in a short period of time which led to loss of jobs and the rise of unemployment.

Already the egalitarian structure of a socialist society was beginning to segregate; expanding to encompass the entire specter of social classes, from the very poor to the very rich, in order to morph into a veritable capitalist society. Obviously, this led to the birth of class hatred that channeled the aversion, previously oriented towards a dictatorial leadership, in the direction of the money flow. Wealth was naturally associated with unorthodox practices, corruption, bribery and nepotism, as these offered a crude but appealing explanation to the ongoing socio-economic divide. The freedom of speech, represented by the media, only fueled the indictments with headlines and disclosures. Soon the political representatives and the administration apparatus were conspicuously linked to every suspicious investment as opportunity facilitators and benefiters. Law making and application was gradually seen as biased and favoring the few at the expense of the majority of people.

Thirdly, there was the transformation of the agriculture. Socialist Romania, through the initial policy of expropriation and nationalization of the land, had an industrialized system of agricultural production. After the change of the political regime, the land was claimed and, through of series of laws, was granted back to the original owners or their successors. The highly acclaimed decision of land restoration had the most unexpected effect as most of the agricultural production went bankrupt. The infrastructure and means of production were divided also amongst the recipients of the repossession acts, many of whom were not working in the agriculture or not having interest in it. So, some of the people previously working the land and not being formerly owners were forced to seek means of existence other than the disorganized agricultural production. Especially in the rural areas, immediately after the passing of the land repossession laws, there was a substantial migration to the cities or abroad. The phenomenon was also largely perceived as capitalist inequity and suspected of corruption and abuse.

Finally, after about 10 to 12 years of democracy, the main conditions for a radical urban transformation were in place. The early years in 2000 came with a real-estate boom. Businesses were already making the transition from formerly heavy plants to smaller more adaptive units of production. Commerce was orienting towards a consumer society and the new industry of services was gaining momentum. There was also cash flowing into a supposed developing economy from the international community in the form of private investments. The joint ventures and stock companies were multiplying thus creating a flourishing business environment with higher wages. The workforce previously engaged in agricultural and industrial activities was adapting by flooding the great cities where the new economy was being born. Pressure was put into new residential developments as much as into representative buildings for the new production and consumption. On the one hand, there was an equally high demand for residential units, office buildings and shopping malls. On the other, not everybody was able to adapt to the change, so there was still a rise in unemployment and occupational cross border migration. Consequently, the past equalitarian society was dividing into poorer and richer classes and communities.

Initially the building industry targeted the city fringe by expanding peri-urban areas with the demand for western suburban life clichés. Owning an individual house seemed to be enough of a certification of capitalism for the medium-high income average family. This quickly put high pressure on the transportation infrastructure, already designed for high density urban structures, instead of sprawl friendly solutions. On the contrary, the businesses targeted the higher density areas and the city centers already dealing with the decay that resulted from the migration of the better remunerated population to the suburbs.

The Re-branding Cycle

Overall, the impact on the high density, Communist districts was minimal since the original design, generally collective housing blocks with commercial ground floors, boulevards with large pathways, and rationally distributed public places easily allowed the development of businesses. Things were different though for the older neighborhoods, including the city centers. These were already experiencing the third stage in the urban cycle (Klaassen et al. 1981, Champion

2001). As defined by Champion, the four stages in the cyclic urban transformation are: (1) urbanization, (2) suburbanization, (3) disurbanization, and (4) reurbanization. Therefore, in some manner, there is some predefined order in the evolution of cities.

A lot of effort is being put in conserving the historical sites, in most of the cases synonymous with the city centers, in order to stop the cycle. There's a global trend in the developed world to limit the intervention on sites that hold built heritage and there are local and international organization supporting it. However, regulations don't solve the large range of problems arising from the property rights, ownership and ultimately, the financial capabilities of both the municipal administration and the private sector. These problems create an unstable balance of the transformation-conservation relationship. Even if public-private financial partnerships are often sought, this doesn't always have the intended outcome. The more interests, the more issues there are to compromise on, not to neglect the risk of regulation bending, casual partaking or misused public funds. In other cases there's the usual pushing and pulling negotiation that would allow new developments in protected areas.

On the one hand, there is an understandable pressure associated with the renewal interventions since the targeted sites benefit from their location, public amenities, ongoing trades and, most importantly, the unique character and ambient value that ensures a constant flow of pedestrians and tourists, all of them potential consumers. On the other hand, the city centers have always been associated with the business activities. This led to their perception of Central Business Districts that grow by pushing against the surrounding urban mass if the economic environment permits it. Theoretically this creates urban evolution, renewal, gentrification, but in reality, there are also discontent, community uprisings, media coverage and public inquiries associated. Many of the global trade and financial cities, having already dealt with this, moved the CBD's from downtown to remote locations where they can evolve independently. Other cities with less financial activities, and this is the normal case with the post-communist developing economies, still keep the trade in the traditional location. As a result of this, unable to expand because of the hard shell created by neighborhoods surrounding them, the CBD cannibalizes the buildings that cannot accommodate the required office and shopping space thus transforming and replacing bits and pieces of a former untainted urban tissue.

Sold as a solution to urban decay, as a mean to achieve the modern lifestyle or advocating the need for jobs, the entrepreneurial image is promoted as a cosmopolitan western like urban representation. Even less important features, such as the benefits of new ground floor stores or parking lots, are capitalized upon in order to appeal to the daily needs of the local communities. But in reality the new *logo buildings* pretend to have an elevated and upgraded status and are not really concerned with trivialities such as integration and cohesion. They tend to strike and wow, dazzling with shiny facades, flashy commercials and oversized corporate logos, that don't quite show concern with trivialities such as integration and cohesion. Otherwise, these are just the visual and compositional elements that you would expect to fragment a coherent urban structure that has a unique identity, yet is being piggybacked by global, not local, identities that are leveling the dialogue with the urban fabric for the universal consumer.

As much as the local specificity adapts to the presence of globalization, sometimes with a loss for its own identity, the global ventures and the multi-national corporations are forced to adapt to the indigenous context. What is derived from this is a peculiar mix, easy digestible by the urban consumer, but with a disappearing structural identity. Sometimes the appearances are being kept as new businesses are installing themselves in existing buildings. Logos and mottos will appear, with no regard for the visual consistency, as a sign of the company's worldwide spread and guarantee for the same quality of services everywhere. In many cases it's almost impossible to have a logo-building implanted, so the oversized logo and the flashy posters will do the job.

This type of *cannibalistic architecture* aims at the transformation of crippled sites that often have intrinsic value. These may be derelict historical buildings, unplanned strategic sites or even good condition iconic buildings belonging to past regimes whose existence is being contested. Also, it takes advantage of the gaps in urban management by targeting unprotected high potential sites and buildings. This is obviously a rebranding. So, in terms of changing urban identity, let's paraphrase Champion (2001) by redefining the cycle to: (1) branding, (2) TOAD-ing (*Temporary, Obsolete, Abandoned and Derelict*), (3) de-branding, and (4) re-branding. Yes, sometimes the rebranding doesn't happen without changing the status of certain spaces to TOAD. This requires elaborated strategies in order to turn a functional building or even public space into a potentially 'unable to keep, must be replaced' site.

The rebranding cycle of the urban tissue is, in its essence, the very natural process of urban evolution, which renewed the cities throughout history. The urban environment was always considered a place of the 'new', the big cities setting the pace of the trends in current, style, norms and image. This resulted in overlapping layers of architectural information that concurred in defining the cities individual characteristic, or their 'brand'. This would have been hardly possible without the regular 'toading' of old urban tissue parts. The process allowed the renewal of outdated and derelict buildings and the reuse of their site for 'better', up to date purposes. There are several types of re-branding involving accidental or deliberate 'toading': (1) cases of decay resulted from ownership neglect, (2) large scale urban restructuring, such as Haussmann's mid-19th century Paris renovation or Cerdà's initial 'Eixample' for Barcelona, (3) post-conflict and post-calamity reconstructions, (4) ideology reflecting urban remodeling, such as Marcello Piacentini or Albert Speer's monumental projects, and (5) dogmatic utter replacement of the urban tissue, like in the case of communist common housing districts. All the above cases of 'toading' are supported by necessity or particular cultural understanding of the urban environment. Their common denominator is that, generally, they are carried out with financial efforts that do not expect immediate or no pecuniary gains, but rather superior comfort, clearer urban structure or some political justified 'proper' urban image.

This brings us to the last type of re-branding, which solely follows the cash flow, seeking to gain the upmost financial benefices from the re-branding of frail locations. Though this is a current practice in long-established capitalist environments, in the particular case of an 'emerging economy' it might be perceived as a callous and unwanted interference, or even as a brutal post-colonial display of financial superiority. The visible facet of this is the abovementioned *cannibalistic architecture* that has no regard, or at most a mocking approach, for the surrounding urban setting. Given the particular case of post-communist cities that lost a large amount of their built heritage during the large scale 1980s urban remodeling, the potential resuming of culture loss through unclear and often undisclosed architectural replacement and infill, constitutes a delicate state of things that is addressed differently by all the urban actors involved.

For now, there's just one element left out of the re-branding cycle. This has the potential to render it ineffective, for it is oriented towards the preservation of the constituted urban identity. It is the public opinion which has simply gone bananas (Taylor 1991, Burns 2003). BANANAs, acronym for *Build Absolutely Nothing Anywhere Near Anyone* are public opinion driven activist groups who oppose site operations and are unwilling to compromise on the issue. They are somehow of novelty in the post-communist urban landscape. Considering the fact that in the past regime the public opinion was censured, when not absolutely silenced, the new democracy has given the BANANAs a voice which is louder and more radical then the outdated, moderate, self-interested LULUs (*Locally Unwanted Land Use*) and NIMBYs (*Not In My Back Yard*). Anyways these seem to have changed focus on different agendas, such as air pollution, landfill locations or waste leakages. The BANANAs are generally FRUITs (*Fear of Revitalization, Urban-Infill and Towers*) who often receive help from the anarchist CAVEs (*Citizens Against Virtually Anything*) that are willing to oppose anything as long as there's protesting that can be hijacked for political purposes. Sadly, this usually discredits the BANANA's attempts.

As the Communist era put effort into dividing the urban communities through population mixing, large scale demolitions and mutual distrust, the recent revival of the communities' cohesion raises again the interest for the common good. Their arguments regarding the infill of new buildings in the traditional urban fabric is that they damage the urban identity, elevate the built density and create more pressure on the transportation network and amenities. Moreover, when this is done with the replacement of old buildings there's the risk that 'what's lost will be lost forever', causing a change that is an irreversible loss for the entire city and also for the future generations. Ultimately, the BANANAs are trying to keep a predefined order that equals from their perspective the established identity of the place.

The Branding of Bucharest in the 19th Century

Figure 1:
Early 20th Century Vintage Postcard Showing Calea Victoriei Boulevard.

Figure 2:
Early 20th Century Vintage Postcard Showing the Royal Palace Square.

Bucharest was first mentioned in an official document written by Vlad Ţepeş, the Valachian Prince, in 1459. In 17th century Bucharest was known as the most prolific trade market in Valachia and, therefore, in 1698 it was chosen as the capital of the region. In 1861, after the Union of Moldavia with Valachia, it was proclamed the capital of the new born state of Romania (Iorga 1939). Because of its new status, Bucharest faced a new era of urban development and transformations as its population grew considerably. After the Independence War, in 1877-1878, Romania was no longer under the Ottoman Empire's influence and it began its persuit for modernity and the research for succesfull western patterns and models (Djuvara 1989). The model adopted for Bucharest was the city of Paris as the French *savoir faire* and culture were considered suitable guidelines for the transformation of the capital city and its society.

The first stage in this complex development process was the urban modernization based on Parisian regulations and laws that were slightly adapted for Bucharest. It consisted of opening new major arterial streets and boulevards, the adjustment of Dâmboviţa River's course, the change of alignments and street enlargements (Fezi 2005) etc.

The second stage of the process, from 1880 to 1910, consisted of the construction of several public edifices and private villas in the romantic style of the eclectic French architecture. The new buildings were designed, almost exclusevely, by French or Romanian architects that had completed their studies at the Ecole des Beaux Arts in Paris (Zahariade 2006). The magnitude of the eclectic movement in Bucharest is certified by the extent of the influence it generated over the social and cultural life of Bucharest as well as upon the legistation, urban planning, artistic expression and architecture. French was considered a semi-official language at the end of the 19th century in Romania (Eliade 1982).

The cultural import and the transformation of Bucharest towards modernity and towards the Western world were legitimate reactions against the Oriental domination. That particular moment in the history of Bucharest, at the turn of the centuries, could be considered the first branding of the city. There was no case for a previous de-branding since although Bucharest experienced first-hand the Ottoman and Phanariot rule, their mark on the architectural and urban context was minimal and only further reflected the 'balkanic' image of the region. Overlapping the French eclectic style onto an already melting pot of cultural characteristics came as a natural, largely accepted and even desired process. It drew a new stylistic direction but did not erase the already established ambiance of the city, which came to be popularly addressed to as 'Little Paris'. Overtime the coined name became 'double-bladed', stating as appropriate both the presence of the western-like style, as deference and its cheap imitation, as ridicule.

Rebranding Examples: Bucharest in the 21st Century

After the fall of the Communist regime Bucharest was left with a number of structural compromise situations. The socialist agenda was to replace the traditional fabric with the more dramatic functionalist one, where the urban choreography would stage compositional axes, great built assemblies and grandiose public edifices that would reflect the supremacy of the ideology. By 1989 this was only half way completed, thus leaving many areas in a limbo state between vacancy and future reassignment. This left several low rise residential areas, already vacated by the previous owner in order to be soon demolished, in a state of uncertainty and devastation. The renewal policy concentrated all the effort in new buildings thus leaving deliberately the old ones to degrade.

Out of numerous cases as such, some were solved by returning the building to the rightful owners through repossession. Lacking the capital to restore or build, the properties began to change hands until an investor would take the risk to slalom the conservation regulations in order to profit as much as possible from the investments. The successful ones were pushing the limits so hard that peculiar compromises began to appear as a result of legislation bending. Mainly they fall into three typologies. First there is 'the rider' which pretends to be a new modern extension but is actually a parasitic structure attached to or on top of an old building considered to still have esthetic values that deserve to be kept. Often what are kept from the old structure are only the general silhouette and the decorations, the insides being replaced by interior spaces that would better suit the new function. Secondly, there are the 'embezzlement' cases where a new building would target an empty lot near a landmark building in order to profit from its notoriety. Most commonly these are commercial or office buildings that need to gain reputation. Sometimes they go so far that they would incorporate in their logos and marketing strategies the initial landmark as a reference. Thirdly, and this is the most curious case, there are the impersonations. These are places that act as a symbolic landmark because of their history, even if this is about an iconic building that doesn't exist anymore but is still preserved in the collective memory of the community. 'The impersonator' is willing to bring back from oblivion and to recreate parts of the original structure in order to appeal to the memory and emotions of the community and municipality that would, thereby, be more tolerant to what is the main objective.

The Rider

Figure 3: Sarroglia Hotel. (Authors)

Figure 4: The Original House. (Art Historia blog,
http://art-historia.blogspot.com, 18.08.2011)

The example (Figure 4) belongs to the end of the 19th century when it was built to house a family in the immediate vicinity of the historic center of Bucharest. It probably had many owners over a century, but it managed to survive until 2008 when it was time for a change. It changed image, function and perspective due to a large investment that transformed it into a four star hotel in July 2011 (Figure 3). The steps of the transformation were often seen before, around the historic center of Bucharest: abandon or destruction, followed by a variety of modern upgrades contributing to the constant metamorphosis of the historic urban tissue. In this particular case, we are probably dealing with a 'cohabitation' of the new building and the old one, although the former house was rendered an empty shell. Or, from another point of view, "a perfect mixture between old and new, tradition and innovation with special attention paid to each detail"[2].

The urban context and atmosphere of the street are strongly influenced by this intervention because of the uncertain message that it transmits. The new part of the building 'feeds' on the core of the old one and it suppresses it with its dominant steel structure and dark grey metallic finishes. The old building doesn't benefit from this cannibalistic intervention and surprisingly enough nor does the new edifice constructed on top of it.

This was a typical evasive maneuver of the private investor regarding the local regulations that were meant to create some limitations regarding the interventions in the historical part of Bucharest. It is in fact a lax, but legal, interpretation of the very general guidelines given by the public authorities in charge of built heritage. It is not a classical 'façadism' style intervention, though, even if some of the old building was kept because the proportion between the old volume, the 'active archive' (Augustin 2006) and the new structure seems intentionally unrestrained and intrepid. The spirit of the place was completely ignored in this case as well as the impact this new building had on the surroundings. It is a living proof that there are situations when the partial conservation of an object can generate ludicrous contexts.

---

2   Cited from the website of the Sarroglia Hotel, available from http://www.sarrogliahotel.com, 25.10.2011.

The Embezzler

Figure 5:   Saint Joseph Catholic Cathedral
and Cathedral Plaza. (Authors)

Figure 6:   The Armenian Church and Millennium Business Center. (Authors)

Some churches in Bucharest seem to have not only a troubled past but also an unfortunate present. During the Communist period, when religion was seen as undermining the official ideology, a few churches were literally relocated to remote and obscure places to escape demolition or were simply surrounded in order to be concealed. That is why we can sometimes find them behind blocks of flats or inside their courtyards. Now the church is once again the symbol of spiritual beliefs and it is generally respected as such. In some cases though, churches get to relive the experience of more than twenty years ago not because religion is a problem of the present society, but because the area around them happens to be centrally located and, therefore, very profitable.

The two cases (Figure 5 and 6) in the images above are similar. Office skyscrapers are erected in the protected areas of two important historical monuments and overtake by far the height of the neighboring buildings. *Cathedral Plaza* is not completely finished yet and considering the countless lawsuits its developers have with the Catholic Church, it will probably stay that way for a while. The other office building, adjacent to the Armenian Church, suspiciously caught fire and was partially damaged in 2009 and has been abandoned ever since.

We can probably question not only the lack of respect regarding the historical surroundings, but also the validity of the permits given by the authorities. These cases were eventually turned into media scandals because of high visual impact of the developments and, equally, because of the communities involved in the cases. The Armenian ethnics and the Catholics expressed themselves loudly against these edifices, backed up by NGOs such as 'Save Bucharest', 'Asociaţia 21 Decembrie' and 'Bucharest Group'. In the case of the Catholic Cathedral the protests even motivated the public stand of officials in the European Parliament and the Vatican. According to the 2002 census 1,780 persons declared themselves as being Armenian ethnics, in Bucharest and Constanta County, while the Catholic denomination was appreciated at 4.7%, the majority of Catholics being set in Transylvania. Paradoxically, even though the cases involved a minor ethnic group and a minor denomination in a long-established Orthodox area, this attracted notable coverage, due to the 'exotic' side and the feel of 'political correctitude'. Furthermore, by now this led to administrative inquiries and a temporary halt of the developments until a final court decision is made.

The Impersonator

Figure 7:   1939 Vintage Postcard Showing the
                National Theatre on Calea Victoriei.

Figure 8:   The Contemporary Novotel
                Hotel. (Authors)

The old National Theatre (Figure 7) was demolished a few years after it was bombarded and partially destroyed in 1944. It opened its doors for the first time in 1852. The original building was a predominantly baroque in style and had luxurious Carrara marble staircases. The large balcony over the main entrance was an iconic location in Bucharest which served as the tribune for the announcement of many important cultural and mundane events, for nearly a century. However, it was demolished in 1947 (Ionescu 1981) and its site remained unfilled until recently.

In 2007 a new hotel was erected on the empty lot of the former theater. Since Calea Victoriei is still an important artery of Bucharest, the project was thoroughly discussed within the municipality and the Commission for Historic Monuments. It appears that this array (Figure 8) was considered the best solution for this particular case. The new steel and glass building was destined to receive in front of it a small souvenir which is the theater's portico. This was reproduced by contemporary craftsmen with contemporary materials and is reflected now in the glass screen behind it that marks the main entrance to the hotel.

Even if the intentions are clear to strike a sensible cord regarding the flourishing 'la belle époque' Bucharest, this is nothing more than a urban hoax that doesn't solve the integration in the context of an important historic boulevard. The strength and legitimacy of the message sent by the new building is unclear and founded on false premises that could somehow justify the presence of a glass and steel alien structure in the middle of the historic part of the city.

Conclusion

It would seem that the BANANAs struggles have little effect in preventing the rebranding of historical places. It's true that the intruders would use superior weaponry like ownership, funding, lobbying or time, or that they would profit from ambiguous regulations, corruption and the relative lack of professionals in the administrative apparatus to their advantage. However, the opposing party also evolves and profits from the media's appetite for conflicts. Although the opposition lacks funds and are poorly organized for intervention, they gain political advantage from the growing interest shown by local communities and, hence, public figures.

Even if battles are lost over the historical cultural values and the identity of the place that create a 'honeycomb' attraction for cannibal architecture, the BANANAs have their own strategies. Usually, they target high profile cases and with every reputed victory, no matter how small, they are scaring away other plans to alter the built heritage with the fear of exposure, stalling and, ultimately, financial loss. However, taking into account that the targets are often derelict cases, we can't neglect the hypocritical side of the protests that target the transformations but forfeit restoration and conservation goals. No wonder there is growing hatred between the promoters of cannibal architecture and the BANANAs. Therefore, they vilify each other with the first accused of maiming the urban legacy and the second of stemming the progress, in a battle with yet undecided odds.

References

Augustin, I. (2006): Une obsession autochtone: L'architecture au «spécifique national»? In: Augustin, I. (ed.): Influences françaises dans l'architecture et l'art de la Roumanie des XIXe et XXe siècles. Bucharest: Institutul Cultural Român, 82-96.

Burns, K. (2003): Can't see the point of new buildings? You're bananas. In: Sunday Times of London, July 6.

Champion, T. (2001): Urbanization, suburbanization, counter urbanization and reurbanization. In: Paddison, R. (ed.): Handbook of urban studies, London: Sage, 143-161.

Dame, F. (1907): Bucharest en 1906. Bucharest: Socec.

Djuvara, N. (1989): Le pays roumain entre Orient et Occident: Les Principautés danubiennes au début du XIXe siècle. Cergy-Pontoise: Publications Orientalistes de France.

Eliade, P. (1982, reprint of 1898): De l'influence française sur l'esprit public en Roumanie. Paris: Kessinger Publishing.

Epron, J.P. (1991): Comprendre l'eclectisme. Nancy: Institut Français d'Architecture, Ecole d'Architecture de Nancy.

Fezi, B.A. (2005): Bucarest et l'influence française: Entre modèle et archétype urbain, 1831-1921. Paris: L'Harmattan.

Ionescu, G. (1981): Arhitectura pe teritoriul României de-a lungul veacurilor. Bucharest: Ed. Academiei Romane.

Iorga, N. (1918): Histoire des relations entre la France et les roumains. Paris: Librairie Payot et Cie.

Klaassen, L., Molle, W. and Paelinck, J. (1981): Dynamics of urban development. New York: St. Martin's Press.

Taylor, D. (1991): Nowhere, no time. In: The Sydney Morning Herald, January 21.

Zahariade, A.M. (2006): Influences françaises sur l'architecture de la Roumanie. In: Augustin, I. (ed.): Influences françaises dans l'architecture et l'art de la Roumanie des XIXe et XXe siècles. Bucharest: Institutul Cultural Român, 9-36.

Syntax of Intervention in Historically Significant Public Open Urban Spaces

Stefanie Leontiadis

This research aims at presenting a methodological way of breaking down syntactic spatial concepts of public open urban space for envisioning architectural interventions that will harmoniously fit into existing historical urban compositions. This takes place through means of branding, using keywords of syntactic expression. These will suggest contemporary ways of *composition, perception* and *representation* in reference to existing ones. Some of the syntactic spatial concepts that are studied include *concept* and *theme, historical layering, signs, symbolism,* and *structure.* The study demonstrates this on a couple of historically important spaces and conceptually explains as well as illustrates methods of new architectural interventions.

The concluding result provides a better understanding for the fluid intervention of newly marked architectural elements inside public open urban spaces as our existence in the contemporary world calls for new stylistic elements in the field of vision of a specific theme. The different styles and chronological executions, when sharing a common internal structure of elements and more essential aspects of visual reality, may blend harmoniously and introduce new fields of intellectual continuity in the history of architectural creation and conceptual innovation of paradigmatic times.

Background Theory and Critical Synthesis

Historical spaces of momentousness, sometimes categorized in the preservation categories of World Heritage Sites, are spatial *compositions* of memory and urban identification of adorning affiliation and reference to the past. They are branded spaces that *represent* and *mark* the cultural, technological and even spiritual mindset of people of certain times and extract themes that fall into the categories of virtual, temporal or mobile times, spaces and existences. It may be argued that historical spaces express important evolutional moments of humanity, expressed in an almost virtual, three-dimensional manner exposing levels of artistic or literary brilliance of man at one point in time. When this combat with memory and virtual reality takes place in public open urban spaces, the question rises whether it is equally important to act similarly in pursuit of three dimensional excursions into *perceiving* the present and future, taking place inside the same historical public open urban space. In doing so, the visual *education* does not only hold significance towards the past, but also references the present reality and future aspirations, as it is important not to worship the ancestral accomplishments exclusively, but also to find ways for processions that are innovative means of human representation.

Imperative in this consideration is Françoise Choay's point of view on the heritage concept of the civic space, on which she speaks in her paper *Questioning the Heritage Concept: A Polemic Anthology* (Choay 2009). Choay speculates the meaning of *heritage* in its spatial acceptation beyond the objects that are encompassed in it and from the anthropological point of view, similar to how she studies the concept of *anthropopolis* (versus *technotopia*) in her *Utopies et Réalités* (Choay 1986: 242), where anthropopolis corresponds to the culturalist perception of the public open urban space. This idea associates itself to the spoken existence of the public civic space holding the role of a backdrop against which human life unfolds. This relationship has been theoretically evident through architectural research studies on the civic places and has been evidently visible in cases of cities of the past, along with contemporary historically preserved spaces. However, in the contemporary environment of purely modernistic and undefined approaches, or in places of periodized hybridizations, this relationship is not as clear.

Relating the heritage concept to the definition of the word 'monument' (derived from *monere*: to alert, to recall, to memorize), the concretization of heritage takes the form of living, organic and effective memory of members, persons, events, beliefs, rites or social rules which are components of its identity. It consequently becomes inevitable to translate heritage as a semiotic way to express multiple things, or as Choay (2009: 7) puts it, "it duplicates the symbolic function of language" and to bring together "the dual temporality of humans and nature". Aiming for this intent, one finds the scrutiny of the *historic monument* linked to the examination of *antiquities* (*antiquitates*: to designate all the ancient productions such as language, customs and traditions) which factually led to the seeking of the most ideal methods of civic space creation, an iconographic documentation of the material found, and later on a more epistemological linkage to the natural sciences and their analysis of living forms (Choay 2009: 7). The phenomenon is manifested in the scattered ruins of historical towns, or in *non-place* of urban abolition through time, where the scene documents "a concentration of ancient pain handed down ... the arrogance of the survivor ... [and] a displacement in time which transforms them into myth" (D'Ardia 2009: 2).

The contemporary interventions into the existing heritage of public open urban spaces are a sensitive issue as there is the debate of preservation and non-intervention versus the advocacy of construction progressivism and interventionism. This debate starts with Ruskin's (1849: 1) sentiment that "restoration is the worst form of destruction that a building can possibly suffer" and Viollet-le-Duc's (1868: 14) surmise that "restoring an edifice ... means restoring it to a complete state that may never have existed".

However, through the use of branding by means of consistent themes, historical layers, allegorical symbolism and structural consistency, topics discussed here, the architectural outcome from a perceptive point of view becomes stronger with this consequent development of branded rhythms and patterns. This sense of organic fluidity through thought and time is also mentioned by Christopher Alexander (1979: ix): "It is a process which brings order out of nothing but ourselves; it cannot be attained, but it will happen of its own accord, if we will only let it." This is especially a challenge within the expanding city of a historically important node such as the city of Milan for example with a very strong central core and more confusing surroundings. The city, in an effort to keep up with European and global upgrading, development and technological standards, easily loses the meaning of a valid pattern that unifies the scattered pieces of significance. Alexander's explanation of the pattern is what establishes a city as alive, time by time, proving that every place is given its character by certain patterns of events that keep occurring at that point of time, while governed by certain geometric structures in space. Converting this into a scientific metaphor of logic, patterns are the atoms and molecules from which buildings and towns are made and should be remembered in the acts of interventions through historical importance.

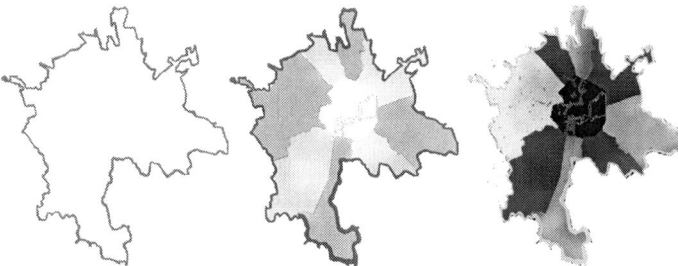

Figure 1:   The City's Border Outline, from the Map of 1860. (Author)

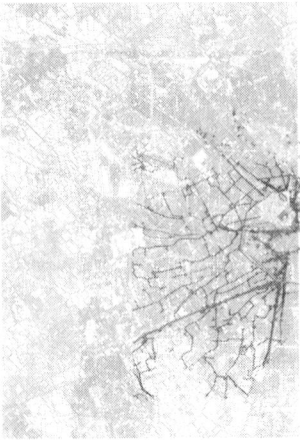

Figure 2:   Western Milan Region, Historical Origins and Infrastructural
               Expansion. (Author)

Figure 3:   Map of 1860 Overlaid with City-Borders, Infrastructural Expansion
               and Built Construction Orienting the Radial 'Leakage'. (Author)

This kind of artful consideration, in order to be technically correct and comprehensive, must draw its roots into history, especially when trying to tackle a philosophical problem and propose a new solution, as Ernst Gombrich would suggest. This brings us to the conceptual design of Antonio di Pietro Averlino (better known as *Filarete*, meaning in Greek 'lover of virtue'), the Italian Renaissance architect, sculptor and architectural theorist who designed the ideal city of Sforzinda basing its design on keywords of *sign, allegory, archetype, conflict* and *monarchy*. More specifically, it follows the radial symmetry of the eight point star, prone to representing an ancient magic sign where the circular shape is divided into compartments, each of which containing a Virtue and the corresponding Vice, or even the allegory of uncertainties of Fortune shown in the Middle Ages as a wheel. The circular choice of the urban plan represents the archetype of the humanist city of the High Renaissance hinting to the perfect form that a society (Kostof 1997) should hold which obviously conflicts reality-issues of despotism and monarchy (Alighieri 1312).

The design of Filarete is a typical example of the city designed as an iconology of ideals and morals where the images and the form of the whole become an allegory that mark its identity, forming a means of symbolism, and representation of the 'invisible world of ideas'. The image becomes part of the history of representation, and what is yielded to the receivers of this imaging is a *psychology of perception*, not only from the point of view of the designer, but of the likenesses, tastes and moral awareness and beliefs proposing what Gombrich would call, 'categories of expression', a term referring to various stylistic devices and traditions in parallel with psychological effects. The city of Filarete is an important mention due to the influence of the designer's theories on constructions of medieval cities, and on ideological typologies, affecting the development of environmental perception, and the patterns of spaces that we see today.

But as artful and geometrically sophisticated that an urban plan may be, the conditions of modern urban expansion and the phenomenon of sprawl often 'disorganize' the standards of the traditional city, in a tendency to change the hierarchical radii of the urban structures in an unplanned and uncongenial manner. Figure 1-3 represent the origins and structural system of the rigidity of Milan, along with the public activities and open spaces that remain neutral, with the function of public parks, and accompanying gardens/piazzas to important buildings. Furthermore, they illustrate the relationship of this rigidity to the 'looseness' of the composition as the range from the center increases, with the establishment of more grand and modern units of urban public settlements (stadium, cemetery, Fiera Campionaria, Hippodrome, EXPO 2015), some of which represent the more 'unconventional' activities. Perhaps the task of designing outside the rigidity of the rings is more arduous because the aim to also create some logical continuation of structure for the city is a difficult and convoluted task. However, the creation of *civic art* is just as hard within the traditional rigid setting, as the typological styles may easily come in conflict with the original *perceptual concepts* that once branded the area which may still be unknown. Thus, the city as a whole becomes a *mosaic* of missing pieces where the task of 'filling in the gaps' to create a complete work of *civic art* becomes the task of each architect who undertakes a city's commission.

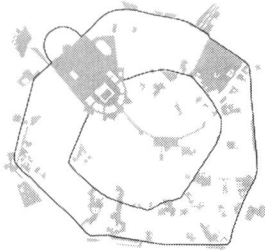

Figure 4:   Public Open Spaces along Milan's Major Rings. The highlighted locations are parks, piazzas and in some cases, loosely designed green areas/voids. (Author)

With the above reactions, analogies and thoughts, we can only stress the complexity of the morphological theory behind urban analysis and design. Guya Bertelli (2009) in her article *Description and Interpretation of the Architectonic, Urban and Environmental Forms: Theories and Techniques* rightly stresses three important solutions to help with the awareness of these complex situations of branding identification: the knowledge of historical data, the surveys and analysis of the elements that compose the area, and finally direct acquaintance with the site. To mention 'composition' of design, one does not simply speak for the sake of artistic improvisation, innovation and imagination, but furthermore, about a multivalent process of multiple steps and interpretations that lead to the final and most difficult passage. Particularly one should define a master plan, study the constructive and structural system as well as study the details (Bertelli 2009).

Figure 5:   Milan's Rings in Relation to the Public Open Spaces (Blue) and Public Activities (Orange: Stadium, Cemetery, Fiera Campionaria, Hippodrome). There is an emphasis of structural rigidity versus activity looseness. (Author)

Figure 6:   Forms and Orientations of Paths and Districts, Referencing to Field Forces of Repulsion and Attraction. This supports studies by Arnheim (1977) for the use of conceptual building morphologies in directing fields. (Author)

More absolute in the attitude of distinction is Kevin Lynch (1970) stressing imageability and independence from practical functionality as well as the will of meaning and symbolization. His theory of constructing *mental maps* inspires art proposed as a sort of grid made up by reference points independent from aesthetical or ideological evaluations within the city. In this case, a web of associations overlapping an urban tissue by means of an artistic project creates an important base for appropriation of a place. Taking this further in 1981 with his book *Good City Form*, Lynch (1981) proposes a model analogous to branding based more on perceptual motivation of the city rather than political or economic reasoning by establishing descriptions of urban civic art through his "normative models" (Lynch 1981) of *the cosmic model, the practical model* and *the organic model*, hence describing more tightly the relationship between the history of urban form and the reasoning behind it.

These considerations not only provide a mental image of the environment to support the behaviour of the city but also provide feedback in the understanding of urban activities that come from identifying certain pattern behaviours. In understanding the composition of commonly held urban images, we speculate important variables of the vicinity and grasp the nature of social experience that might take place in the context of our design. The goal is perhaps similar to that of painting where a kind of illusion is desired with the contemplation between form and content. We borrow from the conceptual forms of the surroundings in order to create a new kind of content, a more modern one. In the effort to create this kind of civic art where the public open environment starts embodying aspects of the fine arts, those of compositional tricks and illusionary concepts, one might argue on the purity of design similarly to how Plato objected upon the sacrifices of illusion and might have strongly criticized those few artists who discovered new effects to increase illusion and lifelikeness, such as Myron, Phidias, Zeuxis and Apelles (Gombrich 1960: 141).

This illusion and borrowing from the extension of directions and forms of the vicinity is demonstrated in Figure 7 and 8 which illustrate a master plan intervention in the centre of Milan. The design teaches the visitor to particularize, to articulate, and to make a distinction where before there was only an undifferentiated mass. It brings forth a questionable level of expectation as to what comes next because the exterior scenery constantly changes, in volume and hierarchy thus providing continuing waves of fulfillment, right guesses, and wrong moves, just as the entry into the second level will bring the anticipating viewer diagonally into the adjacent pavilion of the next nation. There is a constant playfulness of 'mental sets'. Shown more specifically in Figure 8, the design of the exterior and interior public open urban spaces express a situation of *emergence* in relation to the surrounding building masses and among the spaces within the compositional layout. One space blends into the other under a common *structural orientation* that borrows the *directional paths* of perceptual imagery and memory from the surrounding situation of *historical significance*. Also observing the design from a three-dimensional point of view (Figure 9 and 10), first from a bird's-eye view from the West end of the site (Figure 9) and then from a more grounded view (Figure 10), we are able to analyze the structure of the composition, the means of orientation, and the paths that are extracted by the surrounding site.

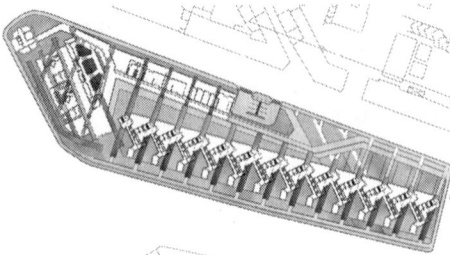

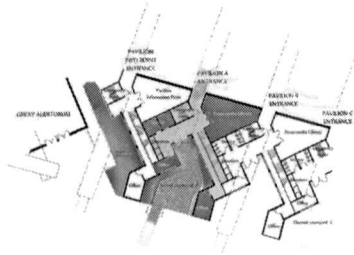

Figure 7:   Master Plan Intervention in Milan's Center. (Author)

Figure 8:   A Closer Look of the First Floor Plan. (Author)

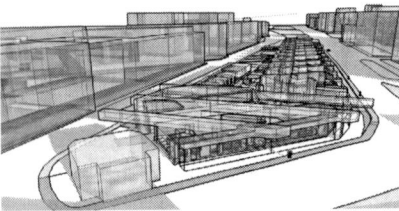

Figures 9:   Birds-Eye View from the West End of the Site. (Author)

Figure 10:   A More Grounded View of the Site. (Author)

'Figures' of the Transcription: Ruins, Signs, Traces

Ruins, signs and traces are not only elements to be considered in the analysis of the morphology of a map but also elements that play a great role in the creation of a certain atmosphere, to mark a certain location. As the creation of a certain 'locus' is the result of many synthetic elements and figures that make a unified conceptual whole, it is important to study and analyze what makes a place feel like an identifiable and resonating environment, and how the elements of the urban space make the inhabitants feel at 'home'. As Edmund Gustav Albrecht Husserl (1977) talks about structures of consciousness, he implies that the phenomena which appear are acts of consciousness, and objects of systematic reflection and analysis. In fact, he believed that phenomenology could provide firm basis for all human knowledge, including scientific knowledge, and could establish philosophy as a 'rigorous science'. Taking this further by a German theorist who studied Husserl's philosophy, Martin Heidegger (1927) stated that all investigations of being have historically focused on particular entities and their properties, or have treated being itself as an entity, or substance with properties. He firmly supported the importance of psychology in the study of urban spaces and environments of existential importance which is explained by his doctoral thesis in *psychologism*, a field where psychology is considered to play a central role in grounding or explaining some other non-psychological type of fact or law.

This brings us to Christian Norberg-Schulz, the Norwegian architect, architectural historian and theorist who deals with the phenomenology of place. What is important about Norberg-Schulz's claims on the public 'locus', particularly in his book *Genius Loci: Towards a Phenomenology of Architecture* that relates to the exploration of 'ruins, signs and traces' of professor Bertelli's theory, is the concept of 'dwelling'. Although dwelling was a word initially analyzed by Martin Heidegger as 'a thing that gathers world', Norberg-Schulz (1991: 19) uses the concept to analyze the meaning further, always giving full credit to the borrowed thought processes and analysis of his primary reference author, Heidegger. Norberg-Schulz, therefore, explains that a dwelling is an *'existential foothold'*, a place where man can *orient* himself, where he can identify himself with an environment, where the 'locus' becomes something more than just a 'shelter', and where it is composed by spaces where life occurs as 'places' in the true sense of the word. In his book, he writes that in order for a man to 'dwell' in a space, he must locate himself in space and expose to a certain environmental character. The two psychological functions involved may be called "orientation" and "identification" (Norberg-Schulz 1991: 19). In other words, in order for a man to feel at home with his environment, he must be able to recognize fundamental *traces* of his surroundings, and also be able to identify what he sees by certain signs, and recognizable elements.

Ruins introduce a different dimension with time and connect the past with the present. One may refer to an architect's intimate association with a site as knowledge that holds ruins of the past, converting a contemporary situation to a past memory and offering a sense of orientation and identification on the site. Without a certain *ruin* there would be no memory and nothing to assist the urbanite with finding connections in a certain location. Ruins are concrete environmental properties that create semiotic relationships in architectural designs (Norberg-Schulz 1991: 21).

The traces of a public open urban space are the *schemata* that come up in the architect's mind because of the pavement that he sees. A different interpretation may be that the trace is not the single element of an object alone, but that the semiotic object alone provides the *clue* of the schemata, or figures and shapes that make up the larger composition of the space. The object within the space that represents the ruin restores the meaning and identity of each part of the larger space and, although, it is a 'static' figure, it traces the route of a larger 'dynamic principle'. Such traces not only help acquaint with the surroundings but also develop perceptual schemata which determine all future experiences. Again, as Norberg-Schulz (1991: 21) says, "the schemata comprise universal structures which are inter-human, as well as locally determined and culturally conditioned structures. Evidently every human being has to possess schemata of orientation as well as identification."

Finally, a sign may create a verbal expression, a symbol that creates a point of reference as a geometric sign of point, line, or surface. A sign on the larger scale of an urban design should be something which shouts from a distance, and creates symbolism without further questioning and cryptographic meanings. But in the case of a demolished city where little of identity is left, a sign may be something as little as a pavement, a hierarchical tree in a plaza, a boulder, or a bench.

In the case of a historical public open urban space analysis, it is important to study the various elements and visual identification to its deeper roots in order to establish and maintain continuity in the urban identity of a historical space. Similarly to the reference on memory, cultural memory and genetic memory (Bertelli 2009), it is vital to analyze *layers* of different kinds of meanings in order to lay out the foundation of our work for any kind of future redevelopment. All this includes the *knowledge* which consists of references, physical objects and elements, the *events* occurring in the space and memorized in time, and the *deep marks* that sign the land of the history.

The example of Barcelona brings forward the situation of a historical and metropolitan city consisting of layers of renewed cities that "… followed one another, that were born and died over time" (Bertelli 2009). In pursuit of intervention inside a major public open urban space, one must look for the signs of the Barrio Gotico, the perfect quadrilateral of the Royal Square, the open spaces of the more recent city, the Casco Antiguo, the expansions of the Raval, Pouble Nou and Barceloneta, the new Museum of Contemporary Art (MACBA) by Richard Meier, the S. Caterina Market by Miralles-Tagliabue, the new Rambla of Raval, to name perhaps the most important ones, and moving on with history, the later projects of the Miro Park, Calle Arago, Calle Enric Granados, Calle Lanca e Marina, and the projects for the redesign of the Gran Via and the Paseos of Gracia and Sant Joan.

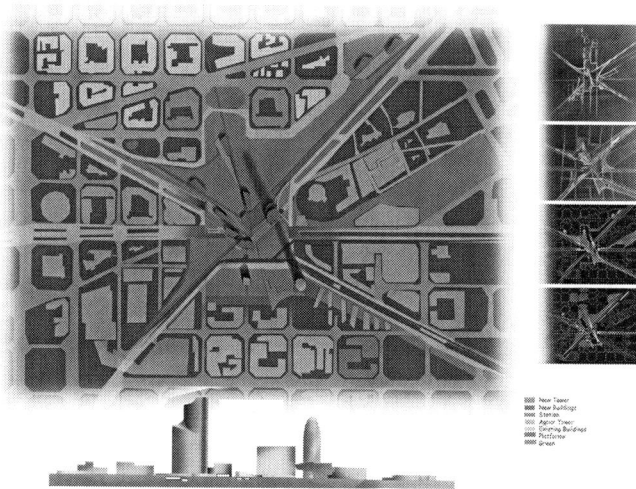

Figure 11:   Master Plan of an Experimental Project in Barcelona.
(Author)

Figure 11 depicts a proposal of an intermodal junction of Barcelona's 'Placa de les Glories Catalanes', embellishing on the above mentioned concepts of traces, expansion and rarefaction in a synthesis of conceptualizing the most important morphological elements that marked the formation of the city, based on natural borders, major infrastructure, important nodes, fundamental settlements and grid establishment for city organization. More specifically, the final master plan of Figure 11 is a result of the natural limits on either side of the territory, the natural limits on the north of historic villages that formed early settlements, the intersecting character of major infrastructural roads of the Gran Via, the Meridiana and the Diagonal, the historical city of Barcelona on the south part of the territory, and the regular design of Plan Cerda marking the new planning rule of the modern contemporary city.

Conclusion

Conclusively from this study, and for all speculations of the thesis, in the contemporary world of loss of references, of loss of ground, and of an ever yet desire to represent, rises the goal of interpretation and syntactic considerations of importance through project case studies which demonstrate an effort to brand locations by means of references to ruins, evolution layering, thematic consistency and an ever yet desire to elaborate on existing themes that mark a place. Faced with the reality of contemporary condition and 'the death of God', the aim perhaps touches upon a means of modern enlightenment, relevant to secular theism, and hope to discover possibilities of an absolute reality in which the construction of public open urban spaces and the art that goes within them will be concretized on the basis of universal rationality, similar to the views of Friedrich Nietzsche's philosophical considerations of modernism and the exhaustion of something that still inspires (De Sola-Morales et al. 1997: 59).

This method supports a systematic philosophy of human culture speculation that also Ernst Cassirer speaks about in which the contemplation of individual parts of a three dimensional space gather their meaning solely from the *place* in which they stand, their historical context, evolution and meaning, "a system in which the content and significance of each form would be characterized by the richness and specific quality of the relations and concatenations in which it stands with other spiritual energies and ultimately with totality" (Cassirer 1955: 82).

References

Alexander, C. (1979): Timeless way of building. New York: Oxford University Press.
Alighieri, D. (1312): De Monarchia. Firenze: Nabu Press.
Arnheim, R. (1977): The dynamics of architectural forum. Berkeley: University of California Press.
Bertelli, G. (2009): Description and interpretation of the architectonic, urban and environmental forms: Theories and techniques. Milan: Politecnico di Milano Lecture.
Cassirer, E. (1955): The philosophy of symbolic forms, volume I: Language. New Haven: Yale University Press.
Choay, F. (2009): Questioning the heritage concept: A polemic anthology. Milan: Politecnico di Milano Seminar.
Choay, F. (1986): Urbanism in question. In: Gottdiener, M. and Lagopoulos, A. (eds.): The city and the sign: An introduction to urban semiotics. New York: Columbia University Press, 241-258. First published (1965): L'Urbanisme: Utopies et Réalités: Un Anthologie. Paris: Seuil.

D'Ardia, G. (2009): On injured bodies: Thoughts for forgotten landscape. Pescara: Sala Editori.

De Sola-Morales, I., Thompson, G. and Whiting, S. (1997): Differences: Topographies of contemporary architecture. Boston: MIT Press.

Gombrich, E.H. (1960): Art and illusion: A study in the psychology of pictorial representation. London: Phaidon.

Heidegger, M. (1927): Being and time: Harper perennial modern classics, 2008 reprint edition. London: Harper Collins.

Husserl, E. and Cairns, D. (1977): Cartesian meditations: An introduction to phenomenology. Boston: Martinus Nijhoff Pub.

Kostof, S. (1997): The city assembled: The elements of urban form through history. London: Thames and Hudson Ltd.

Lynch, K. (1981): A theory of good city form. Cambridge: The MIT Press.

Lynch, K. (1960): The image of the city. Cambridge: The MIT Press.

Norberg-Schulz, C. (1980): Genius Loci: Towards a phenomenology of architecture. New York: Rizzoli.

Ruskin, J. (1849): The lamp of memory, in the seven lamps of architecture, section XVIII. London: Dover Publications.

Viollet-le-Duc, E. (1868): Dictionnaire Raisonné de l'Architecture Française. Paris: Libraires, Imprimeries Reunites.

Branding as Enabling Knowledge Creation: The Role of Space and Cognition in Branding Processes

Markus F. Peschl / Thomas Fundneider

This paper introduces the concept of *enabling,* as opposed to managing or controlling, as a key characteristic and attitude for designing spaces which are supposed to have a 'branding effect'. In our case we will focus on a very specific notion of branding or branded spaces; namely, spaces that are branded for creating (new) knowledge. It can be seen easily that this is a very generic understanding of brand that can be applied to many domains. In other words, we see a brand not primarily as a product, but as a state of knowledge.

In such a view, branding is about creating a specific knowledge state in the user of a particular brand or 'branded space'. This implies that branding is the process that leads to a certain branded space which sets the boundary conditions for an individual knowledge state of the perceiver. One of our key assumptions is that *branding is about (co-)creating new knowledge.* We are suggesting to *enable* such knowledge creation processes instead of pushing the user in a particular state of mind by trying to manipulate or gain control over his or her mind. It will be shown that state-of-the-art knowledge creation approaches can teach us a lot about enabling processes of knowledge creation and, hence, about branding (spaces).

In the first part of this paper we will develop the theoretical concept of enabling and its implications for processes of knowledge creation and branding. The second part is concerned with spaces that follow this approach of enabling. We refer to them as *Enabling Spaces* that facilitate knowledge (creation) processes by providing a framework of constraints. Finally we will discuss the implications for branding.

Branding as Enabling

Cognitive Science and Epistemological Considerations

Is branding about controlling, influencing, manipulating, or modulating our minds? We suggest to approach branding from the perspective of cognitive science, for example, Brook and Stainton (2000), Clark (2001), and Friedenberg and Silverman (2006) and of creating (new) knowledge and innovations according to authors such as Amabile (1996), Fagerberg and Verspagen (2009), Krogh et al. (2000), Nonaka et al. (2008), and Peschl and Fundneider (2008). As an implication of the mentioned scientific foundations, *branding has something to do with creating a more or less well defined knowledge state or knowledge dynamics in the user* or the perceiver of a particular brand. In other words, branding is supposed to *create* some kind of *new knowledge* in the perceiver. This knowledge is the foundation of a particular 'brand experience' including emotional states, sensory states, social or cultural aspects, etc. Thus, the guiding question is how do we have to design a branded space for enabling the user that he or she is triggered in such a way that he/she may create new knowledge around the brand in an autonomous manner.

This leads us directly into two very old debates in epistemology and cognitive science: (i) (How) Can we specify desired states or dynamics of knowledge by external stimuli? (ii) (How) Can we produce new knowledge in a deterministic or rule-based manner? Question (i) concerns the debate between realism and antirealism/constructivism (Glasersfeld 1984, 1991, Maturana 1970, Varela et al. 1991). From the perspective of epistemology, systems theory, and of cognitive (neuro-)science it is clear that the environment does *not* completely determine the mental state or the knowledge of a cognitive system (Peschl 1997, 2001). The internal knowledge dynamics is only *modulated* by the environmental dynamics. This is due to the fact that we do not only find bottom-up connections, in the sense of projecting from the sensory system to the brain connections, but also a considerable multitude of top-down or outward connections projecting from the inside of the brain to the outside (Varela et al. 1991, Roth 2009, Peschl 2001, 1997, Goldstein 2002). According to the constructivist perspective this implies that external environmental stimuli only "perturbate" (Maturana 1970) or modulate the internal knowledge dynamics, but they cannot determine it. In this perspective, the goal of every cognitive system is to compensate for these perturbations and to try to get into a stable coupling, both physically and epistemologically, with the environment. For question (i) above, this implies (not only for the process of branding) that we cannot assume that it is such a simple task to influence the users' knowledge dynamics or experience just by providing the 'right' set of stimuli. The effects of these stimuli will be rather limited or will not always evoke the expected change.

What about question (ii) concerning the possibility of mechanistically producing new knowledge? If we are assuming that branding has something to do with creating new knowledge in the user's or perceiver's mind, we have to admit that, as an implication of our answer to question (i), we will have to seriously question a mechanistic understanding of creating new knowledge. Specifically, there must be the idea that rules, algorithms, or mechanisms exist describing the process of successfully producing new knowledge. This means that we have to challenge the assumption that if one applies these rules faithfully this will lead to new knowledge in a *deterministic* manner. For our question of branding as knowledge creation, this implies that we will most probably fail if we think that we can bring about new knowledge in a mechanistic manner. What are the alternatives?

Attitude of Enabling

While in the classical perspective the attitude of control and manipulation was in the fore, the authors suggest to replace this position with the approach of *enabling*. What does 'enabling' mean in the context of generating new knowledge? The answer covers two aspects that are crucial: (a) On the one hand we have to give up on the regime of control, determinism, and making. (b) On the other hand enabling implies to *provide a set of constraints* or a *facilitating framework* supporting the *processes of bringing forth new knowledge*, hence to facilitate the creation of brands in the perceiver's mind. This can be best thought of in a metaphor of a force field in which the constraints are realized as attractors and repellers. While the constraints are responsible for modulating, they do not determine the knowledge dynamics because knowledge dynamics is driven both by its internal dynamics and is carried by the forces of the attractors/repellers. These attractors and repellers act as a framework of constraints modulating the knowledge dynamics. Stokes (2007) and Onarheim (2012) show impressively the importance of constraints in processes of knowledge creation. New knowledge or innovation can only be brought forth in an environment that is not completely free and 'empty'; rather a set and framework of constraints is necessary in order to support these creation processes which – in some cases – themselves might change the constraints.

What are the implications of this approach of enabling for knowledge creation? First of all, it has to be clear that this is not only an abstract and cognitive concept. Second, enabling is mainly a question of *attitude, habitus* or a paradigm of thinking and acting. Unfortunately, the enabling paradigm is a rather '*poor*' and *weak* concept because one has to give up control and let things go and let things develop. Of course this is not a very comfortable position especially in a business environment where everything has to be efficient, determined, calculable, 'managed', and predictable.

However, the enabling attitude is a consequence of having to admit that we are not in (total) control especially when being engaged in knowledge creation activities. It seems to be more sensible to 'surrender' than to invest too much energy and resources into an epistemological battle which we will never be able to win. However, enabling does not imply that we are only passively sitting there waiting for new knowledge to break forth; quite the contrary is true because the real challenge is to create enabling structures in the form of constraints and active interventions which support these highly fragile processes.

As a consequence, the enabling approach requires an alternative set of attitudes, values, habitus/habits, as well as epistemic practices. First of all we have to (re-)acquire 'epistemological virtues' of openness, being able to reflect, to radically question ourselves, and to let go. Furthermore, we have to (re-)learn to listen and observe closely; to let ourselves be impressed, meaning that we are open to something that is changing us even if it means that we have to give up on well-established and dear patterns of thinking. Another attitude concerns the domain of cultivating our patience and our ability to wait for the 'right moment' (kairos) so that we can listen to weak and fragile signals in order to cultivate/incubate them. Finally, we have to learn how to provide an ecosystem or 'living ambiences' of cultivation, facilitation, incubation and enabling, rather than a regime of control and forced change.

What are the implications for the process of branding? Enabling requires a high level of humbleness giving the user priority for a process of knowledge creation 'from within'. For our concept of branding as a process of knowledge creation this implies that branding is not so much concerned with imposing manipulative stimuli from the outside on the user. Rather, in our understanding, the strategy is to provide a framework of enabling constraints that allows and facilitates the emergence of knowledge processes 'from within'. In other words, from our perspective, branding is about triggering a *latent knowledge* which is already there but not yet recognized and which is still 'dormant' and must be activated. In this sense branding is closely related to recent approaches in the field of knowledge creation, such as Scharmer's (2001, 2007) Theory-U or Peschl and Fundneider's (2008) Emergent Innovation approach. Hence, branding is not so much about manipulating the user's knowledge with brute force, such as exposing him/her to repetitive slogans, logos, ads, etc.; rather, *branding is about taking him or her on a joint journey of co-creation involving the user(s), the brand itself (as a process), networks, peers, as well as implicitly the brand (co-)designers.* During such a journey the user cultivates his or her latent knowledge and the *brand acts as an enabler for this process of activation.*

As a consequence, we need such enablers. It is interesting to see that a brand can act as an enabler (for knowledge creation) and on the other side, can be enabled by other enablers (technological, social, cultural, etc.). We refer to these knowledge creation eco-systems (Krippendorff 2006, 2011) as *Enabling Spaces* (Peschl 2007, Peschl and Fundneider 2012). They represent a rather generic form of branded spaces, namely spaces enabling processes of *knowledge co-creation*.

Enabling Spaces

Enabling Spaces are conceived as multi-dimensional spaces that are orchestrated in an integrated manner in order to best possibly support processes of collaborative and individual knowledge creation. We are proposing a rather broad understanding of space involving several dimensions, such as an architectural, social, emotional, epistemological, technological dimension, etc. Hence, space is understood as an environment or a *container* providing a set of *constraints* which is responsible for holding this container together as well as giving it a minimal structure and dynamics. It is a space providing enabling structures, elements that facilitate and smoothly intervene, as well as constraints allowing knowledge processes to flow and to develop their own dynamics in such a way that radically new knowledge may break forth in the sense of bringing in-potentia knowledge into action (see Peschl and Fundneider 2012).

Enabling Spaces are interdisciplinary in their nature. It is necessary to consider *constraints* and forms of *enabling interventions* from many different disciplines, such as social, emotional, cognitive, cultural, technological, epistemological, organizational, and, of course architectural constraints and interventions. The challenge is to integrate these aspects into a holistic ensemble which functions as an Enabling Space. It is the *interdisciplinary* interaction between these elements that brings about a seamless flow of knowledge and interaction between the participating cognitive systems and their environment. This is a typical *design process/task* which does not have a single 'best solution', but has to be approached in a 'designerly manner' (Dorst 2003, 2006, Glanville 1998, 2007, Gedenryd 1998).

Integrating Dimensions of Knowledge Processes and Structures

As opposed to many other approaches the crucial point of Enabling Spaces is to *integrate* knowledge *processes* and *structures*/constraints in a highly consistent manner. This can only be achieved if one assumes a radical epistemological perspective; namely, one *starts* with studying the processes of *knowledge creation* which are involved in the prospective Enabling Space. Beyond that it is necessary to dive into the culture and the internal structures of the organization in order to gain a profound understanding of its *core* and its brand. The core and the brand are closely related to each other. While the core characterizes the inner workings and structures of an organization, the brand represents the *interface* of the organization towards the outside. This core is the foundation for developing a model of the organization's core processes and, on their basis, *design patterns* (Alexander et al. 1977) which are a first step toward an integration of processes and structures.

The framework of Enabling Spaces acts as a container holding knowledge creation processes and activities. The Enabling Space is designed as a multi-dimensional space in which architectural/physical, social, cognitive, techno-logical, epistemological, cultural, intellectual, emotional and other factors are considered and integrated with the aim to support knowledge creation activities. In the following sections, these dimensions will be described.

Architectural and Physical Space

This dimension refers to the physical space or the Euclidean space in which the knowledge processes are taking place. It is an intentionally designed and built physical environment that surrounds the users with its concrete physical structure(s). These structures comprise all elements in the space and its context, be it walls, furniture, windows, its material dimension, etc. This space is mainly characterized by two elements of architecture (as built structures) and design. Examples of what the authors see as architectural spaces are: offices, spaces for creative and knowledge work, workshops, (knowledge) ateliers, concrete physical places as branded spaces, urban places, or even urban settlements.

The challenge is to design this space in such a way that the flow of knowledge and social interaction is supported in the best possible way for the specific (knowledge or brand creation) task at stake. In many cases today's architecture leads to 'disabling spaces' rather than enabling or even actively supporting knowledge creation processes. Allen and Henn (2007), Krogh et al. (2000), and many others give good examples of how to solve this architectural design challenge. Allen and Henn (2007), for example, show impressively how the social coherence and communication patterns and behaviors are influenced by the physical architecture. Furthermore, they show that the design of physical space is an intrinsic part of management tasks and has similar importance as, for instance, the organizational structure and processes.

Social, Cultural, and Organizational Space

Knowledge (creation) processes are always embedded in social processes; social interaction is a *conditio sine qua non* for the emergence of new knowledge in a collaborative setting. As is shown in the field of, for instance, science and technology studies (House 2003, Latour 1987, Cole and Derry 2005) or of creativity (Kelley 2004, Peschl 2009, Sternberg 2005) and by many others, social groups are essential for bringing forth new knowledge. Therefore, there has to be a 'social container', a (social) atmosphere in which these processes can develop their own dynamics in order to gain their own strength. Apart from other aspects, trust and openness are key enablers for the social dimension which have to be established before any kind of knowledge creation work or branding can start.

Above that, knowledge creation is always embedded in the culture and organizational structures of an organization. They heavily influence the enabling or disabling effects on knowledge creation processes and have to be considered and designed accordingly.

Cognitive Space

Every process of knowledge creation has its origin in the individual brain and in cognitive processes. Cognition (and its interaction with the environment; e.g., Clark's (2008) extended cognition approach) is the source of new knowledge. Hence, it is the cognitive space which has to be taken into account when thinking about Enabling Spaces. What are the key cognitive enablers among the cognitive activities which are provided by our brain? Among them are the cognitive abilities to observe closely, to "listen to what wants to emerge" (Scharmer 2007: 13 and 201), to reflect one's premises, to sense and to understand one's own patterns of thinking and perception, to enter into a 'real' dialogue (Bohm 1996, Isaacs 1999), practical intelligence/phronesis (φρόνησις) (Nonaka et al. 2008), or learning processes in a prototyping setting, etc.

Emotional Space

Cognition is always embedded into *emotional states* and this applies especially to branded spaces. For example, the state of fear will, in most cases, neither trigger nor support a creative process. An Enabling Space has to take into consideration this dimension and offer features triggering emotional states supporting processes of knowledge creation, such as security, protection, openness, etc. However, the emotional dimension of Enabling Spaces is not only about 'feeling well'. In some cases it is necessary to push oneself into an emotionally *uncomfortable* situation in order to leave behind one's well-established and dear patterns of thought and perception.

Epistemological Space

Dealing with knowledge creation processes always involves a wide spectrum of different types, categories, styles, or genres of knowledge processes. There is a huge difference between the knowledge being involved and created in a process of ideation, of close observation, of intuitive reasoning, of deep understanding, of sense making, of prototyping, of letting-come, of reflecting, of implementing, of executing a routine, etc.

Hence, in order to establish an epistemologically enabling eco-system, one has to first identify the knowledge processes which are relevant for the particular phase of the knowledge creation process (compare also the organizational epistemology approach by Tsoukas (2005) showing how different types of knowledge processes are intertwined in organizations). One has to understand the very nature of these processes. Finally, it is necessary to create an enabling environment in the sense of boundary conditions, constraints, attractors, etc. in which this knowledge dynamics can develop, can grow and flow. From these considerations it becomes clear that the resulting spaces will look very different according to the supported knowledge process and the organizational culture and social setting. For example, we worked with several corporate IT-departments and, although one would assume that the core processes are the same, they were quite different in their physical layouts, in their technological support as well as in their organizational processes.

Technological and Virtual Space

Knowledge creation processes are always embedded in a technological environment. This comprises a wide range of technological means ranging from 'low-tech' tools such as white boards, flip charts, light ambiences, etc. to high-tech tools such as computers, the internet, social media, (knowledge) visualization tools, simulations, complex software, knowledge displays, etc. (Shneiderman 2007). In most knowledge creation processes, technological support from the area of *design (thinking)* has turned out to be highly productive (Brown 2009, Sanders and Stappers 2008). These tools comprise mapping technologies, knowledge technologies, observation technologies, or simulation and prototyping technologies.

Designing Branded Spaces as Enabling Spaces

As we are dealing with a rather broad concept of space here, it is clear that these dimensions cannot be seen separately. Rather, the very goal of Enabling Spaces consists of *integrating* these aspects in a *radically interdisciplinary* manner of an integrated design, a whole, like a composition, or a piece of art ('Gesamtkunstwerk' in German). Especially in the context of collaborative processes of knowledge creation we see the necessity of integrating social, cultural, emotional, physical/architectural, as well as epistemological issues. Consequently bringing forth new knowledge is a highly fragile knowledge process which is about intuition, listening to weak signals, deep thinking and understanding, incubating vague knowledge, etc. Due to the fragility and vulnerability of these processes, it is necessary to create a kind of *container*, an Enabling Space, providing *qualities* like offering an environment of *protection*, of being able to hold and cultivate epistemological and social fragility, of enabling the free flow of knowledge, of silence, of openness for error, openness for change, etc.

These design qualities have to be translated into integrated and interdisciplinary concepts, which in their wholeness form a concrete Enabling Space. In this context this means that *trust* is a major issue. Trust is needed not only between the team members, i.e., in the concrete social domain, but also as a cultural value in the organization, which does not only exist on paper, but is practiced in every routine and social interaction. Furthermore, there has to be established an (epistemological) understanding that the knowledge and processes, which the team is dealing with here, are highly fragile and need completely different mindsets and attitudes: a different mode of operating, of talking, 'negotiating' meaning, dialoguing, and interacting with each other, novel criteria of evaluating and judging, etc. Furthermore, the (interior) design of this space has to reflect this vulnerability and fragility on the one and the openness on the other hand.

Hence, the challenge is how to *design* such a complex high dimensional space that, despite its diversity and dynamics, maintains its unity. The goal of the Enabling Spaces design process/approach is to devise and develop architectural design concepts for spaces cultivating and supporting processes of knowledge creation and innovation. This whole process is based on a *profound understanding of the organization and/or brand*. Starting with an extensive research phase, the organization's and brand's core knowledge processes as well as its cultural, organizational, and structural parameters are identified. This is achieved by means of a wide variety of participatory and ethnographic qualitative and quantitative observation methods (how are users interacting, how are particular spaces being used, etc.). The experiences and perspectives of a selected variety of stakeholders are studied through qualitative, generative in-depth interviews (depending on the size of the project 15-40 interviews). Furthermore, the behaviors and needs of a systemically wide stakeholder group are identified by using a comprehensive quantitative online questionnaire. The observation/research phase is completed by ethnographic studies as well as by observing and collecting artifacts, processes, etc.

In the next step, the 'sense-making phase', this systemic multi-perspective and multi-stakeholder view, is condensed into a so-called 'core-process model' illustrating the research findings in a highly concentrated manner. In this phase, the observation results are analyzed, described, and checked for patterns, (hidden) assumptions, polarities, discrepancies, and potentials in a qualitative inductive process so that a comprehensive overall profile being based on a profound understanding of the organization/brand can be developed. These core processes represent the essence of the organization and the brand. They act as a solid theoretical foundation for all subsequent design as well as for decision-making processes.

This abstract model is then transformed into *design patterns* describing and explicating *design qualities*. Their function is to provide the foundation for translating and transforming these abstract core knowledge processes into concepts for concrete (materialized) structures and processes. They are a necessary prerequisite for understanding and realizing the various (architectural, social, technological, organizational, etc.) dimensions of the Enabling Space. On the basis of these design patterns, a holistic design concept is co-developed in interdisciplinary workshops bringing together experts from different fields, such as architecture, design, sociology, information and communication technology, etc. The result of a design concept goes far beyond architectural aspects and, in many cases, brings about changes in the organizational and social structures, processes, and culture. Architecture transforms and shapes organizations/brands and vice versa.

Design Principles for Branded Enabling Spaces

Several principles and implications can be derived from Enabling Spaces that are relevant for the design of branded spaces:

Primacy of enabling (vs. controlling): Instead of designing systems which try to mechanically create new knowledge or manipulate the user of a branded space, it is necessary to think about such systems in terms of a set of subtle and well-balanced constraints and interventions facilitating and supporting the cognitive and social processes of knowledge creation. They can be thought of as a structured container providing the necessary conditions for *emergent* processes of knowledge (co-)creation. They leave room for and trust in the emerging knowledge dynamics and in the processes of social interaction. This attitude of enabling is probably the most important principle which should be present in every design decision as it gives the knowledge creation process a whole new character and dynamics.

Trust as primary epistemic virtue: Both branded spaces and Enabling Spaces build on and at the same time should support and enable 'epistemic virtues' but first and foremost *trust*. Trust is the social and epistemic driver and conditio sine qua non for any process of collaborative knowledge creation as well as for any process of branding. It is necessary to establish both a social and an epistemological atmosphere supporting these highly fragile processes being involved in generating new knowledge. In classical knowledge creation or innovation settings this can be achieved by systematic teambuilding activities, by creating awareness about the fragility of these intuitive processes, by an architectural design inducing an atmosphere of protection, by establishing rules (of conduct), ethical principles, or policies both for the face-to-face and the virtual domain. An atmosphere of trust allows for several other epistemic competencies which are highly valuable for the process of knowledge creation: openness, transparency, sharing of knowledge and intuitions, reflectiveness, openness to challenging one's own assumptions and deep knowledge/attitudes, etc.

Taking epistemology seriously: Experience from a large number of projects with Enabling Spaces has shown that it is essential to use knowledge processes as the point of departure. Apart from classical parameters, such as organizational structures, emotional and cultural processes and characteristics, or social issues, knowledge processes reveal the very deep 'secrets' of the brand and the organization. A *profound understanding* of the content, the assumptions, etc. is a key for designing such enabling environments. This can only be achieved by an in-depth qualitative analysis, especially, if one wants to use such environments as a chance for 'branding' users' minds.

Interdisciplinarity: Such spaces are interdisciplinary in nature, in their design and their knowledge results. In most cases the new emerges at the borders of disciplines and is the result of friction between these borders (Eigenbrode et al. 2007). In this context one has to emphasize the increasing importance of the approaches and skills provided by the humanities (e.g., tools for reflection, sense making, or creation of meaning) and arts (e.g., design thinking, Brown 2008, 2009).

Integration of social, epistemological, as well as technological issues: According to Krippendorff (1989, 2006, 2011) innovations are artifacts; they themselves are produced by cognitive systems using artifacts supporting knowledge creation processes. Branded spaces as well as Enabling Spaces have to be seen as technologies integrating various fields of epistemology, social systems, cultural and architectural matters, and ICT. They are an ecology of artifacts (Krippendorff and Butter 2007: 5) and *socio-epistemological technologies* that enable collaborative creation of new knowledge.

Primacy of interactivity and interface: Following Norman's (1991) suggestion that we should not misunderstand (cognitive) artifacts as tools primarily amplifying already existing cognitive (creative) abilities, we should start understanding both Enabling Spaces and branded spaces as spaces facilitating a change in the mode of knowledge creation and perception. It is the *interaction* between the enabling artifacts and the participating cognitive systems that give rise to a change in the way of bringing forth new knowledge and finally of perceiving the world.

Furthermore, it is not primarily the materiality of Enabling Spaces, including information and communication tools, but its *social utilization* by *interacting* with them that is of importance (Krippendorff 2011). We have to focus on the process and the functionality of an *interface* which is offered by this integration of tools forming an Enabling/branded Space. They act as an *interface* enabling a smooth interaction with the user and potential new knowledge. Therefore, it is not only about an interface in the sense of a human-computer interface, but about the *whole branded space as an interface* coupling the users, technology, physical and non-physical structures, his/her cognition with the knowledge about the brand.

Importance of physical space: Physical space is not only about the (social) quality of face-to-face collaboration and communication, but also about the epistemological quality in the processes of knowledge creation. As we have seen, it is the enabling quality of the surrounding artifacts which 'extends' our cognitive abilities (Clark 2008, Menary 2010) in processes of knowledge creation. It is in the nature of our mind as well as of the epistemological domain that we need some *direct* input as well as 'resistance' from the environment as opposed to purely virtual experiences thereof. This is well known from (philosophy of) science. Whenever we are doing empirical experiments we are confronted with the limits of reality and, by 'colliding with reality', we are learning and creating new knowledge through applying a trial-and-error strategy.

This process of verification/falsification (Popper 1959, 1962) is at the heart of any process of knowledge creation. In most cases these things cannot be solved by only applying virtual methods (e.g., simulations), as the experience of the 'resistance' is rather limited in the virtual realm. These things have to be done in 'real world' environments. Ideally, it is a well-balanced combination of real and virtual enablers that support the processes for knowledge creation necessary for brand creation best.

Conclusion

One of the premises of this paper was that branding is based on a process of knowledge (co-)creation. This process is part of emotional binding, as well as social and cultural issues. It has been shown that the perspective of a mechanistic knowledge production has to be replaced by an attitude of *enabling*. In the context of knowledge creation enabling means to *provide a set of constraints*. For instance, Stokes (2007) or Onarheim (2012) show the importance of constraints in knowledge creation processes and/or of a *facilitating framework* for supporting these *processes of bringing forth new knowledge*. We have seen that the enabling approach requires an alternative set of attitudes, values, as well as epistemic practices: openness, being able to reflect, to radically question ourselves and our assumptions, and to let go. Furthermore, we have to acquire basic epistemic practices that are necessary prerequisites for successful work in knowledge creation.

   As a consequence, we had to ask ourselves how this set of enabling constraints and interventions as well as the resulting epistemic practices could be realized. Which environments are necessary that these processes can come about? We referred to these environments as *Enabling Spaces*. It is obvious that cognition is at the heart of every process of knowledge creation. Nevertheless cognition is always embedded and situated in the body and in its environment (Clark 2008, Menary 2010, Varela et al. 1991). The concept of Enabling Spaces is a result of taking seriously that knowledge creation is not only a cognitive activity being located inside the brain or purely virtual between people, but it is intrinsically coupled with the environment that includes the social environment. Enabling Spaces provide such an extended cognitive environment that holds, incubates, and cultivates these fragile processes of knowledge creation. It has been shown that Enabling Spaces comprise several dimensions which have to be integrated into an interdisciplinary design. The main point is the *radical integration* of knowledge *processes* with architectural, social, cognitive, emotional, etc. *structures*. It is this delicate balance between controlling the processes of knowledge creation and letting them follow their own flow which represents the quality of a well-designed Enabling Space.

As for branded spaces our considerations concerning Enabling Spaces have several implications. One important dimension of branded spaces is that new (brand-)knowledge is (co-)created in the user of such spaces by providing a specific environment and by interacting with the brand (see extended cognition approach). Co-Creation happens in several ways: between the user and the brand artifacts, social interaction between users, and interaction between an enabling branded space and the user. Hence, what we have learned in Enabling Spaces about facilitating processes of knowledge co-creation also can be applied in the context of branded spaces. Furthermore, Enabling Spaces themselves can be used as source for creating brands and branded spaces.

If branded spaces are about supporting processes of knowledge creation, we suggest that the strategy is to provide a framework of enabling constraints that allows and facilitates the emergence of knowledge processes 'from within'. This means that they should be designed in such a way that they trigger *latent knowledge* which is already there and which has not been recognized yet, which is still 'dormant' and which has to be activated. Here we can learn a lot from recent approaches in the field of knowledge creation, such as Scharmer's (2001, 2007) Theory-U or Peschl and Fundneider's (2008) Emergent Innovation approach. In such a perspective branding and branded spaces are not so much about influencing or manipulating the user. Rather, branding is about taking the user on a *joint journey of (knowledge) co-creation* during which his or her latent knowledge becomes cultivated and the *brand acts as an enabler for this process of activation.*

References

Alexander, C., Ishikawa, S. and Silverstein, M. (1977): A pattern language: Towns, buildings, construction. Oxford: Oxford University Press.

Allen, T.J. and Henn, G.W. (2007): The organization of architecture and innovation: Managing the flow of technology. Amsterdam: Butterworth-Heinemann Elsevier.

Amabile, T. (1996): Creativity in context. Boulder: Westview Press.

Bohm, D. (1996): On dialogue. London: Routledge.

Brook, A. and Stainton, R.J. (2000): Knowledge and mind: A philosophical introduction. Cambridge, MA: MIT Press.

Brown, T. (2008): Design thinking. In: Harvard Business Review, 86(6), 84-93.

Brown, T. (2009): Change by design: How design thinking transforms organizations and inspires innovation. New York, NY: Harper Collins.

Clark, A. (2001): Mindware: An introduction to the philosophy of cognitive science. New York: Oxford University Press.

Clark, A. (2008): Supersizing the mind: Embodiment, action, and cognitive extension. Oxford: Oxford University Press.

Cole, M. and Derry, J. (2005): We have met technology and it is us. In: Sternberg, R.J. and Preiss, D. (eds.): Intelligence and technology: The impact of tools on the nature and development of human abilities. Hillsdale, NJ: Lawrence Erlbaum Associates, 209-227.

Dorst, K. (2003): The problem of design problems. In: Cross, N. and Edmonds, E. (eds.): Expertise in design. Sydney: Creativity and Cognition Studio Press, 135-147.

Dorst, K. (2006): Design problems and design paradoxes. In: Design Issues, 22(3), 4-17.

Eigenbrode, S.D., O'Rourke, M., Wulfhorst, J.D., Althoff, D.M., Goldberg, C.S., Merrill, K., Morse, W., Nielsen-Pincus, M., Stephens, J., Winowiecki, L. and Bosque-Pérez, N.A. (2007): Employing philosophical dialogue in collaborative science. In: Bioscience, 57(1), 55-64.

Fagerberg, J. and Verspagen, B. (2009): Innovation studies: The emerging structure of a new scientific field. In: Research Policy, 38, 218-233.

Friedenberg, J. and Silverman, G. (2006): Cognitive science: An introduction to the study of the mind. Thousand Oaks, CA: Sage Publications.

Gedenryd, H. (1998): How designers work. Lund, Sweden: Lund University Cognitive Studies.

Glanville, R. (1998): Re-searching design and designing research. In: Design Issues, 15(2), 88-91.

Glanville, R. (2007): Try again. Fail again. Fail better: The cybernetics in design and the design in cybernetics. In: Kybernetes: The International Journal of Systems and Cybernetics, 36(9/10), 1173-1206.

Glasersfeld, E. v. (1984): An introduction to radical constructivism. In: Watzlawick, P. (ed.): The invented reality. New York: Norton, 17-40.

Glasersfeld, E. v. (1991): Knowing without metaphysics: Aspects of the radical constructivist position. In: Steier, F. (ed.): Research and reflexivity. London: SAGE Publishers, 12-29.

Goldstein, E.B. (2002): Sensation and perception. Pacific Grove, CA: Wadsworth Publishing Company.

House, N.A. Van (2003): Science and technology studies and information studies. In: Cronin, B. (ed.): Annual review of information science and technology, 38, 3-86.

Isaacs, W.N. (1999): Dialogue and the art of thinking together: A pioneering approach to communicating in business and life. New York: Doubleday Currency.

Kelley, T. (2004): The art of innovation: Lessons in creativity from IDEO, America's leading design firm. London: Profile Books.

Krippendorff, K. (1989): On the essential contexts of artifacts or on the proposition that 'design is making sense (of things)'. In: Design Issues, 5(2), 9-39.

Krippendorff, K. (2006): The semantic turn: A new foundation for design. Boca Raton, FL: Taylor and Francis CRC Press.

Krippendorff, K. (2011): Principles of design and a trajectory of artificiality. In: Journal of Product Innovation Management, 28(3), 411-418.

Krippendorff, K. and Butter, R. (2007): Semantics: Meanings and contexts of artifacts. In: Schifferstein, H.N.J. and Hekkert, P. (eds.): Product experience. New York: Elsevier, 1-25.

Krogh, G. v., Ichijo, K. and Nonaka, I. (2000): Enabling knowledge creation: How to unlock the mystery of tacit knowledge and release the power of innovation. New York: Oxford University Press.

Latour, B. (1987): Science in action: How to follow scientists and engineers through society. Milton Keynes: Open University Press.

Maturana, H.R. (1970): Biology of cognition. In: Maturana, H.R. and Varela, F.J. (eds.): Autopoiesis and cognition: The realization of the living. Dordrecht, Boston: Reidel Publishing, 2-60.

Menary, R. (2010) (ed.): The extended mind. Cambridge, MA: MIT Press.

Nonaka, I., Toyama, R. and Hirata, T. (2008): Managing flow: A process theory of the knowledge based firm. Basingstoke, New York: Palgrave Macmillan.

Norman, D.A. (1991): Cognitive artifacts. In: Carroll, J.M. (ed.): Designing interaction: Psychology at the human-computer interface. New York, NY: Cambridge University Press, 17-38.

Onarheim, B. (2012): Creativity from constraints in engineering design: Lessons learned at Coloplast. In: Journal of Engineering Design, 23(4), 323-336.

Peschl, M.F. (1997): The representational relation between environmental structures and neural systems: Autonomy and environmental dependency in neural knowledge representation. In: Nonlinear Dynamics, Psychology, and Life Sciences (NDPSFS), 1(2), 99-121.

Peschl, M.F. (2001): Constructivism, cognition, and science: An investigation of its links and possible shortcomings. In: Foundations of Science, 6(1), 125-161.

Peschl, M.F. (2007): Enabling spaces: Epistemologische Grundlagen der Ermöglichung von Innovation und knowledge creation. In: Gronau, N. (ed.): Professionelles Wissensmanagement: Erfahrungen und Visionen. Berlin: GITO, 362-372.

Peschl, M.F. (2009): Innovation as a socio-epistemological technology. In: Hornung-Prähauser, V. and Luckmann, M. (eds.): Creativity and innovation competencies on the Web: How does the 'new' emerge with support of Web technologies? Salzburg: Salzburg Research, 46-56.

Peschl, M.F. and Fundneider, T. (2008): Emergent innovation and sustainable knowledge co-creation: A socio-epistemological approach to 'innovation from within'. In: Lytras, M.D., Carroll, J.M. and Damiani, E. (eds.): The open knowledge society: A computer science and information systems manifesto. New York: Springer, 101-108.

Peschl, M.F. and Fundneider, T. (2012): Spaces enabling game-changing and sustaining innovations: Why space matters for knowledge creation and innovation. In: Journal of Organisational Transformation and Social Change (OTSC), 9(1), 41-61.

Popper, K.R. (1962): Conjectures and refutations: The growth of scientific knowledge. New York: Basic Books.

Popper, K.R. (1959): The logic of scientific discovery. London: Hutchinson.

Roth, G. (2009): Aus der Sicht des Gehrins. Frankfurt am Main: Suhrkamp.

Sanders, E.B.-N. and Stappers, P.J. (2008): Co-creation and the new landscapes of design. In: CoDesign, 4(1), 5-18.

Scharmer, C.O. (2001): Self-transcending knowledge: Sensing and organizing around emerging opportunities. In: Journal of Knowledge Management, 5(2), 137-150.

Scharmer, C.O. (2007): Theory U: Leading from the future as it emerges: The social technology of presencing. Cambridge, MA: Society for Organizational Learning.

Shneiderman, B. (2007): Creativity support tools: Accelerating discovery and innovation. In: Communications of the ACM, 50, 20-32.

Sternberg, R.J. (2005): Creativity or creativities? In: International Journal of Human-Computer Studies, 63(4/5), 370-382.

Stokes, P.D. (2007): Using constraints to generate and sustain novelty. In: Psychology of Aesthetics, Creativity, and the Arts, 1(2), 107-113.

Tsoukas, H. (2005): Complex knowledge: Studies in organizational epistemology. Oxford: Oxford University Press.

Varela, F.J., Thompson, E. and Rosch, E. (1991): The embodied mind: Cognitive science and human experience. Cambridge, MA: MIT Press.

About the Authors

Nicholas Adjouri, born 1965 in Helsinki/Finland, studied branding and communication at the University of Arts in Berlin and Innovation Management at the Technical University Berlin. He received a doctorate in branding at the Free University of Berlin in 1993. From 1989 on he worked as a creative director for several advertising and design companies. In 1995 he founded his own brand and design consultancy located in Berlin/Germany. He holds a professorship at the Stralsund University of Applied Sciences since 2010. Nicholas Adjouri has written several books about branding.
adjouri@adjouri.com

Prof. Dr. Bernd Ankenbrand is Professor of Constructivist Finance at the Karlshochschule International University and managing director at MOSAIG oHG. His research activities and teaching is clustered around Business Model Innovation, Behavioral Economics, and various valuation topics, especially brand values and naming rights. Prof. Ankenbrand has studied economics and business at Witten/Herdecke University and at Stockholm University. His professional experience includes positions at Kienbaum Management Consultants, Arthur Andersen, PricewaterhouseCoopers Corporate Finance and gexid.
bankenbrand@karlshochschule.de

Dr. Laura Baker was a speech language pathologist and school administrator in the USA. In 1997 she set up and promoted the first bilingual grade school in Graz, Austria. Since 2005 with a PhD in psycholinguistics, she teaches at FH Joanneum University of Applied Sciences in Industrial/International Management. Her teaching and research interests as well as publications include intercultural communication and competence, co-creativity and team building plus English as a second language. Exploration of synergy in the co-creative process of team work is seen as a part of branded spaces management.
laura.baker@fh-joanneum.at

Melodena Stephens Balakrishnan is an Associate Professor in the Faculty of Business and Management, University of Wollongong in Dubai and is President and Founder of the Academy of International Business Middle East North Africa Chapter. She is the Regional Editor for Emerging Markets Case Studies Collection and has lived in India, USA, Taiwan and UAE. She has over sixteen years of industry and education experience.
melodenabalakrishnan@uowdubai.ac.ae

Thomas Bezold is Professor of Sport Management at the Reinhold Würth University of the University of Heilbronn. He holds two master degrees in sports economics and European sport management. From the University of Bayreuth he received his PhD in sports science, marketing and general management. Thomas has published several books and articles on sports marketing and branding. In addition to academia he worked as a Director of Sports in the Department of the City of Bayreuth and has held senior consulting activities in the field of sports marketing. His focus in research and teaching includes sports marketing, brand management and international sports management.
thomas.bezold@fh-heilbronn.de

Prof. Dr. Louise Bielzer is Professor of Communication and Strategic Management at Karlshochschule International University, Karlsruhe. She is Head of the MEEC (Meetings, Exhibitions, Events and Conventions) Management Studies. Additionally, she is an elected member of the Karlshochschule Senate. She is regularly invited as a guest lecturer at the Università Cattolica del Sacro Cuore in Milan, Italy and the Fachhochschule Kufstein, Austria, where she was awarded a Guest Professorship in Summer Term 2011. Before assuming the professorship at Karlshochschule in September 2007, Louise Bielzer worked as senior consultant at SYMBIOS AG for six years.
lbielzer@karlshochschule.de

Jörg Dauscher works as a self-employed consultant and writer. After studying literature, he joined Töchter und Söhne as a copywriter. Thereafter, he was employed as a consultant for Hill&Knowlton and then worked as co-owner of brot+salz. His focus as a consultant is on setting off, structuring and guiding creative processes. In 2010 he was invited by the Goethe Institut to give lectures on creative writing processes at Tirana University. His publications are *Nach Albanien: Bericht einer Reise* (2nd edition 2009), *Der Sommer in K: Erzählung* *aus einem russischen Dorf* (2009), *Die Invasion der Träume: Versuch über Berlin* (2012).

joerg@ideenhandlung.de

Frank Otto Dietrich's work and research interests center on brands that function successfully in identity construction for media presence and as an interface for business models. He has worked within agencies in the area of planning/strategy for national and international brands. After working at GREY Worldwide, Frank Otto Dietrich went on to study Communications, Strategic Marketing, Sociology and Politics. He holds a Master's degree from Berlin University of the Arts. Together with Ralf Schmidt-Bleeker, he developed the concept of *Narrative Brand Planning* and at the start of 2012 they founded the advertising agency *WAALD*. Today, Narrative Brand Planning provides the core methodology for their work.

frank.otto.dietrich@waald.com

Christoph Engl is the director of Südtirol Marketing Gesellschaft (South Tyrol Marketing Group). The company has been given the mandate of strengthening South Tyrol's image and desirability as a tourist destination. Christoph Engl comes from a legal background and has had a somewhat unusual career path: He started out working for a number of South Tyrol's employers' associations and later became the director of the region's 5,000-member-strong association of hoteliers. It was in 2001 that he finally made the switch to marketing and received his appointment at the South Tyrol Marketing Group. In his role as director, Christoph Engl spearheaded the introduction of the South Tyrol umbrella brand.

smg.direction@suedtirol.info

Thomas Fundneider is founder and CEO of the innovation agency theLivingCore (www.theLivingCore.com), specializing in the areas of strategy, innovation and transformation. Having his background in landscape architecture, his focus for many years is on establishing an innovative and entrepreneurial culture and mindset in organizations. Moreover, Thomas Fundneider is lecturing at several universities in Europe on the topics of (game-changing) innovation, entrepreneurship and Enabling Spaces. He is member of the Board of the Austrian chapter of the PDMA, the world's largest support organization for product development and innovation.

Fundneider@theLivingCore.com

Prof. Dr. **Werner Gronau** functions as Director of the 'Tourism & Transport Research Center' of the University of Nicosia/Cyprus and also holds the position as Professor for Tourism, Travel & Transport at the University of Stralsund/Germany. He holds a German degree in Human Geography from the Technical University of Munich and a PhD in Tourism Studies ('Leisure Mobility and Leisure Style') from the University of Paderborn. His research interests focus on sustainable Destination Development and Management. He has worked in several research projects granted by different institutions as for example the German Ministry of Research or the European Commission and presented the results on international conferences as well as in various journals and books.
werner.gronau@fh-stralsund.de

Dr. **Sonja Kastner** studied Communication in Social and Economic Contexts at Berlin University of the Arts (UdK). She worked as a conceptual designer and copywriter at the internet agency Pixelpark Berlin for global brands. Her dissertation is about the design process of sonic branding. She is professor for 'Strategic Communication' at Hochschule für Technik und Wirtschaft Berlin (HTW).
kastner@htw-berlin.de

Greg Kerr is a lecturer in marketing at the University of Wollongong. His career history includes local government as well as business development. He has been a board member of tourist associations as well as a credit union and a chamber of commerce. Greg has held a number of governance roles at UOW including Head of Marketing and is Chair of the Commerce and Sydney Business School Alumni.
gkerr@uow.edu.au

Michael Klein is an architect and researcher based in Vienna, Austria. He studied architecture at Vienna University of Technology and the École Spéciale d'Architecture in Paris and graduated from the Academy of Fine Arts Vienna in 2007. Since then, he has been working in the field of architecture, landscape architecture and urbanism. From 2009 on, Michael has been lecturing and teaching design classes at Vienna University of Technology. His theoretical research interest focuses on how political thinking plus its practices and economic conditions affect design, architecture and the urban environment.
mk@scibe.eu

Stefanie Leontiadis completed her PhD with Merit in Urban and Architectural Design in 2012 at the Politecnico di Milano, supervised by Ilaria Valente, while also receiving the European Doctorate title, focusing on syntactic representations and theories of the architecture of public open urban spaces in the contemporary city. She has presented in various conferences, highlighted by an international distinction of the 'IPHS Young Researchers' Session Achievement Award in Research 2010' by the International Planning History Society. Currently she is involved as a Research Associate in the ATRIUM project (Architecture of Totalitarian Regimes of the 20th century in Urban Management) of the South East Europe Transnational Cooperation Programme.

stefanie.leontiadis@gmail.com

Erica Liu is the principal lecturer and programme leader of BA (Hons) Interior Architecture & Design in the University of Hertfordshire, UK. Before joining the university, Erica was an interior and exhibition designer in the Far East for over 10 years. She also acts as a consultant for the Pinkspiration Social Enterprise. Erica is the external examiner for two universities' degree courses. She has a PhD in Cultural Studies and her research projects included place branding and Kansei design theory.

erica.liu.interior.design@gmail.com

Steven Miles is Professor in Urban Culture at the University of Brighton, and author of *Spaces for Consumption: Pleasure and Placelessness in the Post-Industrial City* (Sage, 2010). His key publications include *Consumerism as a Way of Life* (Sage, 1998) and *Youth Lifestyles in a Changing World* (OUP, 2000) and he is co-author of *Consuming Cities* (Palgrave Macmillan, 2004) with Malcolm Miles. He is the Editor-in-Chief of the *Journal of Consumer Culture*.

s.miles2@brighton.ac.uk

Florin Mureşanu is an architect with a master degree in Integrated Urban Planning at the 'Ion Mincu' University of Architecture and Urbanism in Bucharest, where he is now teaching urban planning and design as a lecturer. With a PhD in urban sciences, he is currently a postdoctoral fellow in history and cultural studies at the 'Babes-Bolyai' University in Cluj-Napoca.

gomarchgo@yahoo.com

Monica Mureşanu is an architect with a master degree in Conservation and Rehabilitation of Built Heritage at the 'Ion Mincu' University of Architecture and Urbanism, Bucharest and a research master degree in Cultural and Social History of Architecture and Urban Forms centuries from École Nationale Superieure d'Architecture de Versailles. She is currently a PhD candidate in Architecture and Building Restoration at the 'Ion Mincu' University of Architecture and Urbanism, Bucharest.
monicamuresanu@yahoo.com

Sven Mussler is Managing Partner of Mussler Consulting GmbH in Hamburg, Germany, a boutique consultancy focusing on brand and marketing strategy, brand value management, and intellectual property valuation. Sven has helped numerous clients in linking brand and financial metrics to measure brand and business value and to support strategic decision making processes. Sven previously worked for Unilever in sales and marketing, PwC's advisory practice, and for WPP/ Millward Brown in Germany and the U.K. Sven published numerous articles and frequently speaks on conferences and seminars.
sven.mussler@mussler-consulting.de

Timo Mussler is a managing partner of 'Publik. Agentur für Kommunikation'. He consults for companies in the field of the development of communication strategies and its creative implementation in the domains public relations, sponsoring and event marketing. He studied Business Economics with the focus on Marketing. In 1999 he started his professional career in the Haniel group. Within this service company he acquired eight years experience in the field of marketing and sales by, for example, leading the Customer Relationship Management. In 2006 he started as a managing partner of the family-owned company Mussler Communication. Since the merger with 'Publik. Agentur für Kommunikation' in 2012, Mussler Communication exists as its own trademark of the new Company Publik.
mussler@mussler-communication.de

Garyfalia Palaiologou is a PhD candidate at the Bartlett School of Graduate Studies, University College London, supported by an EPSRC studentship. Her research focuses on the evolutionary processes and the urban transformations that characterise the interface between the public and private realm. She is an architect by training (NTUA) and has a Master's Degree in Advanced

Architectural Studies (MSc AAS) at the Bartlett School of Graduate Studies, University College London.

g.palaiologou@ucl.ac.uk

Professor **Alan Penn** is the Dean of the Bartlett faculty of the Built Environment, an HEFCE Business Fellow and a founding director of Space Syntax Ltd. He is a member of the Space Group, an EPSRC Platform funded research group. His research focuses on understanding the way that the design of the built environment affects the patterns of social and economic behaviour of organisations and communities. Current research includes the development of agent based simulations of human behaviour, the development of spatio-temporal representations of built environments, investigations of urban spatial networks and the application of these techniques in studies of urban sustainability.

a.penn@ucl.ac.uk

Markus F. Peschl is Professor for Cognitive Science and Philosophy of Science at the University of Vienna. In his research he focuses on the transdisciplinary fields of innovation, cognition, and on designing spaces for knowledge creation ('Enabling Spaces'). He has published more than 120 papers and 6 books.

franz-markus.peschl@univie.ac.at

Andreas Rumpfhuber is an architect and researcher, and founder of Expanded Design which is a design research office based in Vienna, Austria. Currently he is the principal investigator of the Viennese part of SCIBE (Scarcity and Creativity in the Built Environment) and project leader of the Austrian Science Foundation-funded research project 'Architecture of Cybernetics of Organization' (fwf.ac.at).

ar@expandeddesign.net

Ralf Schmidt-Bleeker's work focuses on complex aspects of brand meaning and their management. He is particularly fascinated by the conflicts and ambivalences that make brands exciting and successful. Ralf Schmidt-Bleeker worked for the WPP agency Arthur Schlovsky, among others, in the area of planning/strategy for national and international brands. He initially came to the industry from a visual perspective as a trained media designer before completing a Master's degree in Communications, Strategic Marketing, Sociology and

Politics at Berlin University of the Arts. Together with Frank Otto Dietrich, he developed the concept of *Narrative Brand Planning* and at the start of 2012 they founded the advertising agency WAALD. Today, Narrative Brand Planning provides the core methodology for their work.

ralf.schmidt-bleeker@waald.com

Stephan Sonnenburg is Professor for Creativity and Transformative Management at the Karlshochschule International University in Karlsruhe, Germany. He is Dean of the Faculty 'Management and Performance'. Stephan Sonnenburg has broad research interests in the field of creativity, branding and management within which he examines the performative and transformative potential. One of his latest publications together with Sangeeta Singh in the Journal of Interactive Marketing is *Brand Performances in Social Media*.

ssonnenburg@karlshochschule.de

Jan Specht studied architecture followed by a Master of Business Administration. He worked as researcher and lecturer at different European universities and on international real estate projects. Since 2009 Jan has been attending a PhD program at the International Graduate School of Girona, Spain, investigating the impacts of contemporary architecture on tourism destinations. He is a fellow of the EU Science and Technology Programme China, doing research and teaching at Sun Yat-Sen University, Guangzhou.

jan@specht.com

Prof. Dr. **Antti Vihinen** is Professor of Cultural Theory and Destination Management at the Karlshochschule International University in Karlsruhe, Germany. He is the former Managing Director of the Sibelius Hall Lahti, Chairman of the Board of the Lahti Travel Ltd, Finland, and was an AIPC Board Member 2002-2008. His research focuses on city branding, destination image, politics and culture as well as arts management. He published on Sibelius, Wagner, music, politics and culture.

avihinen@karlshochschule.de

420 547

Printed by Printforce, the Netherlands